The Conspiracy of Pontiac and the Indian War

Francis Parkman

THE

CONSPIRACY OF PONTIAC

AND THE

INDIAN WAR

AFTER

THE CONQUEST OF CANADA.

BY

FRANCIS PARKMAN.

EIGHTH EDITION, REVISED, WITH ADDITIONS.

Vol. I.

BOSTON:
LITTLE, BROWN, AND COMPANY.
1877.

CAMBRIDGE:

PRESS OF JOHN WILSON AND SON.

TO

JARED SPARKS, LL.D.,

PRESIDENT OF HARVARD UNIVERSITY

THESE VOLUMES ARE DEDICATED

AS A TESTIMONIAL OF HIGH PERSONAL REGARD,

AND A TRIBUTE OF RESPECT

FOR HIS DISTINGUISHED SERVICES TO

AMERICAN HISTORY.

PREFACE

TO THE SIXTH EDITION.

———

I CHOSE the subject of this book as affording better opportunities than any other portion of American history for portraying forest life and the Indian
character; and I have never seen reason to change
this opinion. In the nineteen years that have
passed since the first edition was published, a considerable amount of additional material has come
to light. This has been carefully collected, and is
incorporated in the present edition. The most
interesting portion of this new material has been
supplied by the Bouquet and Haldimand Papers,
added some years ago to the manuscript collections
of the British Museum. Among them are several
hundred letters from officers engaged in the Pontiac
war, some official, others personal and familiar,
affording very curious illustrations of the events of
the day and of the characters of those engaged in
them. Among the facts which they bring to light,
some are sufficiently startling; as, for example, the
proposal of the Commander-in-Chief to infect the

hostile tribes with the small-pox, and that of a distinguished subordinate officer to take revenge on the Indians by permitting an unrestricted sale of rum.

The two volumes of the present edition have been made uniform with those of the series " France and England in North America." I hope to continue that series to the period of the extinction of French power on this continent. " The Conspiracy of Pontiac" will then form a sequel; and its introductory chapters will be, in a certain sense, a summary of what has preceded. This will involve some repetition in the beginning of the book, but I have nevertheless thought it best to let it remain as originally written.

Boston, 16 September, 1870.

PREFACE

TO THE FIRST EDITION.

————

THE conquest of Canada was an event of moment-ous consequence in American history. It changed the political aspect of the continent, prepared a way for the independence of the British colonies, rescued the vast tracts of the interior from the rule of military despotism, and gave them, eventually, to the keeping of an ordered democracy. Yet to the red natives of the soil its results were wholly disastrous. Could the French have maintained their ground, the ruin of the Indian tribes might long have been postponed; but the victory of Quebec was the signal of their swift decline. Thence-forth they were destined to melt and vanish before the advancing waves of Anglo-American power, which now rolled westward unchecked and unop-posed. They saw the danger, and, led by a great and daring champion, struggled fiercely to avert it. The history of that epoch, crowded as it is with scenes of tragic interest, with marvels of suffering and vicissitude, of heroism and endurance, has been, as yet, unwritten, buried in the archives of governments, or among the obscurer records of private adventure. To rescue it from oblivion is the object of the following work. It aims to portray the American forest and the American Indian at the period when both received their final doom.

It is evident that other study than that of the closet is indispensable to success in such an attempt. Habits of early reading had greatly aided to prepare me for the task; but necessary knowledge of a more practical kind has been supplied by the indulgence of a strong natural taste, which, at various intervals, led me to the wild regions of the north and west. Here, by the camp-fire, or in the canoe, I gained familiar acquaintance with the men and scenery of the wilderness. In 1846, I visited various primitive tribes of the Rocky Mountains, and was, for a time, domesticated in a village of the western Dahcotah, on the high plains between Mount Laramie and the range of the Medicine Bow.

The most troublesome part of the task was the collection of the necessary documents. These consisted of letters, journals, reports, and despatches, scattered among numerous public offices, and private families, in Europe and America. When brought together, they amounted to about three thousand four hundred manuscript pages. Contemporary newspapers, magazines, and pamphlets have also been examined, and careful search made for every book which, directly or indirectly, might throw light upon the subject. I have visited the sites of all the principal events· recorded in the narrative, and gathered such local traditions as seemed worthy of confidence.

I am indebted to the liberality of Hon. Lewis Cass for a curious collection of papers relating to the siege of Detroit by the Indians. Other important contributions have been obtained from the state paper offices of London and Paris, from the archives of New York, Pennsylvania, and other states, and from the manuscript collections of several historical societies. The late William L. Stone, Esq., commenced an elaborate biography of Sir William Johnson, which it is much to be lamented he did not live to complete. By the kindness of Mrs. Stone, I was permitted to copy from his extensive collection of documents such portions as would serve the purposes of the following History.

To President Sparks of Harvard University, General Whiting, U. S. A., Brantz Mayer, Esq., of Baltimore, Francis J. Fisher, Esq., of Philadelphia, and Rev. George E. Ellis, of Charlestown, I beg to return a warm acknowledgment for counsel and assistance. Mr. Benjamin Perley Poore and Mr. Henry Stevens procured copies of valuable documents from the archives of Paris and London. Henry R. Schoolcraft, Esq., Dr. Elwyn, of Philadelphia, Dr. O'Callaghan, of Albany, George H. Moore, Esq., of New York, Lyman C. Draper, Esq., of Philadelphia, Judge Law, of Vincennes, and many others, have kindly contributed materials to the work. Nor can I withhold an expression of thanks to the aid so freely rendered in the dull task of proof-reading and correction.

The crude and promiscuous mass of materials presented an aspect by no means inviting. The field of the history was uncultured and unreclaimed, and the labor that awaited me was like that of the border settler, who, before he builds his rugged dwelling, must fell the forest-trees, burn the undergrowth, clear the ground, and hew the fallen trunks to due proportion.

Several obstacles have retarded the progress of the work. Of these, one of the most considerable was the condition of my sight. For about three years, the light of day was insupportable, and every attempt at reading or writing completely debarred. Under these circumstances, the task of sifting the materials and composing the work was begun and finished. The papers were repeatedly read aloud by an amanuensis, copious notes and extracts were made. and the narrative written down from my dictation. This process, though extremely slow and laborious, was not without its advantages; and I am well convinced that the authorities have been even more minutely examined, more scrupulously collated, and more thoroughly digested, than they would have been under ordinary circumstances.

In order to escape the tedious circumlocution, which, from the nature of the subject, could not otherwise have been avoided, the name English is applied, throughout the volume, to the British American colonists, as well as to the people of the mother country. The necessity is somewhat to be regretted, since, even at an early period, clear distinctions were visible between the offshoot and the parent stock.

Boston, August 1, 1851.

CONTENTS OF VOL. I.

CHAPTER I.

INTRODUCTORY. — INDIAN TRIBES EAST OF THE MISSISSIPPI.

CHAPTER II.

1663–1763.

FRANCE AND ENGLAND IN AMERICA.

CHAPTER III.

1608–1763.

The French, the English, and the Indians.

CHAPTER IV.

1700–1755.

Collision of the Rival Colonies.

CHAPTER V.

1755–1763.

THE WILDERNESS AND ITS TENANTS AT THE CLOSE OF THE FRENCH WAR.

CHAPTER VI.

1760

THE ENGLISH TAKE POSSESSION OF THE WESTERN POSTS.

CHAPTER VII.

1760–1763.

ANGER OF THE INDIANS. — THE CONSPIRACY

CHAPTER VIII.

1763.

INDIAN PREPARATION.

CHAPTER IX.

1763, APRIL.

THE COUNCIL AT THE RIVER ECORCES.

CHAPTER X.

1763, MAY.

DETROIT.

CHAPTER XI.

1763.

TREACHERY OF PONTIAC.

CHAPTER XII.

1763.

PONTIAC AT THE SIEGE OF DETROIT.

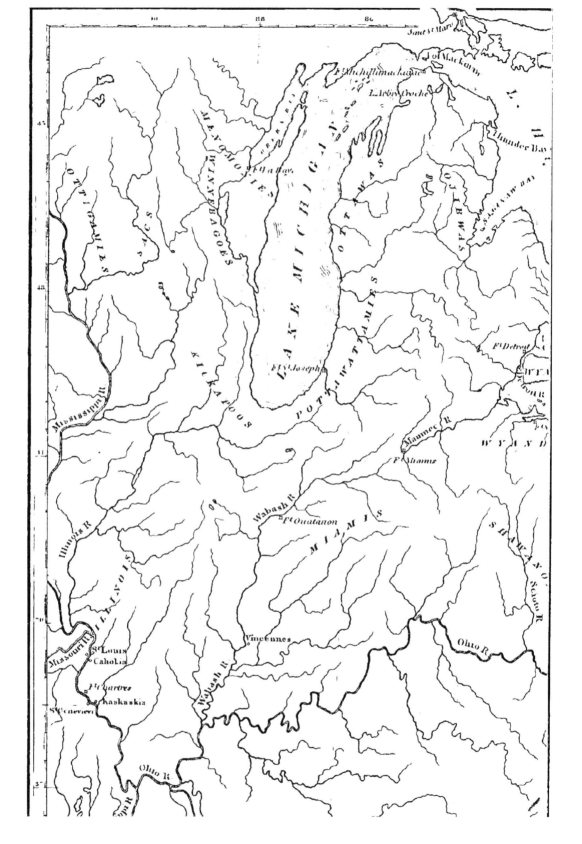

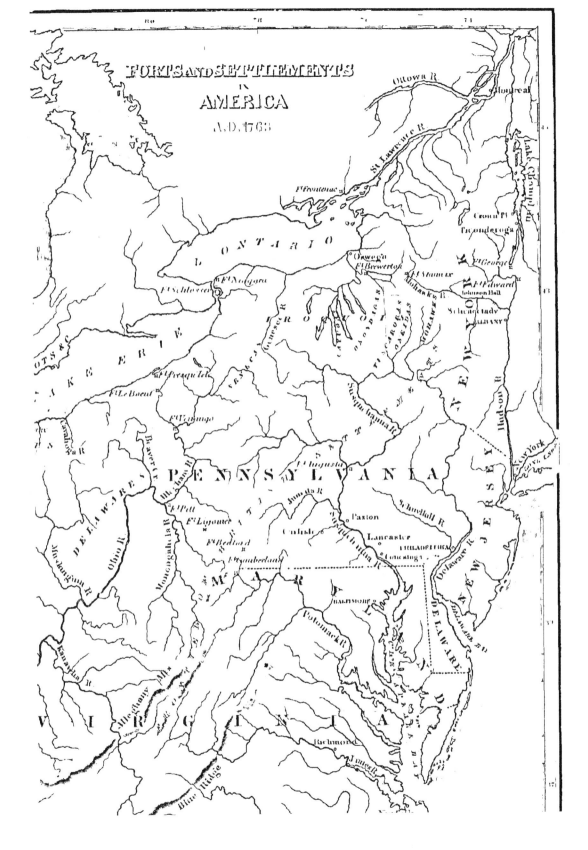

THE

CONSPIRACY OF PONTIAC.

——◆——

CHAPTER I.

INTRODUCTORY.—INDIAN TRIBES EAST OF THE
MISSISSIPPI.

THE Indian is a true child of the forest and the
desert. The wastes and solitudes of nature are his
congenial home. His haughty mind is imbued
with the spirit of the wilderness, and the light of
civilization falls on him with a blighting power.
His unruly pride and untamed freedom are in harmony with the lonely mountains, cataracts, and
rivers among which he dwells; and primitive
America, with her savage scenery and savage men,
opens to the imagination a boundless world, un-
matched in wild sublimity.

The Indians east of the Mississippi may be divided into several great families, each distinguished
by a radical peculiarity of language. In their
moral and intellectual, their social and political
state, these various families exhibit strong shades

1

of distinction ; but, before pointing them out, I shall indicate a few prominent characteristics, which, faintly or distinctly, mark the whole in com mon.

All are alike a race of hunters, sustaining life wholly, or in part, by the fruits of the chase. Each family is split into tribes ; and these tribes, by the exigencies of the hunter life, are again divided into sub-tribes, bands, or villages, often scattered far asunder, over a wide extent of wilderness. Unhappily for the strength and harmony of the Indian race, each tribe is prone to regard itself, not as the member of a great whole, but as a sovereign and independent nation, often arrogating to itself an importance superior to all the rest of mankind ;[1] and the warrior whose petty horde might muster a few scores of half-starved fighting men, strikes his hand upon his heart, and exclaims, in all the pride of patriotism, " I am a *Menomone*."

In an Indian community, each man is his own master. He abhors restraint, and owns no other authority than his own capricious will ; and yet this wild notion of liberty is not inconsistent with certain gradations of rank and influence. Each tribe has its sachem, or civil chief, whose office is in a manner hereditary, and, among many, though by no means among all tribes, descends in the female line ; so that the brother of the incumbent, or the son of his sister, and not his own son, is the right-

---

[1] Many Indian tribes bear names which in their dialect signify *men*, indicating that the character belongs, *par excellence*, to them. Sometimes the word was used by itself, and sometimes an adjective was joined with it, as *original men, men surpassing all others.*

ful successor to his dignities.[1]   If, however, in the
opinion of the old men and subordinate chiefs, the
heir should be disqualified for the exercise of the
office by cowardice, incapacity, or any defect of
character, they do not scruple to discard him, and
elect another in his place, usually fixing their
choice on one of his relatives.   The office of the
sachem is no enviable one.   He has neither laws
to administer nor power to enforce his commands.
His counsellors are the inferior chiefs and principal
men of the tribe; and he never sets himself in
opposition to the popular will, which is the sovereign power of these savage democracies.   His
province is to advise, and not to dictate; but, should
he be a man of energy, talent, and address, and
especially should he be supported by numerous
relatives and friends, he may often acquire no small
measure of respect and power.   A clear distinction is drawn between the civil and military authority, though both are often united in the same person.   The functions of war-chief may, for the most
part, be exercised by any one whose prowess and
reputation are sufficient to induce the young men
to follow him to battle; and he may, whenever he
thinks proper, raise a band of volunteers, and go
out against the common enemy.

We might imagine that a society so loosely
framed would soon resolve itself into anarchy; yet
this is not the case, and an Indian village is singu-

[1] The dread of female infidelity has been assigned, and with probable
truth, as the origin of this custom.   The sons of a chief's sister must necessarily be his kindred; though his own reputed son may be, in fact, the
offspring of another.

larly free from wranglings and petty strife. Several causes conspire to this result. The necessities of the hunter life, preventing the accumulation of large communities, make more stringent organiza tion needless; while a species of self-control, inculcated from childhood upon every individual, enforced by a sentiment of dignity and manhood, and greatly aided by the peculiar temperament of the race, tends strongly to the promotion of harmony. Though he owns no law, the Indian is inflexible in his adherence to ancient usages and customs; and the principle of hero-worship, which belongs to his nature, inspires him with deep respect for the sages and captains of his tribe. The very rudeness of his condition, and the absence of the passions which wealth, luxury, and the other incidents of civilization engender, are favorable to internal harmony; and to the same cause must likewise be ascribed too many of his virtues, which would quickly vanish, were he elevated from his savage state.

A peculiar social institution exists among the Indians, very curious in its character; and though I am not prepared to say that it may be traced through all the tribes east of the Mississippi, yet its prevalence is so general, and its influence on political relations so important, as to claim especial attention. Indian communities, independently of their local distribution into tribes, bands, and villages, are composed of several distinct clans. Each clan has its emblem, consisting of the figure of some· bird, beast, or reptile; and each is distinguished by the name of the animal which it thus bears as its device; as, for example, the clan of the Wolf, the Deer, the Otter, or the Hawk. In the language of the Algonquins, these emblems are known by the name of *Totems*.[1] The members of the same clan, being connected, or supposed to be so, by ties of kindred, more or less remote, are prohibited from intermarriage. Thus Wolf cannot marry Wolf; but he may, if he chooses, take a wife from the clan of Hawks, or any other clan but his own. It follows that when this prohibition is rigidly observed, no single clan can live apart from the rest; but the whole must be mingled together, and in every family the husband and wife must be of different clans.

To different totems attach different degrees of rank and dignity; and those of the Bear, the Tortoise, and the Wolf are among the first in honor. Each man is proud of his badge, jealously asserting its claims to respect; and the members of the same clan, though they may, perhaps, speak different dialects, and dwell far asunder, are yet bound together by the closest ties of fraternity. If a man is killed, every member of the clan feels called

---

[1] Schoolcraft, *Oneota*, 172.

The extraordinary figures intended to represent tortoises, deer, snakes, and other animals, which are often seen appended to Indian treaties, are the totems of the chiefs, who employ these devices of their respective clans as their sign manual. The device of his clan is also sometimes tattooed on the body of the warrior.

The word *tribe* might, perhaps, have been employed with as much propriety as that of *clan*, to indicate the totemic division; but as the former is constantly employed to represent the local or political divisions of the Indian race, hopeless confusion would arise from using it in a double capacity.

upon to avenge him; and the wayfarer, the hunter, or the warrior is sure of a cordial welcome in the distant lodge of the clansman whose face perhaps he has never seen. It may be added that certain privileges, highly prized as hereditary rights, sometimes reside in particular clans; such as that of furnishing a sachem to the tribe, or of performing certain religious ceremonies or magic rites.

The Indians east of the Mississippi may be divided into three great families: the Iroquois, the Algonquin, and the Mobilian, each speaking a language of its own, varied by numerous dialectic forms. To these families must be added a few stragglers from the great western race of the Dahcotah, besides several distinct tribes of the south, each of which has been regarded as speaking a tongue peculiar to itself.[1] The Mobilian group embraces the motley confederacy of the Creeks, the crafty Choctaws, and the stanch and warlike Chickasaws. Of these, and of the distinct tribes dwelling in their vicinity, or within their limits, I shall only observe that they offer, with many modifications, and under different aspects, the same essential features which mark the Iroquois and the Algonquins, the two great families of the north.[2] The latter, who were the conspicuous

[1] For an ample view of these divisions, see the *Synopsis* of Mr. Gallatin, *Trans. Am. Ant. Soc.* II.

[2] It appears from several passages in the writings of Adair, Hawkins, and others, that the totem prevailed among the southern tribes. In a conversation with the late Albert Gallatin, he informed me that he was told by the chiefs of a Choctaw deputation, at Washington, that in their tribe were eight totemic clans, divided into two classes, of four each. It is very remarkable that the same number of clans, and the same division into classes, were to be found among the Five Nations or Iroquois.

actors in the events of the ensuing narrative, demand a closer attention.

THE IROQUOIS FAMILY.

Foremost in war, foremost in eloquence, foremost in their savage arts of policy, stood the fierce people called by themselves the *Hodenosaunee*, and by the French the *Iroquois*, a name which has since been applied to the entire family of which they formed the dominant member.[1]　They extended their conquests and their depredations from Quebec to the Carolinas, and from the western prairies to the forests of Maine.[2]　On the south, they forced tribute from the subjugated Delawares, and pierced the mountain fastnesses of the Chero

---

[1] A great difficulty in the study of Indian history arises from a redundancy of names employed to designate the same tribe; yet this does not prevent the same name from being often used to designate two or more different tribes.　The following are the chief of those which are applied to the Iroquois by different writers, French, English, and German:—

Iroquois, Five, and afterwards Six Nations; Confederates, Hodenosaunee, Aquanuscioni, Aggonnonshioni, Ongwe Honwe, Mengwe, Maquas, Mahaquase, Massawomecs, Palenachendchiesktajeet.

The name of Massawomecs has been applied to several tribes; and that of Mingoes is often restricted to a colony of the Iroquois which established itself near the Ohio.

[2] François, a well-known Indian belonging to the remnant of the Penobscots living at Old Town, in Maine, told me, in the summer of 1843, that a tradition was current, among his people, of their being attacked in ancient times by the Mohawks, or, as he called them, Mohogs, a tribe of the Iroquois, who destroyed one of their villages, killed the men and women, and roasted the small children on forked sticks, like apples, before the fire.　When he began to tell his story, François was engaged in patching an old canoe, in preparation for a moose hunt; but soon growing warm with his recital, he gave over his work, and at the conclusion exclaimed with great wrath and earnestness, "Mohog all devil!"

kees with incessant forays.[1]   On the north, they
uprooted the ancient settlements of the Wyandots;
on the west they exterminated the Eries and the
Andastes, and spread havoc and dismay among
the tribes of the Illinois; and on the east, the
Indians of New England fled at the first peal of
the Mohawk war-cry.   Nor was it the Indian race
alone who quailed before their ferocious valor.
All Canada shook with the fury of their onset;
the people fled to the forts for refuge; the blood-
besmeared conquerors roamed like wolves among
the burning settlements, and the colony trembled
on the brink of ruin.

The Iroquois in some measure owed their triumphs to the position of their country; for they
dwelt within the present limits of the State of New
York, whence several great rivers and the inland
oceans of the northern lakes opened ready thoroughfares to their roving warriors through all the adjacent wilderness.   But the true fountain of their
success is to be sought in their own inherent energies, wrought to the most effective action under a
political fabric well suited to the Indian life; in
their mental and moral organization; in their insatiable ambition and restless ferocity.

In their scheme of government, as in their social

---

[1] The tribute exacted from the Delawares consisted of wampum, or
beads of shell, an article of inestimable value with the Indians. "Two
old men commonly go about, every year or two, to receive this tribute;
and I have often had opportunity to observe what anxiety the poor Indians were under, while these two old men remained in that part of the
country where I was.   An old Mohawk sachem, in a poor blanket and a
dirty shirt, may be seen issuing his orders with as arbitrary an authority
as a Roman dictator." — Colden, *Hist. Five Nations*, 4.

customs and religious observances, the Iroquois displayed, in full symmetry and matured strength, the same characteristics which in other tribes are found distorted, withered, decayed to the root, or, perhaps, faintly visible in an imperfect germ. They consisted of five tribes or nations — the Mohawks, the Oneidas, the Onondagas, the Cayugas, and the Senecas, to whom a sixth, the Tuscaroras, was afterwards added.[1] To each of these tribes belonged an organization of its own. Each had several sachems, who, with the subordinate chiefs and principal men, regulated all its internal affairs; but, when foreign powers were to be treated with, or matters involving the whole confederacy required deliberation, all the sachems of the several tribes convened in general assembly at the great council-house, in the Valley of Onondaga. Here ambassadors were received, alliances were adjusted, and all subjects of general interest discussed with exemplary harmony.[2] The order of debate was

[1] The following are synonymous names, gathered from various writers : —

Mohawks, Anies, Agniers, Agnierrhonons, Sankhicans, Canungas, Mauguawogs, Ganeagaonoh.

Oneidas, Oneotas, Onoyats, Anoyints, Onneiouts, Oneyotecaronoh, Onoiochrhonons.

Onondagas, Onnontagues, Onondagaonohs.

Cayugas, Caiyoquos, Goiogoens, Gweugwehonoh.

Senecas, Sinnikes, Chennessies, Genesees, Chenandoanes, Tsonnontouans, Jenontowanos, Nundawaronoh.

[2] "In the year 1745, August Gottlieb Spangenburg, a bishop of the United Brethren, spent several weeks in Onondaga, and frequently attended the great council. The council-house was built of bark. On each side six seats were placed, each containing six persons. No one was admitted besides the members of the council, except a few, who were particularly honored. If one rose to speak, all the rest sat in profound

piescribed by time-honored customs, and, in the fiercest heat, of controversy, the assembly maintained its self-control.

But the main stay of Iroquois polity was the system of *totemship*. It was this which gave the structure its elastic strength; and but for this, a mere confederacy of jealous and warlike tribes must soon have been rent asunder by shocks from without or discord from within. At some early period, the Iroquois probably formed an individual nation; for the whole people, irrespective of their separation into tribes, consisted of eight totemic clans; and the members of each clan, to what nation soever they belonged, were mutually bound to one another by those close ties of fraternity which mark this singular institution. Thus the five nations of the confederacy were laced together by an eight-fold band; and to this hour their slender remnants cling to one another with invincible tenacity.

It was no small security to the liberties of the Iroquois — liberties which they valued beyond any

silence, smoking their pipes. The speaker uttered his words in a singing tone, always rising a few notes at the close of each sentence. Whatever was pleasing to the council was confirmed by all with the word Nee, or Yes. And, at the end of each speech, the whole company joined in applauding the speaker by calling Hoho. At noon, two men entered bearing a large kettle filled with meat, upon a pole across their shoulders, which was first presented to the guests. A large wooden ladle, as broad and deep as a common bowl, hung with a hook to the side of the kettle, with which every one might at once help himself to as much as he could eat. When the guests had eaten their fill, they begged the counsellors to do the same. The whole was conducted in a very decent and quiet manner. Indeed, now and then, one or the other would lie flat upon his back to rest himself, and sometimes they would stop, joke, and laugh heartily." — Loskiel, *Hist. Morav. Miss.* 138.

other possession — that by the Indian custom of
descent in the female line, which among them was
more rigidly adhered to than elsewhere, the office
of the sachem must pass, not to his son, but to his
brother, his sister's son, or some yet remoter kinsman.   His power was constantly deflected into the
collateral branches of his family; and thus one of
the strongest temptations of ambition was cut off.[1]
The Iroquois had no laws; but they had ancient
customs which took the place of laws.   Each man,
or rather, each clan, was the avenger of its own
wrongs; but the manner of the retaliation was
fixed by established usage.   The tribal sachems,
and even the great council at Onondaga, had no
power to compel the execution of their decrees;
yet they were looked up to with a respect which
the soldier's bayonet or the sheriff's staff would
never have commanded; and it is highly to the

[1] The descent of the sachemship in the female line was a custom
universally prevalent among the Five Nations, or Iroquois proper.   Since,
among Indian tribes generally, the right of furnishing a sachem was
vested in some particular totemic clan, it results of course that the descent
of the sachemship must follow the descent of the totem; that is, if the
totemship descend in the female line, the sachemship must do the same.
This custom of descent in the female line prevailed not only among the
Iroquois proper, but also among the Wyandots, and probably among the
Andastes and the Eries, extinct members of the great Iroquois family.
Thus, among any of these tribes, when a Wolf warrior married a Hawk
squaw, their children were Hawks, and not Wolves.   With the Creeks
of the south, according to the observations of Hawkins (*Georgia Hist.
Coll.* III 69), the rule was the same; but among the Algonquins, on the
contrary, or at least among the northern branches of this family, the
reverse took place, the totemships, and consequently the chieftainships,
descending in the male line, after the analogy of civilized nations.   For
this information concerning the northern Algonquins, I am indebted to
Mr Schoolcraft, whose opportunities of observation among these tribes
have surpassed those of any other student of Indian customs and character

honor of the Indian character that they could exert so great an authority where there was nothing to enforce it but the weight of moral power.[1]

The origin of the Iroquois is lost in hopeless obscurity. That they came from the west; that they came from the north; that they sprang from the soil of New York, are the testimonies of three conflicting traditions, all equally worthless as aids to historic inquiry.[2] It is at the era of their confederacy — the event to which the five tribes owed all their greatness and power, and to which we need assign no remoter date than that of a century before the first arrival of the Dutch in New York — that faint rays of light begin to pierce the gloom, and the chaotic traditions of the earlier epoch mould themselves into forms more palpable and distinct.

Taounyawatha, the God of the Waters — such is the belief of the Iroquois — descended to the earth

[1] An account of the political institutions of the Iroquois will be found in Mr. Morgan's series of letters, published in the *American Review* for 1847. Valuable information may also be obtained from *Schoolcraft's Notes on the Iroquois*.

Mr. Morgan is of opinion that these institutions were the result of "a protracted effort of legislation." An examination of the customs prevailing among other Indian tribes makes it probable that the elements of the Iroquois polity existed among them from an indefinite antiquity; and the legislation of which Mr. Morgan speaks could only involve the arrangement and adjustment of already existing materials.

Since the above chapter was written, Mr. Morgan has published an elaborate and very able work on the institutions of the Iroquois. It forms an invaluable addition to this department of knowledge

[2] Recorded by Heckewelder, Colden, and Schoolcraft That the Iroquois had long dwelt on the spot where they were first discovered by the whites, is rendered probable by several circumstances. See Mr. Squier's work on the *Aboriginal Monuments of New York*.

to instruct his favorite people in the arts of savage life; and when he saw how they were tormented by giants, monsters, and evil spirits, he urged the divided tribes, for the common defence, to band themselves together in an everlasting league. While the injunction was as yet unfulfilled, the sacred messenger was recalled to the Great Spirit; but, before his departure, he promised that another should appear, empowered to instruct the people in all that pertained to their confederation. And accordingly, as a band of Mohawk warriors was threading the funereal labyrinth of an ancient pine forest, they heard, amid its blackest depths, a hoarse voice chanting in measured cadence; and, following the sound, they saw, seated among the trees, a monster so hideous, that they stood benumbed with terror. His features were wild and frightful. He was encompassed by hissing rattlesnakes, which, Medusa-like, hung writhing from his head; and on the ground around him were strewn implements of incantation, and magic vessels formed of human skulls. Recovering from their amazement, the warriors could perceive that in the mystic words of the chant, which he still poured forth, were couched the laws and principles of the destined confederacy. The tradition further declares that the monster, being surrounded and captured, was presently transformed to human shape, that he became a chief of transcendent wisdom and prowess, and to the day of his death ruled the councils of the now united tribes. To this hour the presiding sachem of the council at

Onondaga inherits from him the honored name of Atotarho.[1]

The traditional epoch which preceded the auspicious event of the confederacy, though wrapped in clouds and darkness, and defying historic scrutiny, has yet a character and meaning of its own. The gloom is peopled thick with phantoms; with monsters and prodigies, shapes of wild enormity, yet offering, in the Teutonic strength of their conception, the evidence of a robustness of mind unparalleled among tribes of a different lineage. In these evil days, the scattered and divided Iroquois were beset with every form of peril and disaster. Giants, cased in armor of stone, descended on them from the mountains of the north. Huge beasts trampled down their forests like fields of grass. Human heads, with streaming hair and glaring eye balls, shot through the air like meteors, shedding pestilence and death throughout the land. A great horned serpent rose from Lake Ontario; and only the thunder-bolts of the skies could stay his ravages, and drive him back to his native deeps. The skeletons of men, victims of some monster of the forest, were seen swimming in the Lake of Teungk-too; and around the Seneca village on the Hill of Genundewah, a two-headed serpent coiled himself, of size so monstrous that the wretched people were unable to ascend his scaly sides, and perished in

---

[1] This preposterous legend was first briefly related in the pamphlet of Cusick, the Tuscarora, and after him by Mr. Schoolcraft, in his *Notes* The curious work of Cusick will again be referred to.

multitudes by his pestilential breath. Mortally wounded at length by the magic arrow of a child, he rolled down the steep, sweeping away the forest with his writhings, and plunging into the lake below, where he lashed the black waters till they boiled with blood and foam, and at length, exhausted with his agony, sank, and perished at the bottom. Under the Falls of Niagara dwelt the Spirit of the Thunder, with his brood of giant sons; and the Iroquois trembled in their villages when, amid the blackening shadows of the storm, they heard his deep shout roll along the firmament.

The energy of fancy, whence these barbarous creations drew their birth, displayed itself, at a later period, in that peculiar eloquence which the wild democracy of the Iroquois tended to call forth, and to which the mountain and the forest, the torrent and the storm, lent their stores of noble imagery. That to this imaginative vigor was joined mental power of a different stamp, is witnessed by the caustic irony of Garangula and Sagoyewatha, and no less by the subtle policy, sagacious as it was treacherous, which marked the dealings of the Iroquois with surrounding tribes.[1]

[1] For traditions of the Iroquois see Schoolcraft, *Notes*, Chap. IX. Cusick, *History of the Five Nations*, and Clark, *Hist. Onondaga*, I.

Cusick was an old Tuscarora Indian, who, being disabled by an accident from active occupations, essayed to become the historian of his people, and produced a small pamphlet, written in a language almost unintelligible, and filled with a medley of traditions in which a few grains of truth are inextricably mingled with a tangled mass of absurdities. He relates the monstrous legends of his people with an air of implicit faith, and traces the presiding sachems of the confederacy in regular descent from the first Atotarho downwards. His work, which was printed

With all this mental superiority, the arts of life among them had not emerged from their primitive rudeness ; and their coarse pottery, their spear and arrow heads of stone, were in no way superior to those of many other tribes.   Their agriculture deserves a higher praise.   In 1696, the invading army of Count Frontenac found the maize fields extending a league and a half or two leagues from their villages ; and, in 1779, the troops of General Sullivan were filled with amazement at their abundant stores of corn, beans, and squashes, and at the old apple orchards which grew around their settlements.

Their dwellings and works of defence were far from contemptible, either in their dimensions or in their structure ; and though by the several attacks of the French, and especially by the invasion of De Nonville, in 1687, and of Frontenac, nine years later, their fortified towns were levelled to the earth, never again to reappear ; yet, in the works of Champlain and other early writers we find abundant evidence of their pristine condition.   Along the banks of the Mohawk, among the hills and hollows of Onondaga, in the forests of Oneida and Cayuga, on the romantic shores of Seneca Lake and the rich borders of the Genessee, surrounded by waving maize fields, and encircled from afar by the green margin of the forest, stood the ancient strongholds of the confederacy.   The clustering dwellings were

at the Tuscarora village, near Lewiston, in 1828, is illustrated by several rude engravings representing the Stone Giants, the Flying Heads, and other traditional monsters.

encompassed by palisades, in single, double, or triple rows, pierced with loopholes, furnished with platforms within, for the convenience of the defenders, with magazines of stones to hurl upon the heads of the enemy, and with water conductors to extinguish any fire which might be kindled from without.[1]

The area which these defences enclosed was often several acres in extent, and the dwellings, ranged in order within, were sometimes more than a hundred feet in length. Posts, firmly driven into the ground, with an intervening framework of poles, formed the basis of the structure; and its sides and arched roof were closely covered with layers of elm bark. Each of the larger dwellings contained several distinct families, whose separate fires were built along the central space, while compartments on each side, like the stalls of a stable, afforded some degree of privacy. Here, rude couches were prepared, and bear and deer skins spread; while above, the ripened ears of maize, suspended in rows, formed a golden tapestry.[2]

---

[1] Lafitau, *Mœurs des Sauvages Ameriquains*, II. 4–10.

Frontenac, in his expedition against the Onondagas, in 1696 (see Official Journal, *Doc Hist New York*, I 332), found one of their villages built in an oblong form, with four bastions. The wall was formed of three rows of palisades, those of the outer row being forty or fifty feet high. The usual figure of the Iroquois villages was circular or oval, and in this instance the bastions were no doubt the suggestion of some European adviser.

[2] Bartram gives the following account of the great council-house at Onondaga, which he visited in 1743. —

"We alighted at the council-house, where the chiefs were already assembled to receive us, which they did with a grave, cheerful complaisance, according to their custom; they shew'd us where to lay our baggage, and repose ourselves during our stay with them; which was in the two end apartments of this large house. The Indians that came with us

In the long evenings of midwinter, when in the
wilderness without the trees cracked with biting
cold, and the forest paths were clogged with snow,
then, around the lodge-fires of the Iroquois, warriors, squaws, and restless naked children were
clustered in social groups, each dark face brighten-
ing in the fickle firelight, while, with jest and laugh,
the pipe passed round from hand to hand. Perhaps
some shrivelled old warrior, the story-teller of the
tribe, recounted to attentive ears the deeds of ancient heroism, legends of spirits and monsters, or
tales of witches and vampires — superstitions not
less rife among this all-believing race, than among
the nations of the transatlantic world.

The life of the Iroquois, though void of those
multiplying phases which vary the routine of civilized existence, was one of sharp excitement and
sudden contrast. The chase, the war-path, the

were placed over against us   This cabin is about eighty feet long and
seventeen broad, the common passage six feet wide, and the apartments
on each side five feet, raised a foot above the passage by a long sapling,
hewed square, and fitted with joists that go from it to the back of the
house ; on these joists they lay large pieces of bark, and on extraordinary
occasions spread mats made of rushes ᛫ this favor we had ; on these floors
they set or lye down, every one as he will ; the apartments are divided
from each other by boards or bark, six or seven foot long, from the lower
floor to the upper, on which they put their lumber ; when they have eaten
their homony, as they set in each apartment before the fire, they can put
the bowl over head, having not above five foot to reach ; they set on the
floor sometimes at each end, but mostly at one ; they have a shed to put
their wood into in the winter, or in the summer to set to converse or
play, that has a door to the south ; all the sides and roof of the cabin are
made of bark, bound fast to poles set in the ground, and bent round on the
top, or set aflatt, for the roof, as we set our rafters ; over each fireplace
they leave a hole to let out the smoke, which, in rainy weather, they
cover with a piece of bark. and this they can easily reach with a pole to
push it on one side or quite over the hole ; after this model are most of
their cabins built." — Bartram, *Observations*. 40.

dance, the festival, the game of hazard, the race of political ambition, all had their votaries. When the assembled sachems had resolved on war against some foreign tribe, and when, from their great council-house of bark, in the Valley of Onondaga, their messengers had gone forth to invite the warriors to arms, then from east to west, through the farthest bounds of the confederacy, a thousand warlike hearts caught up the summons. With fasting and praying, and consulting dreams and omens; with invoking the war god, and dancing the war-dance, the warriors sought to insure the triumph of their arms; and then, their rites concluded, they began their stealthy progress through the devious pathways of the forest. For days and weeks, in anxious expectation, the villagers awaited the result. And now, as evening closed, a shrill, wild cry, pealing from afar, over the darkening forest, proclaimed the return of the victorious warriors. The village was alive with sudden commotion; and snatching sticks and stones, knives and hatchets, men, women, and children, yelling like fiends let loose, swarmed out of the narrow portal, to visit upon the captives a foretaste of the deadlier torments in store for them. The black arches of the forest glowed with the fires of death; and with brandished torch and firebrand the frenzied multitude closed around their victim. The pen shrinks to write, the heart sickens to conceive, the fierceness of his agony; yet still, amid the din of his tormentors, rose his clear voice of scorn and defiance. The work was done; the blackened trunk was flung to the dogs, and, with clamorous shouts and hootings, the murderers sought to drive away the spirit of their victim.[1]

The Iroquois reckoned these barbarities among their most exquisite enjoyments ; and yet they had other sources of pleasure, which made up in frequency and in innocence what they lacked in intensity. Each passing season had its feasts and dances, often mingling religion with social pastime. The young had their frolics and merry-makings ; and the old had their no less frequent councils, where conversation and laughter alternated with grave deliberations for the public weal. There were also stated periods marked by the recurrence of momentous ceremonies, in which the whole community took part — the mystic sacrifice of the dogs, the orgies of the dream feast, and the loathsome festival of the exhumation of the dead. Yet in the intervals of war and hunting, these resources would often fail ; and, while the women were toiling in the cornfields, the lazy warriors beguiled

---

[1] "Being at this place the 17 of June, there came fifty prisoners from the south-westward. They were of two nations, some whereof have few guns; the other none at all. One nation is about ten days' journey from any Christians, and trade onely with one greatt house, nott farr from the sea, and the other trade onely, as they say, with a black people. This day of them was burnt two women, and a man and a child killed with a stone. Att night we heard a great noyse as if yᵉ houses had all fallen, butt itt was only yᵉ inhabitants driving away yᵉ ghosts of yᵉ murthered.

"The 18ᵗʰ going to Canagorah, that day there were most cruelly burnt four men, four women and one boy. The cruelty lasted aboutt seven hours When they were almost dead letting them loose to the mercy of yᵉ boys, and taking the hearts of such as were dead to feast on." — Greenhalgh, *Journal,* 1677.

the hours with smoking or sleeping, with gambling or gallantry.[1]

If we seek for a single trait preëminently characteristic of the Iroquois, we shall find it in that boundless pride which impelled them to style themselves, not inaptly as regards their own race, " the men surpassing all others."[2] " Must I," exclaimed one of their great warriors, as he fell wounded among a crowd of Algonquins, — " must I, who have made the whole earth tremble, now die by the hands of children ? " Their power kept pace with their pride. Their war-parties roamed over half America, and their name was a terror from the Atlantic to the Mississippi ; but, when we ask the numerical strength of the dreaded confederacy, when we discover that, in the days of their greatest triumphs, their united cantons could not have mustered four thousand warriors, we stand amazed at the folly and dissension which left so vast a region the prey of a handful of bold marauders. Of the cities and villages now so thickly scattered over the lost domain of the Iroquois, a single one might boast a more numerous population than all the five united tribes.[3]

[1] For an account of the habits and customs of the Iroquois, the following works, besides those already cited, may be referred to : —
Charlevoix, *Letters to the Duchess of Lesdiguières*; Champlain, *Voyages de la Nouv. France*; Clark, *Hist. Onondaga*, I., and several volumes of the Jesuit *Relations*, especially those of 1656–1657 and 1659–1660.

[2] This is Colden's translation of the word Ongwehonwe, one of the names of the Iroquois.

[3] La Hontan estimated the Iroquois at from five thousand to seven thousand fighting men ; but his means of information were very imperfect, and the same may be said of several other French writers, who have overrated the force of the confederacy. In 1677, the English sent

From this remarkable people, who with all the ferocity of their race blended heroic virtues and marked endowments of intellect, I pass to other members of the same great family, whose different fortunes may perhaps be ascribed rather to the force of circumstance, than to any intrinsic inferiority.

The peninsula between the Lakes Huron, Erie, and Ontario was occupied by two distinct peoples, speaking dialects of the Iroquois tongue. The Hurons or Wyandots, including the tribe called by the French the Dionondadies, or Tobacco Nation,[1] dwelt among the forests which bordered the eastern shores of the fresh water sea, to which they have left their name; while the Neutral Nation, so called from their neutrality in the war between the Hurons and the Five Nations, inhabited the northern shores of Lake Erie, and even extended their eastern flank across the strait of Niagara.

The population of the Hurons has been variously stated at from ten thousand to thirty thousand souls, but probably did not exceed the former esti-

---

one Greenhalgh to ascertain their numbers. He visited all their towns and villages, and reported their aggregate force at two thousand one hundred and fifty fighting men. The report of Colonel Coursey, agent from Virginia, at about the same period, closely corresponds with this statement. Greenhalgh's Journal will be found in Chalmers's *Political Annals*, and in the *Documentary History of New York*. Subsequent estimates, up to the period of the Revolution, when their strength had much declined, vary from twelve hundred to two thousand one hundred and twenty. Most of these estimates are given by Clinton, in his *Discourse on the Five Nations*, and several by Jefferson, in his *Notes on Virginia*.

[1] Hurons, Wyandots, Yendots, Ouendaets, Quatogies.

The Dionondadies are also designated by the following names: Tionontatez, Petuneux — Nation of Tobacco.

mate. The Franciscans and the Jesuits were early among them, and from their descriptions it is apparent that, in legends and superstitions, manners and habits, religious observances and social customs, they were closely assimilated to their brethren of the Five Nations. Their capacious dwellings of bark, and their palisaded forts, seemed copied after the same model.[1] Like the Five Nations, they were divided into tribes, and cross-divided into totemic clans ; and, as with them, the office of sachem descended in the female line. The same crude materials of a political fabric were to be found in both ; but, unlike the Iroquois, the Wyandots had not as yet.wrought them into a system, and woven them into a harmonious whole.

Like the Five Nations, the Wyandots were in some measure an agricultural people ; they bartered the surplus products of their maize fields to surrounding tribes, usually receiving fish in exchange ; and this traffic was so considerable, that the Jesuits styled their country the Granary of the Algonquins.[2]

Their prosperity was rudely broken by the hostilities of the Five Nations ; for though the conflicting parties were not ill matched in point of numbers, yet the united counsels and ferocious energies of the confederacy swept all before them. In the year 1649, in the depth of winter, their

---

[1] See Sagard, *Hurons*, 115.

[2] Bancroft, in his chapter on the Indians east of the Mississippi, falls into a mistake when he says that no trade was carried on by any of the tribes. For an account of the traffic between the Hurons and Algonquins, see Mercier, *Relation des Hurons*, 1637, p. 171.

warriors invaded the country of the Wyandots, stormed their largest villages, and involved all within in indiscriminate slaughter.[1] The survivors fled in panic terror, and the whole nation was broken and dispersed.

Some found refuge among the French of Canada, where, at the village of Lorette, near Quebec, their descendants still remain; others were incorporated with their conquerors; while others again fled northward, beyond Lake Superior, and sought an asylum among the wastes which bordered on the north-eastern bands of the Dahcotah. Driven back by those fierce bison-hunters, they next established themselves about the outlet of Lake Superior, and the shores and islands in the northern parts of Lake Huron. Thence, about the year 1680, they descended to Detroit, where they formed a permanent settlement, and where, by their superior valor, capacity, and address, they soon acquired an ascendency over the surrounding Algonquins.

The ruin of the Neutral Nation followed close on that of the Wyandots, to whom, according to Jesuit authority, they bore an exact resemblance in character and manners.[2] The Senecas soon found means to pick a quarrel with them; they were assailed by all the strength of the insatiable confederacy, and within a few years their destruction as a nation was complete.

South of Lake Erie dwelt two members of the

[1] See "Jesuits in North America."
[2] According to Lallemant, the population of the Neutral Nation amounted to at least twelve thousand; but the estimate is probably exaggerated. — *Relation des Hurons*, 1641, p. 50.

Iroquois family.   The Andastes built their fortified villages along the valley of the Lower Susquehanna; while the Erigas, or Eries, occupied the borders of the lake which still retains their name. Of these two nations little is known, for the Jesuits had no missions among them, and few traces of them survive beyond their names and the record of their destruction.   The war with the Wyandots was scarcely over, when the Five Nations turned their arms against their Erie brethren.

In the year 1655, using their canoes as scaling ladders, they stormed the Erie stronghold, leaped down like tigers among the defenders, and butchered them without mercy.[1]   The greater part of the nation was involved in the massacre, and the remnant was incorporated with the conquerors, or with other tribes, to which they fled for refuge. The ruin of the Andastes came next in turn; but this brave people fought for twenty years against their inexorable assailants, and their destruction was not consummated until the year 1672, when they shared the fate of the rest.[2]

Thus, within less than a quarter of a century, four nations, the most brave and powerful of the North American savages, sank before the arms of the confederates.   Nor did their triumphs end here.   Within the same short space they subdued

---

[1] The Iroquois traditions on this subject, as related to the writer by a chief of the Cayugas, do not agree with the narratives of the Jesuits. It is not certain that the Eries were of the Iroquois family.   There is some reason to believe them Algonquins, and possibly identical with the Shawanoes.

[2] Charlevoix, *Nouvelle France*, I. 443

their southern neighbors the Lenape,[1] the leading members of the Algonquin family, and expelled the Ottawas, a numerous people of the same lineage, from the borders of the river which bears their name. In the north, the west, and the south, their conquests embraced every adjacent tribe; and meanwhile their war parties were harassing the French of Canada with reiterated inroads, and yelling the war-whoop under the walls of Quebec.

They were the worst of conquerors. Inordinate pride, the lust of blood and dominion, were the mainsprings of their warfare; and their victories were stained with every excess of savage passion. That their triumphs must have cost them dear; that, in spite of their cautious tactics, these multiplied conflicts must have greatly abridged· their strength, would appear inevitable. Their losses were, in fact, considerable; but every breach was repaired by means of a practice to which they, in common with other tribes, constantly adhered. When their vengeance was glutted by the sacrifice of a sufficient number of captives, they spared the lives of the remainder, and adopted them as members of their confederated ·tribes, separating wives from husbands, and children from parents, and distributing them among different villages, in order that old ties and associations might be more completely broken up. This policy is said to have been designated among them by a name which signifies " flesh cut into pieces and scattered among the tribes."

---

[1] Gallatin places the final subjection of the Lenape at about the year 1750 — a printer's error for 1650. — *Synopsis*, 48.

In the years 1714–15, the confederacy received a great accession of strength. Southwards, about the headwaters of the rivers Neuse and Tar, and separated from their kindred tribes by intervening Algonquin communities, dwelt the Tuscaroras, a warlike people belonging to the generic stock of the Iroquois. The wrongs inflicted by white settlers, and their own undistinguishing vengeance, involved them in a war with the colonists, which resulted in their defeat and expulsion. They emigrated to the Five Nations, whose allies they had been in former wars with southern tribes, and who now gladly received them, admitting them as a sixth nation, into their confederacy.

It is a remark of Gallatin, that, in their career of conquest, the Five Nations encountered more stubborn resistance from the tribes of their own family, than from those of a different lineage. In truth, all the scions of this warlike stock seem endued with singular vitality and force, and among them we must seek for the best type of the Indian character. Few tribes could match them in prowess, constancy, moral energy, or intellectual vigor. The Jesuits remarked that they were more intelligent, yet less tractable, than other savages; and Charlevoix observes that, though the Algonquins were readily converted, they made but fickle proselytes; while the Hurons, though not easily won over to the church, were far more faithful in their adherence.[1] Of this tribe, the Hurons or Wyandots, a candid and experienced observer declares,

---

[1] *Nouvelle France,* I. 196

that of all the Indians with whom he was conversant, they alone held it disgraceful to turn from the face of an enemy when the fortunes of the fight were adverse.[1]

Besides these inherent qualities, the tribes of the Iroquois race derived great advantages from their superior social organization. They were all, more or less, tillers of the soil, and were thus enabled to concentrate a more numerous population than the scattered tribes who live by the chase alone. In their well-peopled and well-constructed villages, they dwelt together the greater part of the year; and thence the religious rites and social and political usages, which elsewhere existed only in the germ, attained among them a full development. Yet these advantages were not without alloy, and the Jesuits were not slow to remark that the stationary and thriving Iroquois were more loose in their observance of social ties, than the wandering and starving savages of the north.[2]

THE ALGONQUIN FAMILY.

Except the detached nation of the Tuscaroras, and a few smaller tribes adhering to them, the Iroquois family was confined to the region south of the Lakes Erie and Ontario, and the peninsula east

---

[1] William Henry Harrison, *Discourse on the Aborigines of the Ohio.* See *Ohio Hist. Trans. Part Second,* I. 257.

[2] " Here ye Indyans were very desirous to see us ride our horses, wch wee did · they made great feasts and dancing, and invited us yt when all ye maides were together, both wee and our Indyans might choose such as lyked us to ly with." — Greenhalgh, *Journal*

of Lake Huron. They formed, as it were, an island in the vast expanse of Algonquin population, extending from Hudson's Bay on the north to the Carolinas on the south; from the Atlantic on the east to the Mississippi and Lake Winnipeg on the west. They were Algonquins who greeted Jacques Cartier, as his ships ascended the St. Lawrence. The first British colonists found savages of the same race hunting and fishing along the coasts and inlets of Virginia; and it was the daughter of an Algonquin chief who interceded with her father for the life of the adventurous Englishman. They were Algonquins who, under Sassacus the Pequot, and Philip of Mount Hope, waged war against the Puritans of New England; who dwelt at Penacook, under the rule of the great magician, Passaconaway, and trembled before the evil spirits of the White Hills; and who sang *aves* and told their beads in the forest chapel of Father Rasles, by the banks of the Kennebec. They were Algonquins who, under the great tree at Kensington, made the covenant of peace with William Penn; and when French Jesuits and fur-traders explored the Wabash and the Ohio, they found their valleys tenanted by the same far-extended race. At the present day, the traveller, perchance, may find them pitching their bark lodges along the beach at Mackinaw, spearing fish among the rapids of St. Mary's, or skimming the waves of Lake Superior in their birch canoes.

Of all the members of the Algonquin family, those called by the English the Delawares, by the

French the Loups, and by themselves Lenni Lenape, or Original Men, hold the first claim to
attention ; for their traditions declare them to be
the parent stem whence other Algonquin tribes have
sprung. The latter recognized the claim, and, at
all solemn councils, accorded to the ancestral tribe
the title of Grandfather.[1]

The first European colonists found the conical
lodges of the Lenape clustered in frequent groups
about the waters of the Delaware and its tributary
streams, within the present limits of New Jersey,
and Eastern Pennsylvania. The nation was separated into three divisions, and three sachems formed
a triumvirate, who, with the council of old men,
regulated all its affairs.[2] They were, in some small
measure, an agricultural people ; but fishing and
the chase were their chief dependence, and through
a great part of the year they were scattered abroad,
among forests and streams, in search of sustenance.

When William Penn held his far-famed council
with the sachems of the Lenape, he extended the
hand of brotherhood to a people as unwarlike in
their habits as his own pacific followers. This is
by no means to be ascribed to any inborn love of
peace. The Lenape were then in a state of degrad-
ing vassalage to the Five Nations, who, that they
might drain to the dregs the cup of humiliation,

---

[1] The Lenape, on their part, call the other Algonquin tribes Children,
Grandchildren, Nephews, or Younger Brothers ; but they confess the
superiority of the Wyandots and the Five Nations, by yielding them the
title of Uncles. They, in return, call the Lenape Nephews, or more frequently Cousins.

[2] Loskiel, Part I. 130.

had forced them to assume the name of Women,
and forego the use of arms.[1] Dwelling under the
shadow of the tyrannical confederacy, they were
long unable to wipe out the blot; but at length,
pushed from their ancient seats by the encroachments of white men, and removed westward, partially beyond the reach of their conquerors, their
native spirit began to revive, and they assumed a
tone of defiance. During the Old French War
they resumed the use of arms, and while the Five
Nations fought for the English, they espoused the
cause of France. At the opening of the Revolution, they boldly asserted their freedom from the
yoke of their conquerors; and a few years after,
the Five Nations confessed, at a public council, that
the Lenape were no longer women, but men.[2]
Ever since that period, they have stood in high
repute for bravery, generosity, and all the savage
virtues; and the settlers of the frontier have often
found, to their cost, that the *women* of the Iroquois
have been transformed into a race of formidable
warriors. At the present day, the small remnant
settled beyond the Mississippi are among the bravest
marauders of the west Their war-parties pierce the
farthest wilds of the Rocky Mountains; and the

---

[1] The story told by the Lenape themselves, and recorded with the
utmost good faith by Loskiel and Heckewelder, that the Five Nations
had not conquered them, but, by a cunning artifice, had cheated them
into subjection, is wholly unworthy of credit. It is not to be believed that
a people so acute and suspicious could be the dupes of so palpable a trick;
and it is equally incredible that a high-spirited tribe could be induced, by
the most persuasive rhetoric, to assume the name of Women, which in
Indian eyes is the last confession of abject abasement.

[2] Heckewelder, *Hist. Ind. Nat.* 53.

prairie traveller may sometimes meet the Delaware warrior returning from a successful foray, a gaudy handkerchief bound about his brows, his snake locks fluttering in the wind, and his rifle resting across his saddle-bow, while the tarnished and begrimed equipments of his half-wild horse bear witness that the rider has waylaid and plundered some Mexican cavalier.

Adjacent to the Lenape, and associated with them in some of the most notable passages of their history, dwelt the Shawanoes, the Chaouanons of the French, a tribe of bold, roving, and adventurous spirit. Their eccentric wanderings, their sudden appearances and disappearances, perplex the antiquary, and defy research; but from various scattered notices, we may gather that at an early period they occupied the valley of the Ohio; that, becoming embroiled with the Five Nations, they shared the defeat of the Andastes, and about the year 1672 fled to escape destruction. Some found an asylum in the country of the Lenape, where they lived tenants at will of the Five Nations; others sought refuge in the Carolinas and Florida, where, true to their native instincts, they soon came to blows with the owners of the soil. Again, turning northwards, they formed new settlements in the valley of the Ohio, where they were now suffered to dwell in peace, and where, at a later period, they were joined by such of their brethren as had found refuge among the Lenape.[1]

[1] The evidence concerning the movements of the Shawanoes is well summed up by Gallatin, *Synopsis*, 65. See also Drake, *Life of Tecumseh*, 10

Of the tribes which, single and detached, or co-
hering in loose confederacies, dwelt within the
limits of Lower Canada, Acadia, and New England,
it is needless to speak; for they offered no distinctive traits demanding notice. Passing the country
of the Lenape and the Shawanoes, and descending
the Ohio, the traveller would have found its valley
chiefly occupied by two nations, the Miamis or
Twightwees, on the Wabash and its branches, and
the Illinois, who dwelt in the neighborhood of the
river to which they have given their name, while
portions of them extended beyond the Mississippi.
Though never subjugated, as were the Lenape, both
the Miamis and the Illinois were reduced to the last
extremity by the repeated attacks of the Five Nations; and the Illinois, in particular, suffered so
much by these and other wars, that the population
of ten or twelve thousand, ascribed to them by the
early French writers, had dwindled, during the first
quarter of the eighteenth century, to a few small
villages.[1] According to Marest, they were a people
sunk in sloth and licentiousness; but that priestly
father had suffered much at their hands, and viewed
them with a jaundiced eye. Their agriculture was
not contemptible; they had permanent dwellings
as well as portable lodges; and though wandering
through many months of the year among their
broad prairies and forests, there were seasons when
their whole population was gathered, with feastings

---

[1] Father Rasles, 1723, says that there were eleven. Marest, in 1712,
found only three.

and merry-making, within the limits of their villages.

Turning his course northward, traversing Lakes
Michigan and Superior, and skirting the western
margin of Lake Huron, the voyager would have
found the solitudes of the wild waste around him
broken by scattered lodges of the Ojibwas, Pottawattamies, and Ottawas.   About the bays and rivers
west of Lake Michigan, he would have seen the
Sacs, the Foxes, and the Menomonies; and penetrating the frozen wilderness of the north, he would
have been welcomed by the rude hospitality of the
wandering Crees or Knisteneaux.

The Ojibwas, with their kindred, the Pottawattamies, and their friends the Ottawas, — the latter of
whom were fugitives from the eastward, whence
they had fled from the wrath of the Iroquois, —
were banded into a sort of confederacy.[1]   They
were closely allied in blood, language, manners and
character.   The Ojibwas, by far the most numerous
of the three, occupied the basin of Lake Superior,
and extensive adjacent regions.   In their boundaries, the career of Iroquois conquest found at length
a check.   The fugitive Wyandots sought refuge in
the Ojibwa hunting-grounds; and tradition relates
that, at the outlet of Lake Superior, an Iroquois
war-party once encountered a disastrous repulse.

In their mode of life, they were far more rude
than the Iroquois, or even the southern Algonquin
tribes.   The totemic system is found among them

---

[1] Morse, *Report, Appendix,* 141.

in its most imperfect state. The original clans have become broken into fragments, and indefinitely multiplied; and many of the ancient customs of the institution are but loosely regarded. Agriculture is little known, and, through summer and winter, they range the wilderness with restless wandering, now gorged to repletion, and now perishing with want. In the calm days of summer, the Ojibwa fisherman pushes out his birch canoe upon the great inland ocean of the north; and, as he gazes down into the pellucid depths, he seems like one balanced between earth and sky. The watchful fish-hawk circles above his head; and below, farther than his line will reach, he sees the trout glide shadowy and silent over the glimmering pebbles. The little islands on the verge of the horizon seem now starting into spires, now melting from the sight, now shaping themselves into a thousand fantastic forms, with the strange mirage of the waters; and he fancies that the evil spirits of the lake lie basking their serpent forms on those unhallowed shores. Again, he explores the watery labyrinths where the stream sweeps among pine-tufted islands, or runs, black and deep, beneath the shadows of moss-bearded firs; or he drags his canoe upon the sandy beach, and, while his camp-fire crackles on the grass-plat, reclines beneath the trees, and smokes and laughs away the sultry hours, in a lazy luxury of enjoyment.

But when winter descends upon the north, sealing up the fountains, fettering the streams, and turning the green robed forests to shivering nakedness, then, bearing their frail dwellings on their backs, the Ojibwa family wander forth into the wilderness, cheered only on their dreary track by the whistling of the north wind, and the hungry howl of wolves. By the banks of some frozen stream, women and children, men and dogs, lie crouched together around the fire. They spread their benumbed fingers over the embers, while the wind shrieks through the fir-trees like the gale through the rigging of a frigate, and the narrow concave of the wigwam sparkles with the frost-work of their congealed breath. In vain they beat the magic drum, and call upon their guardian manitoes;—the wary moose keeps aloof, the bear lies close in his hollow tree, and famine stares them in the face. And now the hunter can fight no more against the nipping cold and blinding sleet. Stiff and stark, with haggard cheek and shrivelled lip, he lies among the snow drifts; till, with tooth and claw, the famished wildcat strives in vain to pierce the frigid marble of his limbs. Such harsh schooling is thrown away on the incorrigible mind of the northern Algonquin. He lives in misery, as his fathers lived before him. Still, in the brief hour of plenty he forgets the season of want; and still the sleet and the snow descend upon his houseless head.[1]

I have thus passed in brief review the more prom-

[1] See Tanner, Long, and Henry. A comparison of Tanner with the accounts of the Jesuit Le Jeune will show that Algonquin life in Lower Canada, two hundred years ago, was essentially the same with Algonquin life on the Upper Lakes within the last half century.

inent of the Algonquin tribes; those whose strug
gles and sufferings form the theme of the ensuing
History. In speaking of the Iroquois, some of the
distinctive peculiarities of the Algonquins have
already been hinted at. It must be admitted that,
in moral stability and intellectual vigor, they are
inferior to the former; though some of the most
conspicuous offspring of the wilderness, Metacom,
Tecumseh, and Pontiac himself, owned their blood
and language.

The fireside stories of every primitive people are
faithful reflections of the form and coloring of the
national mind; and it is no proof of sound philosophy to turn with contempt from the study of a
fairy tale. The legendary lore of the Iroquois,
black as the midnight forests, awful in its gloomy
strength, is but another manifestation of that spirit
of mastery which uprooted whole tribes from the
earth, and deluged the wilderness with blood. The
traditionary tales of the Algonquins wear a different aspect. The credulous circle around an Ojibwa
lodge-fire listened to wild recitals of necromancy
and witchcraft — men transformed to beasts, and
beasts transformed to men, animated trees, and
birds who spoke with human tongue. They heard
of malignant sorcerers dwelling among the lonely
islands of spell-bound lakes; of grisly *weendigoes*,
and bloodless *geebi*; of evil *manitoes* lurking in the
dens and fastnesses of the woods; of pygmy champions, diminutive in stature but mighty in soul, who,
by the potency of charm and talisman, subdued the
direst monsters of the waste; and of heroes, who,

not by downright force and open onset, but by subtle strategy, tricks, or magic art, achieved marvellous
triumphs over the brute force of their assailants.
Sometimes the tale will breathe a different spirit,
and tell of orphan children abandoned in the heart
of a hideous wilderness, beset with fiends and cannibals. Some enamored maiden, scornful of earthly suitors, plights her troth to the graceful manito
of the grove ; or bright aerial beings, dwellers of
the sky, descend to tantalize the gaze of mortals
with evanescent forms of loveliness.

The mighty giant, the God of the Thunder, who
made his home among the caverns, beneath the cataract of Niagara, was a characteristic conception
of Iroquois imagination. The Algonquins held a
simpler faith, and maintained that the thunder was
a bird who built his nest on the pinnacle of tow-
ering mountains. Two daring boys once scaled the
height, and thrust sticks into the eyes of the por-
tentous nestlings ; which hereupon flashed forth
such wrathful scintillations, that the sticks were
shivered to atoms.[1]

---

[1] For Algonquin legends, see Schoolcraft, in *Algic Researches* and
Oneota Le Jeune early discovered these legends among the tribes of his
mission Two centuries ago, among the Algonquins of Lower Canada, a
tale was related to him, which, in its principal incidents, is identical with
the story of the "Boy who set a Snare for the Sun," recently found by
Mr. Schoolcraft among the tribes of the Upper Lakes. Compare *Relation*,
1637, p. 172, and *Oneota*, p. 75 The coincidence affords a curious proof
of the antiquity and wide diffusion of some of these tales.

The Dacotah, as well as the Algonquins, believe that the thunder is
produced by a bird. A beautiful illustration of this idea will be found in
Mrs. Eastman's *Legends of the Sioux*. An Indian propounded to Le Jeune
a doctrine of his own According to his theory, the thunder is produced
by the eructations of a monstrous giant, who had unfortunately swallowed

The religious belief of the Algonquins — and the remark holds good, not of the Algonquins only, but of all the hunting tribes of America — is a cloudy bewilderment, where we seek in vain for system or coherency.   Among a primitive and savage people, there were no poets to vivify its images, and no priests to give distinctness and harmony to its rites and symbols.   To the Indian mind, all nature was instinct with deity.   A spirit was embodied in every mountain, lake, and cataract; every bird, beast, or reptile, every tree, shrub, or grass-blade, was endued with mystic influence: yet this untutored pantheism did not exclude the conception of certain divinities, of incongruous and ever shifting attributes.   The sun, too, was a god, and the moon was a goddess.   Conflicting powers of good and evil divided the universe: but if, before the arrival of Europeans, the Indian recognized the existence of one, almighty, self-existent Being, the Great Spirit, the Lord of Heaven and Earth, the belief was so vague and dubious as scarcely to deserve the name.   His perceptions of moral good and evil were perplexed and shadowy; and the belief in a state of future reward and punishment was by no means universal.[1]

Of the Indian character, much has been written foolishly, and credulously believed.   By the rhapsodies of poets, the cant of sentimentalists, and the

a quantity of snakes; and the latter falling to the earth, caused the appearance of lightning. " Voilà une philosophie bien nouvelle!" exclaims the astonished Jesuit.

[1] Le Jeune, Schoolcraft, James, Jarvis, Charlevoix, Sagard, Brébeuf, Mercier, Vimont, Lallemant, Lafitau, De Smet, &c.

extravagance of some who should have known better, a counterfeit image has been tricked out, which might seek in vain for its likeness through every corner of the habitable earth; an image bearing no more resemblance to its original, than the monarch of the tragedy and the hero of the epic poem bear to their living prototypes in the palace and the camp. The shadows of his wilderness home, and the darker mantle of his own inscrutable reserve, have made the Indian warrior a wonder and a mystery. Yet to the eye of rational observation there is nothing unintelligible in him. He is full, it is true, of contradiction. He deems himself the centre of greatness and renown; his pride is proof against the fiercest torments of fire and steel; and yet the same man would beg for a dram of whiskey, or pick up a crust of bread thrown to him like a dog, from the tent door of the traveller. At one moment, he is wary and cautious to the verge of cowardice; at the next, he abandons himself to a very insanity of recklessness; and the habitual self-restraint which throws an impenetrable veil over emotion is joined to the unbridled passions of a madman or a beast.

Such inconsistencies, strange as they seem in our eyes, when viewed under a novel aspect, are but the ordinary incidents of humanity. The qualities of the mind are not uniform in their action through all the relations of life. With different men, and different races of men, pride, valor, prudence, have different forms of manifestation, and where in one instance they lie dormant, in another they are keen-

ly awake.   The conjunction of greatness and little-
ness, meanness and pride, is older than the days of
the patriarchs; and such antiquated phenomena,
displayed under a new form in the unreflecting, un-
disciplined mind of a savage, call for no special
wonder, but should rather be classed with the other
enigmas of the fathomless human heart.   The dis-
secting knife of a Rochefoucault might lay bare
matters of no less curious observation in the breast
of every man.

Nature has stamped the Indian with a hard and
stern physiognomy.   Ambition, revenge, envy, jealousy, are his ruling passions; and his cold temperament is little exposed to those effeminate vices
which are the bane of milder races.   With him
revenge is an overpowering instinct; nay, more, it
is a point of honor and a duty.   His pride sets all
language at defiance.   He loathes the thought of
coercion; and few of his race have ever stooped to
discharge a menial office.   A wild love of liberty,
an utter intolerance of control, lie at the basis of
his character, and fire his whole existence.   Yet,
in spite of this haughty independence, he is a devout hero-worshipper; and high achievement in
war or policy touches a chord to which his nature
never fails to respond.   He looks up with admiring
reverence to the sages and heroes of his tribe; and
it is this principle, joined to the respect for age
springing from the patriarchal element in his
social system, which, beyond all others, contributes
union and harmony to the erratic members of an
Indian community.   With him the love of glory

kindles into a burning passion ; and to allay its
cravings, he will dare cold and famine, fire, tempest,
torture, and death itself.

These generous traits are overcast by much that
is dark, cold, and sinister, by sleepless distrust, and
rankling jealousy. Treacherous himself, he is always suspicious of treachery in others. Brave as
he is, — and few of mankind are braver, — he will
vent his •passion by a secret stab rather than an
open blow. His warfare is full of ambuscade and
stratagem ; and he never rushes into battle with
that joyous self-abandonment, with which the warriors of the Gothic races flung themselves into the
ranks of their enemies. In his feasts and his drinking bouts we find none of that robust and full-toned
mirth, which reigned at the rude carousals of our
barbaric ancestry. He is never jovial in his cups,
and maudlin sorrow or maniacal rage is the sole
result of his potations.

Over all emotion he throws the veil of an iron
self-control, originating in a peculiar form of pride,
and fostered by rigorous discipline from childhood
upward. He is trained to conceal passion, and not
to subdue it. The inscrutable warrior is aptly im-
aged by the hackneyed figure of a volcano covered
with snow ; and no man can say when or where the
wild-fire will burst forth. This shallow self-mastery
serves to give dignity to public deliberation, and
harmony to social life. Wrangling and quarrel are
strangers to an Indian dwelling ; and while an as
sembly of the ancient Gauls was garrulous as a
convocation of magpies, a Roman senate might have

taken a lesson from the grave solemnity of an Indian council. In the midst of his family and friends, he hides affections, by nature none of the most tender, under a mask of icy coldness; and in the torturing fires of his enemy, the haughty sufferer maintains to the last his look of grim defiance.

His intellect is as peculiar as his moral organization. Among all savages, the powers of perception preponderate over those of reason and analysis; but this is more especially the case with the Indian. An acute judge of character, at least of such parts of it as his experience enables him to comprehend; keen to a proverb in all exercises of war and the chase, he seldom traces effects to their causes, or follows out actions to their remote results. Though a close observer of external nature, he no sooner attempts to account for her phenomena than he involves himself in the most ridiculous absurdities; and quite content with these puerilities, he has not the least desire to push his inquiries further. His curiosity, abundantly active within its own narrow circle, is dead to all things else; and to attempt rousing it from its torpor is but a bootless task. He seldom takes cognizance of general or abstract ideas; and his language has scarcely the power to express them, except through the medium of figures drawn from the external world, and often highly picturesque and forcible. The absence of reflection makes him grossly improvident, and unfits him for pursuing any complicated scheme of war or policy.

Some races of men seem moulded in wax, soft
and melting, at once plastic and feeble. Some
races, like some metals, combine the greatest flexi-
bility with the greatest strength. But the Indian
is hewn out of a rock. You can rarely change the
form without destruction of the substance. Races
of inferior energy have possessed a power of expan-
sion and assimilation to which he is a stranger;
and it is this fixed and rigid quality which has
proved his ruin. He will not learn the arts of civilization, and he and his forest must perish together.
The stern, unchanging features of his mind excite
our admiration from their very immutability; and
we look with deep interest on the fate of this irre-
claimable son of the wilderness, the child who
will not be weaned from the breast of his rugged
mother. And our interest increases when we discern in the unhappy wanderer the germs of heroic
virtues mingled among his vices, — a hand boun-
tiful to bestow as it is rapacious to seize, and
even in extremest famine, imparting its last morsel
to a fellow-sufferer; a heart which, strong in
friendship as in hate, thinks it not too much to lay
down life for its chosen comrade; a soul true to
its own idea of honor, and burning with an un-
quenchable thirst for greatness and renown.

The imprisoned lion in the showman's cage differs not more widely from the lord of the desert,
than the beggarly frequenter of frontier garrisons
and dramshops differs from the proud denizen of
the woods. It is in his native wilds alone that the
Indian must be seen and studied. Thus to depict

him is the aim of the ensuing History; and if, from the shades of rock and forest, the savage features should look too grimly forth, it is because the clouds of a tempestuous war have cast upon the picture their murky shadows and lurid fires.

CHAPTER II.

1608–1763.

FRANCE AND ENGLAND IN AMERICA.

The American colonies of France and England grew up to maturity under widely different auspices. Canada, the offspring of Church and State, nursed from infancy in the lap of power, its puny strength fed with artificial stimulants, its movements guided by rule and discipline, its limbs trained to martial exercise, languished, in spite of all, from the lack of vital sap and energy. The colonies of England, outcast and neglected, but strong in native vigor and self-confiding courage, grew yet more strong with conflict and with striving, and developed the rugged proportions and unwieldy strength of a youthful giant.

In the valley of the St. Lawrence, and along the coasts of the Atlantic, adverse principles contended for the mastery. Feudalism stood arrayed against Democracy; Popery against Protestantism; the sword against the ploughshare. The priest, the soldier, and the noble, ruled in Canada. The ignorant, light-hearted Canadian peasant knew nothing and cared nothing about popular rights and civil liberties. Born to obey, he lived in contented submission, without the wish or the capacity for self-rule. Power, centered in the heart of the system, left the masses inert. The settlements along the margin of the St. Lawrence were like a camp, where an army lay at rest, ready for the march or the battle, and where war and adventure, not trade and tillage, seemed the chief aims of life. The lords of the soil were petty nobles, for the most part soldiers, or the sons of soldiers, proud and ostentatious, thriftless and poor ; and the people were their vassals. Over every cluster of small white houses glittered the sacred emblem of the cross. The church, the convent, and the roadside shrine were seen at every turn ; and in the towns and villages, one met each moment the black robe of the Jesuit, the gray garb of the Recollet, and the formal habit of the Ursuline nun. The names of saints, St. Joseph, St. Ignatius, St. Francis, were perpetuated in the capes, rivers, and islands, the forts and villages of the land ; and with every day, crowds of simple worshippers knelt in adoration before the countless altars of the Roman faith.

If we search the world for the sharpest contrast to the spiritual and temporal vassalage of Canada, we shall find it among her immediate neighbors, the Puritans of New England, where the spirit of non-conformity was sublimed to a fiery essence, and where the love of liberty and the hatred of power burned with sevenfold heat. The English colonist, with thoughtful brow and limbs hardened with toil ; calling no man master, yet bowing rev-

erently to the law which he himself had made ;
patient and laborious, and seeking for the solid
comforts rather than the ornaments of life ; no
lover of war, yet, if need were, fighting with a
stubborn, indomitable courage, and then bending
once more with steadfast energy to his farm, or his
merchandise, — such a man might well be deemed
the very pith and marrow of a commonwealth.

In every quality of efficiency and strength, the
Canadian fell miserably below his rival ; but in all
that pleases the eye and interests the imagination,
he far surpassed him.   Buoyant and gay, like his
ancestry of France, he made the frozen wilderness
ring with merriment, answered the surly howling
of the pine forest with peals of laughter, and
warmed with revelry the groaning ice of the St.
Lawrence.   Careless and thoughtless, he lived
happy in the midst of poverty, content if he could
but gain the means to fill his tobacco-pouch, and
decorate the cap of his mistress with a ribbon.
The example of a beggared nobility, who, proud
and penniless, could only assert their rank by
idleness and ostentation, was not lost upon him.
A rightful heir to French bravery and French restlessness, he had an eager love of wandering and
adventure ; and this propensity found ample scope
in the service of the fur-trade, the engrossing occupation and chief source of income to the colony.
When the priest of St. Ann's had shrived him of
his sins ; when, after the parting carousal, he em
barked with his comrades in the deep-laden canoe ;
when their oars kept time to the measured cadence

of their song, and the blue, sunny bosom of the Ottawa opened before them ; when their frail bark quivered among the milky foam and black rocks of the rapid ; and when, around their camp-fire, they wasted half the night with jests and laughter, — then the Canadian was in his element. His foot-steps explored the farthest hiding-places of the wilderness. In the evening dance, his red cap mingled with the scalp-locks and feathers of the Indian braves ; or, stretched on a bear-skin by the side of his dusky mistress, he watched the gambols of his hybrid offspring, in happy oblivion of the partner whom he left unnumbered leagues behind.

The fur-trade engendered a peculiar class of rest-less bush-rangers, more akin to Indians than to white men. Those who had once felt the fascina-tions of the forest were unfitted ever after for a life of quiet labor ; and with this spirit the whole colony was infected. From this cause, no less than from occasional wars with the English, and re-peated attacks of the Iroquois, the agriculture of the country was sunk to a low ebb ; while feudal exactions, a ruinous system of monopoly, and the intermeddlings of arbitrary power, cramped every branch of industry.[1] Yet, by the zeal of priests and the daring enterprise of soldiers and explorers, Canada, though sapless and infirm, spread forts

---

[1] Raynal. *Hist. Indies*, VII. 87 (Lond. 1783).

Charlevoix, *Voyages, Letter* X.

The Swedish traveller Kalm gives an interesting account of manners in Canada, about the middle of the eighteenth century. For the feudal tenure as existing in Canada, see Bouchette, I. Chap XIV. (Lond. 1831), and Garneau, *Hist. Canada*, Book III. Chap. III.

and missions through all the western wilderness. Feebly rooted in the soil, she thrust out branches which overshadowed half America ; a magnificent object to the eye, but one which the first whirl-wind would prostrate in the dust.

Such excursive enterprise was alien to the genius of the British colonies. Daring activity was rife among them, but it did not aim at the founding of military outposts and forest missions. By the force of energetic industry, their population swelled with an unheard-of rapidity, their wealth increased in a yet greater ratio, and their promise of future great-ness opened with every advancing year. But it was a greatness rather of peace than of war. The free institutions, the independence of authority, which were the source of their increase, were ad-verse to that unity of counsel and promptitude of action which are the soul of war. It was far other-wise with their military rival. France had her Canadian forces well in hand. They had but one will, and that was the will of a mistress. Now here, now there, in sharp and rapid onset, they could assail the cumbrous masses and unwieldy strength of their antagonists, as the king-bird attacks the eagle, or the sword-fish the whale. Between two such combatants the strife must needs be a long one.

Canada was a true child of the Church, baptized in infancy and faithful to the last. Champlain, the founder of Quebec, a man of noble spirit, a states-man and a soldier, was deeply imbued with fervid piety. " The saving of a soul," he would often

say, "is worth more than the conquest of an empire;"[1] and to forward the work of conversion,
he brought with him four Franciscan monks from
France. At a later period, the task of colonization would have been abandoned, but for the hope
of casting the pure light of the faith over the
gloomy wastes of heathendom.[2] All France was
filled with the zeal of proselytism. Men and women of exalted rank lent their countenance to the
holy work. From many an altar daily petitions
were offered for the well-being of the mission;
and in the Holy House of Mont-Martre, a nun lay
prostrate day and night before the shrine, praying
for the conversion of Canada.[3] In one convent,
thirty nuns offered themselves for the labors of the
wilderness; and priests flocked in crowds to the
colony.[4] The powers of darkness took alarm; and
when a ship, freighted with the apostles of the
faith, was tempest-tost upon her voyage, the storm
was ascribed to the malice of demons, trembling
for the safety of their ancient empire.

The general enthusiasm was not without its
fruits. The Church could pay back with usury all
that she received of aid and encouragement from
the temporal power; and the ambition of Riche-
lieu could not have devised a more efficient
enginery for the accomplishment of its schemes,

---

[1] Charlevoix, *Nouv. France,* I. 197.

[2] Charlevoix, I. 198

[3] A D 1635 *Relation des Hurons,* 1636, p. 2.

[4] "Vivre en la Nouvelle France c'est à vray dire vivre dans le sein
de Dieu" Such are the extravagant words of Le Jeune, in his report of
the year 1635.

than that supplied by the zeal of the devoted prop-
agandists.   The priest and the soldier went hand
in hand; and the cross and the *fleur de lis* were
planted side by side.

Foremost among the envoys of the faith were
the members of that mighty order, who, in another
hemisphere, had already done so much to turn
back the advancing tide of religious freedom, and
strengthen the arm of Rome.   To the Jesuits was
assigned, for many years, the entire charge of the
Canadian missions, to the exclusion of the Franciscans, early laborers in the same barren field.   Inspired with a self-devoting zeal to snatch souls from
perdition, and win new empires to the cross; casting from them every hope of earthly pleasure or
earthly aggrandizement, the Jesuit fathers buried
themselves in deserts, facing death with the courage
of heroes, and enduring torments with the constancy
of martyrs.   Their story is replete with marvels —
miracles of patient suffering and daring enterprise.
They were the pioneers of Northern America.[1]
We see them among the frozen forests of Acadia,
struggling on snow-shoes, with some wandering
Algonquin horde, or crouching in the crowded
hunting-lodge, half stifled in the smoky den, and
battling with troops of famished dogs for the last
morsel of sustenance.   Again we see the black-
robed priest wading among the white rapids of
the Ottawa, toiling with his savage comrades to

---

[1] See Jesuit *Relations* and *Lettres Edifiantes:* also, Charlevoix, *passim;*
Garneau, *Hist. Canada*, Book IV. Chap. II.; and Bancroft, *Hist. U. S.*
Chap. XX.

drag the canoe against the headlong water.   Again, radiant in the vestments of his priestly office. he administers the sacramental bread to kneeling crowds of plumed and painted proselytes in the forests of the Hurons; or, bearing his life in his hand, carries his sacred mission into the strong-holds of the Iroquois, like one who invades un-armed a den of angry tigers.   Jesuit explorers traced the St. Lawrence to its source, and said masses among the solitudes of Lake Superior, where the boldest fur-trader scarcely dared to fol-low.   They planted missions at St. Mary's and at Michillimackinac; and one of their fraternity, the illustrious Marquette, discovered the Missis-sippi, and opened a new theatre to the boundless ambition of France.

The path of the missionary was a thorny and a bloody one; and a life of weary apostleship was often crowned with a frightful martyrdom.   Jean de Brebeuf and Gabriel Lallemant preached the faith among the villages of the Hurons, when their terror-stricken flock were overwhelmed by an irrup-tion of the Iroquois.   The missionaries might have fled; but, true to their sacred function, they re-mained behind to aid the wounded and baptize the dying.   Both were made captive, and both were doomed to the fiery torture.   Brebeuf, a veteran soldier of the cross, met his fate with an undaunted composure, which amazed his murderers.   With unflinching constancy he endured torments too horrible to be recorded, and died calmly as a martyr of the early church, or a war-chief of the Mohawks.

The slender frame of Lallemant, a man younger in years and gentle in spirit, was enveloped in blazing savin-bark. Again and again the fire was extinguished; again and again it was kindled afresh; and with such fiendish ingenuity were his torments protracted, that he lingered for seventeen hours before death came to his relief.[1]

Isaac Jogues, taken captive by the Iroquois, was led from canton to canton, and village to village, enduring fresh torments and indignities at every stage of his progress.[2] Men, women, and children vied with each other in ingenious malignity. Redeemed, at length, by the humane exertions of a Dutch officer, he repaired to France, where his disfigured person and mutilated hands told the story of his sufferings. But the promptings of a sleepless conscience urged him to return and complete the work he had begun; to illumine the moral darkness upon which, during the months of his disastrous captivity, he fondly hoped that he had thrown some rays of light. Once more he bent his footsteps towards the scene of his living martyrdom, saddened with a deep presentiment that he was advancing to his death. Nor were his forebodings untrue. In a village of the Mohawks, the blow of a tomahawk closed his mission and his life.

Such intrepid self-devotion may well call forth

---

[1] Charlevoix, I. 292.   [2] Charlevoix, I. 238- 276.

our highest admiration; but when we seek for the results of these toils and sacrifices, we shall seek in vain. Patience and zeal were thrown away upon lethargic minds and stubborn hearts. The reports of the Jesuits, it is true, display a copious list of conversions; but the zealous fathers reckoned the number of conversions by the number of baptisms; and, as Le Clercq observes, with no less truth than candor, an Indian would be baptized ten times a day for a pint of brandy or a pound of tobacco. Neither can more flattering conclusions be drawn from the alacrity which they showed to adorn their persons with crucifixes and medals. The glitter of the trinkets pleased the fancy of the warrior; and, with the emblem of man's salvation pendent from his neck, he was often at heart as thorough a heathen as when he wore in its place a necklace made of the dried forefingers of his enemies. At the present day, with the exception of a few insignificant bands of converted Indians in Lower Canada, not a vestige of early Jesuit influence can be found among the tribes. The seed was sown upon a rock.[1]

While the church was reaping but a scanty harvest, the labors of the missionaries were fruitful of profit to the monarch of France. The Jesuit led the van of French colonization; and at Detroit, Michillimackinac, St. Mary's, Green Bay, and other outposts of the west, the establishment of a mission was the precursor of military occupancy. In other

[1] For remarks on the futility of Jesuit missionary efforts, see Halkett, *Historical Notes*, Chap. IV.

respects no less, the labors of the wandering missionaries advanced the welfare of the colony. Sagacious and keen of sight, with faculties stimulated by zeal and sharpened by peril, they made faithful report of the temper and movements of the distant tribes among whom they were distributed. The influence which they often gained was exerted in behalf of the government under whose auspices their missions were carried on; and they strenuously labored to win over the tribes to the French alliance, and alienate them from the heretic English. In all things they approved themselves the stanch and steadfast auxiliaries of the imperial power; and the Marquis du Quesne observed of the missionary Picquet, that in his single person he was worth ten regiments.[1]

Among the English colonies, the pioneers of civilization were for the most part rude, yet vigorous men, impelled to enterprise by native restlessness, or lured by the hope of gain. Their range was limited, and seldom extended far beyond the outskirts of the settlements. With Canada it was far otherwise. There was no energy in the bulk of her people. The court and the army supplied the mainsprings of her vital action, and the hands which planted the lilies of France in the heart of the wilderness had never guided the ploughshare or wielded the spade. The love of adventure, the ambition of new discovery, the hope of military advancement, urged men of place and culture to em-

---

[1] Picquet was a priest of St Sulpice. For a sketch of his life, see *Lett. Edif.* XIV.

bark on bold and comprehensive enterprise. Many a gallant gentleman, many a nobleman of France, trod the black mould and oozy mosses of the forest with feet that had pressed the carpets of Versailles. They whose youth had passed in camps and courts grew gray among the wigwams of savages; and the lives of Castine, Joncaire, and Priber[1] are invested with all the interest of romance.

Conspicuous in the annals of Canada stands the memorable name of Robert Cavelier de La Salle, the man who, beyond all his compeers, contributed to expand the boundary of French empire in the west. La Salle commanded at Fort Frontenac, erected near the outlet of Lake Ontario, on its northern shore, and then forming the most advanced military outpost of the colony. Here he dwelt among Indians, and half-breeds, traders, voyageurs, bush-rangers, and Franciscan monks, ruling his little empire with absolute sway, enforcing respect by his energy, but offending many by his rigor. Here he brooded upon the grand design which had long engaged his thoughts. He had resolved to complete the achievement of Father Marquette, to trace the unknown Mississippi to its mouth, to plant the standard of his king in the newly-discovered regions, and found colonies which should make good the sovereignty of France from the Frozen Ocean to Mexico. Ten years of his

---

[1] For an account of Priber, see *Adair*, 240. I have seen mention of this man in contemporary provincial newspapers, where he is sometimes spoken of as a disguised Jesuit. He took up his residence among the Cherokees about the year 1736, and labored to gain them over to the French interest.

early life had passed, it is said, in connection with
the Jesuits, and his strong mind had hardened to
iron under the discipline of that relentless school.
To a sound judgment, and a penetrating sagacity,
he joined a boundless enterprise and an adamantine
constancy of purpose.   But his nature was stern
and austere; he was prone to rule by fear rather
than by love; he took counsel of no man, and
chilled all who approached him by his cold
reserve.

At the close of the year 1678, his preparations
were complete, and he despatched his attendants to
the banks of the river Niagara, whither he soon
followed in person.   Here he began a little fort of
palisades, and was the first military tenant of a spot
destined to momentous consequence in future wars.
Two leagues above the cataract, on the eastern
bank of the river, he built the first vessel which
ever explored the waters of the upper lakes.[1]   Her
name was the Griffin, and her burden was forty-
five tons.   On the seventh of August, 1679, she
began her adventurous voyage amid the speechless
wonder of the Indians, who stood amazed, alike at
the unwonted size of the wooden canoe, at the flash
and roar of the cannon from her decks, and at the
carved figure of a griffin, which sat crouched
upon her prow.   She bore on her course along the
virgin waters of Lake Erie, through the beautiful
windings of the Detroit, and among the restless
billows of Lake Huron, where a furious tempest
had well nigh ingulphed her.   La Salle pursued

---

[1] Sparks, *Life of La Salle*, 21.

his voyage along Lake Michigan in birch canoes, and after protracted suffering from famine and exposure reached its southern extremity on the eighteenth of October.[1]

He led his followers to the banks of the river now called the St. Joseph. Here, again, he built a fort; and here, in after years, the Jesuits placed a mission and the government a garrison. Thence he pushed on into the unknown region of the Illinois; and now dangers and difficulties began to thicken about him. Indians threatened hostility; his men lost heart, clamored, grew mutinous, and repeatedly deserted; and worse than all, nothing was heard of the vessel which had been sent back to Canada for necessary supplies. Weeks wore on, and doubt ripened into certainty. She had foundered among the storms of these wilderness oceans; and her loss seemed to involve the ruin of the enterprise, since it was vain to proceed farther without the expected supplies. In this disastrous crisis, La Salle embraced a resolution characteristic of his intrepid temper. Leaving his men in charge of a subordinate at a fort which he had built on the river Illinois, he turned his face again towards Canada. He traversed on foot more than a thousand miles of frozen forest, crossing rivers, toiling through snow-drifts, wading ice-encumbered swamps, sustaining life by the fruits of the chase, and threatened day and night by lurking enemies. He gained his destination, but it was only to encounter a fresh storm of calamities. His enemies had been busy in his absence; a malicious

[1] Hennepin. *New Discovery* 98 (Lond 1698.)

report had gone abroad that he was dead; his
creditors had seized his property; and the stores on
which he most relied had been wrecked at sea, or
lost among the rapids of the St. Lawrence. Still
he battled against adversity with his wonted vigor,
and in Count Frontenac, the governor of the province, — a spirit kindred to his own, — he found a
firm friend. Every difficulty gave way before him;
and with fresh supplies of men, stores, and ammunition, he again embarked for the Illinois. Rounding the vast circuit of the lakes, he reached the
mouth of the St. Joseph, and hastened with anxious
speed to the fort where he had left his followers.
The place was empty. Not a man remained.
Terrified, despondent, mutinous, and embroiled in
Indian wars, they had fled to seek peace and
safety, he knew not whither.

Once more the dauntless discoverer turned back
towards Canada. Once more he stood before Count
Frontenac, and once more bent all his resources
and all his credit to gain means for the prosecution
of his enterprise. He succeeded. With his little
flotilla of canoes, he left his fort, at the outlet of
Lake Ontario, and slowly retraced those intermi-
nable waters, and lines of forest-bounded shore,
which had grown drearily familiar to his eyes. Fate
at length seemed tired of the conflict with so stubborn an adversary. All went prosperously with the
voyagers. They passed the lakes in safety, crossed
the rough portage to the waters of the Illinois, followed its winding channel, and descended the turbid
eddies of the Mississippi, received with various welcome by the scattered tribes who dwelt along its

banks. Now the waters grew bitter to the taste; now the trampling of the surf was heard; and now the broad ocean opened upon their sight, and their goal was won. On the ninth of April, 1682, with his followers under arms, amid the firing of musketry, the chanting of the *Te Deum*, and shouts of " Vive le roi," La Salle took formal possession of the vast valley of the Mississippi, in the name of Louis the Great, King of France and Navarre.[1]

The first stage of his enterprise was accom plished, but labors no less arduous remained behind. Repairing to the court of France, he was welcomed with richly merited favor, and soon set sail for the mouth of the Mississippi, with a squadron of vessels freighted with men and material for the projected colony. But the folly and obstinacy of a jealous naval commander blighted his fairest hopes. The squadron missed the mouth of the river; and the wreck of one of the vessels, and the desertion of the commander, completed the ruin of the expedition. La Salle landed with a band of half-famished followers on the coast of Texas; and, while he was toiling with untired energy for their relief, a few vindictive miscreants conspired against him, and a shot from a traitor's musket closed the career of the iron-hearted discoverer.

It was left with another to complete the enterprise on which he had staked his life; and, in the year 1699, Lemoine d'Iberville planted the germ whence sprang the colony of Louisiana.[2]

---

[1] *Procès Verbal*, in appendix to Sparks's *La Salle*.
[2] Du Pratz, *Hist. Louisiana*, 5. Charlevoix, II. 259.

Years passed on. In spite of a vicious plan of government, in spite of the bursting of the memorable Mississippi bubble, the new colony grew in wealth and strength. And now it remained for France to unite the two extremities of her broad American domain, to extend forts and settlements across the fertile solitudes between the valley of the St. Lawrence and the mouth of the Mississippi, and intrench herself among the forests which lie west of the Alleghanies, before the swelling tide of British colonization could overflow those mountain barriers. At the middle of the eighteenth century, her great project was fast advancing towards completion. The lakes and streams, the thoroughfares of the wilderness, were seized and guarded by a series of posts distributed with admirable skill. A fort on the strait of Niagara commanded the great entrance to the whole interior country. Another at Detroit controlled the passage from Lake Erie to the north. Another at St. Mary's debarred all hostile access 'to Lake Superior. Another at Michillimackinac secured the mouth of Lake Michigan. A post at Green Bay, and one at St. Joseph, guarded the two routes to the Mississippi, by way of the rivers Wisconsin and Illinois; while two posts on the Wabash, and one on the Maumee, made France the mistress of the great trading highway from Lake Erie to the Ohio. At Kaskaskia, Cahokia, and elsewhere in the Illinois, little French settlements had sprung up; and as the canoe of the voyager descended the Mississippi, he saw, at rare intervals, along its swampy margin, a few small stockade forts, half buried amid the redundancy of forest vegetation, until, as he approached Natchez, the dwellings of the *habitans* of Louisiana began to appear.

The forest posts of France were not exclusively of a military character. Adjacent to most of them, one would have found a little cluster of Canadian dwellings, whose tenants lived under the protection of the garrison, and obeyed the arbitrary will of the commandant; an authority which, however, was seldom exerted in a despotic spirit. In these detached settlements, there was no principle of increase. The character of the people, and of the government which ruled them, were alike unfavorable to it. Agriculture was neglected for the more congenial pursuits of the fur-trade, and the restless, roving Canadians, scattered abroad on their wild vocation, allied themselves to Indian women, and filled the woods with a mongrel race of bush-rangers.

Thus far secure in the west, France next essayed to gain foothold upon the sources of the Ohio; and about the year 1748, the sagacious Count Galissonnière proposed to bring over ten thousand peasants from France, and plant them in the valley of that beautiful river, and on the borders of the lakes.[1] But while at Quebec, in the Castle of St. Louis, soldiers and statesmen were revolving schemes like this, the slowly-moving power of England bore on with silent progress from the east. Already the

---

[1] Smith, *Hist. Canada*, I. 208.

British settlements were creeping along the valley of the Mohawk, and ascending the eastern slopes of the Alleghanies.   Forests crashing to the axe, dark spires of smoke ascending from autumnal fires, were heralds of the advancing host ; and while, on one side of the mountains, Celeron de Bienville was burying plates of lead, engraved with the arms of France, the ploughs and axes of Virginian woodsmen were enforcing a surer title on the other.   The adverse powers were drawing near.   The hour of collision was at hand.

CHAPTER III.

1608–1763.

THE FRENCH, THE ENGLISH, AND THE INDIANS.

THE French colonists of Canada held, from the beginning, a peculiar intimacy of relation with the Indian tribes. With the English colonists it was far otherwise; and the difference sprang from several causes. The fur-trade was the life of Canada; agriculture and commerce were the chief sources of wealth to the British provinces. The Romish zealots of Canada burned for the conversion of the heathen; their heretic rivals were fired with no such ardor. And finally while the ambition of France grasped at empire over the farthest deserts of the west, the steady industry of the English colonists was contented to cultivate and improve a narrow strip of seaboard. Thus it happened that the farmer of Massachusetts and the Virginian planter were conversant with only a few bordering tribes, while the priests and emissaries of France were roaming the prairies with the buffalo-hunting Pawnees, or lodging in the winter cabins of the Dahcotah; and swarms of savages, whose uncouth names were strange to English ears, descended

5

yearly from the north, to bring their beaver and otter skins to the market of Montreal.

The position of Canada invited intercourse with the interior, and eminently favored her schemes of commerce and policy. The river St. Lawrence, and the chain of the great lakes, opened a vast extent of inland navigation; while their tributary streams, interlocking with the branches of the Mississippi, afforded ready access to that mighty river, and gave the restless voyager free range over half the continent. But these advantages were well nigh neutralized. Nature opened the way, but a watchful and terrible enemy guarded the portal. The forests south of Lake Ontario gave harborage to the five tribes of the Iroquois, implacable foes of Canada. They waylaid her trading parties, routed her soldiers, murdered her missionaries, and spread havoc and woe through all her settlements.

It was an evil hour for Canada, when, on the twenty-eighth of May, 1609,[1] Samuel de Champlain, impelled by his own adventurous spirit, departed from the hamlet of Quebec to follow a war-party of Algonquins against their hated enemy, the Iroquois. Ascending the Sorel, and passing the rapids at Chambly, he embarked on the lake which bears his name, and with two French attendants, steered southward, with his savage associates, toward the rocky promontory of Ticonderoga. They moved with all the precaution of Indian warfare; when,

---

[1] Champlain, *Voyages*, 136 (Paris 1632). Charlevoix, I. 142.

at length, as night was closing in, they descried a band of the Iroquois in their large canoes of elm bark approaching through the gloom. Wild yells from either side announced the mutual discovery. The Iroquois hastened to the shore, and all night long the forest resounded with their discordant war-songs and fierce whoops of defiance. Day dawned, and the fight began. Bounding from tree to tree, the Iroquois pressed forward to the attack ; but when Champlain advanced from among the Algon-quins, and stood full in sight before them, with his strange attire, his shining breastplate, and features unlike their own,— when they saw the flash of his arquebuse, and beheld two of their chiefs fall dead, — they could not contain their terror, but fled for shelter into the depths of the wood. The Algon-quins pursued, slaying many in the flight, and the victory was complete.

Such was the first collision between the white men and the Iroquois ; and Champlain flattered himself that the latter had learned for the future to respect the arms of France. He was fatally deceived. The Iroquois recovered from their terrors, but they never forgave the injury ; and yet it would be unjust to charge upon Champlain the origin of the desolating wars which were soon to scourge the colony. The Indians of Canada, friends and neighbors of the French, had long been har-assed by inroads of the fierce confederates, and under any circumstances the French must soon have become parties to the quarrel.

Whatever may have been its origin, the war

was fruitful of misery to the youthful colony. The passes were beset by ambushed war-parties. The routes between Quebec and Montreal were watched with tiger-like vigilance. Bloodthirsty warriors prowled about the outskirts of the settlements. Again and again the miserable people, driven within the palisades of their forts, looked forth upon wasted harvests and blazing roofs. The Island of Montreal was swept with fire and steel. The fur-trade was interrupted, since for months together all communication was cut off with the friendly tribes of the west. Agriculture was checked; the fields lay fallow, and frequent famine was the necessary result.[1] The name of the Iroquois became a by-word of horror through the colony, and to the suffering Canadians they seemed troops of incarnate fiends. Revolting rites and monstrous superstitions were imputed to them; and, among the rest, it was currently believed that they cherished the custom of immolating young children, burning them, and drinking the ashes mixed with water to increase their bravery.[2] Yet the wildest imaginations could scarcely exceed the truth. At the attack of Montreal, they placed infants over the embers, and forced the wretched mothers to turn the spit;[3] and those who fell within their clutches endured torments too hideous for description. Their ferocity was equalled only by their courage and address.

[1] Vimont, Colden, Charlevoix, *passim.*
[2] Vimont seems to believe the story. — *Rel. de la N. F.* 1640, **195**
[3] Charlevoix, I. 549.

At intervals, the afflicted colony found respite from its sufferings ; and, through the efforts of the Jesuits, fair hopes began to rise of propitiating the terrible foe.   At one time, the influence of the priests availed so far, that under their auspices a French colony was formed in the very heart of the Iroquois country ; but the settlers were soon forced to a precipitate flight, and the war broke out afresh.[1]   The French, on their part, were not idle ; they faced their assailants with characteristic gallantry.   Courcelles, Tracy, De la Barre, and De Nonville invaded by turns, with various success, the forest haunts of the confederates ; and at length, in the year 1696, the veteran Count Frontenac marched upon their cantons with all the force of Canada.   Stemming the surges of La Chine, gliding through the romantic channels of the Thousand Islands, and over the glimmering surface of Lake Ontario, and trailing in long array up the current of the Oswego, they disembarked on the margin of the Lake of Onondaga ; and, startling the woodland echoes with the clangor of their trumpets, urged their march through the mazes of the forest.   Never had those solitudes beheld so strange a pageantry.   The Indian allies, naked to the waist and horribly painted, adorned with streaming scalp-locks and fluttering plumes, stole crouching among the thickets, or peered with lynx-eyed vision through the labyrinths of foliage. Scouts and forest-rangers scoured the woods in front and flank of the marching columns — men

[1] A. D. 1654-1658. — *Doc. Hist. N. Y.* I. 47.

trained among the hardships of the fur-trade, thin, sinewy, and strong, arrayed in wild costume of beaded moccason, scarlet leggin, and frock of buck-skin, fantastically garnished with many-colored embroidery of porcupine. Then came the levies of the colony, in gray capotes and gaudy sashes, and the trained battalions from old France in cuirass and head-piece, veterans of European wars. Plumed cavaliers were there, who had followed the standards of Condé or Turenne, and who, even in the depths of a wilderness, scorned to lay aside the martial foppery which bedecked the camp and court of Louis the Magnificent. The stern commander was borne along upon a litter in the midst, his locks bleached with years. but his eye kindling with the quenchless fire which, like a furnace, burned hottest when its fuel was almost spent. Thus, beneath the sepulchral arches of the forest, through tangled thickets, and over prostrate trunks, the aged nobleman advanced to wreak his vengeance upon empty wigwams and deserted maize-fields.[1]

Even the fierce courage of the Iroquois began to quail before these repeated attacks, while the gradual growth of the colony, and the arrival of troops from France, at length convinced them that they could not destroy Canada. With the opening of the eighteenth century, their rancor showed signs of abating ; and in the year 1726, by dint of skilful intrigue, the French succeeded in establishing a permanent military post at the important pass of

---

[1] Official Papers of the Expedition. —·*Doc. Hist. N. Y.* I. 323.

Niagara, within the limits of the confederacy.[1]
Meanwhile, in spite of every obstacle, the power
of France had rapidly extended its boundaries in
the west. French influence diffused itself through
a thousand channels, among distant tribes, hostile,
for the most part, to the domineering Iroquois.
Forts, mission-houses, and armed trading stations
secured the principal passes. Traders, and *coureurs de bois* pushed their adventurous traffic into
the wildest deserts ; and French guns and hatchets,
French beads and cloth, French tobacco and
brandy, were known from where the stunted Es-
quimaux burrowed in their snow caves, to where
the Camanches scoured the plains of the south with
their banditti cavalry. Still this far-extended commerce continued to advance westward. In 1738,
La Verandye essayed to reach those mysterious
mountains which, as the Indians alleged, lay beyond the arid deserts of the Missouri and the Sas-
katchawan. Indian hostility defeated his enterprise,
but not before he had struck far out into these
unknown wilds, and formed a line of trading posts,
one of which, Fort de la Reine, was planted on
the Assinniboin, a hundred leagues beyond Lake
Winnipeg. At that early period, France left her
footsteps upon the dreary wastes which even now
have no other tenants than the Indian buffalo-
hunter or the roving trapper.

The fur-trade of the English colonists opposed
but feeble rivalry to that of their hereditary foes.
At an early period, favored by the friendship of

[1] *Doc. Hist. N. Y.* I. 446.

the Iroquois, they attempted to open a.traffic with the Algonquin tribes of the great lakes ; and in the year 1687, Major McGregory ascended with a boat load of goods to Lake Huron, where his appearance excited great commotion, and where he was seized and imprisoned by the French.[1] From this time forward, the English fur-trade languished, until the year 1725, when Governor Burnet, of New York, established a post on Lake Ontario, at the mouth of the river Oswego ; whither, lured by the cheapness and excellence of the English goods, crowds of savages soon congregated from every side, to the unspeakable annoyance of the French.[2] Meanwhile, a considerable commerce was springing up with the Cherokees and other tribes of the south ; and during the first half of the century, the people of Pennsylvania began to cross the Alleghanies, and carry on a lucrative traffic with the tribes of the Ohio. In 1749, La Jonquière, the Governor of Canada, learned, to his great indignation, that several English traders had reached Sandusky, and were exerting a bad influence upon the Indians of that quarter;[3] and two years later, he caused four of the intruders to be seized near the Ohio, and sent prisoners to Canada.[4]

These early efforts of the English, considerable as they were, can ill bear comparison with the vast extent of the French interior commerce. In

---

[1] La Hontan, *Voyages*, I. 74.   Colden, *Memorial on the Fur-Trade.*
[2] *Doc. Hist. N. Y.* I. 444.
[3] Smith, *Hist. Canada*, I. 214.
[4] *Précis des Faits*, 89.

respect also to missionary enterprise, and the political influence resulting from it, the French had every advantage over rivals whose zeal for conversion was neither kindled by fanaticism nor fostered by an ambitious government. Eliot labored within call of Boston, while the heroic Brebeuf faced the ghastly perils of the western wilderness ; and the wanderings of Brainerd sink into insignificance compared with those of the devoted Rasles. Yet, in judging the relative merits of the Romish and Protestant missionaries, it must not be forgotten that while the former contented themselves with sprinkling a few drops of water on the forehead of the proselyte, the latter sought to wean him from his barbarism and penetrate his savage heart with the truths of Christianity.

In respect, also, to direct political influence, the advantage was wholly on the side of France. The English colonies, broken into separate governments, were incapable of exercising a vigorous and consistent Indian policy ; and the measures of one government often clashed with those of another. Even in the separate provinces, the popular nature of the constitution and the quarrels of governors and assemblies were unfavorable to efficient action ; and this was more especially the case in the province of New York, where the vicinity of the Iroquois rendered strenuous yet prudent measures of the utmost importance. The powerful confederates, hating the French with bitter enmity, naturally inclined to the English alliance ; and a proper treatment would have secured their firm and lasting friendship. But, at the early periods of her history, the assembly of New York was made up in great measure of narrow-minded men, more eager to consult their own petty interests than to pursue any far-sighted scheme of public welfare.[1] Other causes conspired to injure the British interest in this quarter. The annual present sent from England to the Iroquois was often embezzled by corrupt governors or their favorites.[2] The proud chiefs were disgusted by the cold and haughty bearing of the English officials, and a pernicious custom prevailed of conducting Indian negotiations through the medium of the fur-traders, a class of men held in contempt by the Iroquois, and known among them by the significant title of " rum carriers."[3] In short, through all the counsels of the province Indian affairs were grossly and madly neglected.[4]

With more or less emphasis, the same remark holds true of all the other English colonies.[5] With

[1] Smith, *Hist. N Y. passim.*

[2] *Rev Military Operations, Mass. Hist Coll 1st Series*, VII 67.

[3] Colden, *Hist. Five Nat.* 161.

[4] *MS. Papers of Cadwallader Colden. MS. Papers of Sir William Johnson.*

" We find the Indians, as far back as the very confused manuscript records in my possession, repeatedly upbraiding this province for their negligence, their avarice, and their want of assisting them at a time when it was certainly in their power to destroy the infant colony of Canada, although supported by many nations ; and this is likewise confessed by the writings of the managers of these times." — *MS. Letter — Johnson to the Board of Trade, May 24,* 1765.

[5] " I apprehend it will clearly appear to you, that the colonies had all along neglected to cultivate a proper understanding with the Indians, and from a mistaken notion have greatly despised them, without considering that it is in their power to lay waste and destroy the frontiers. This opinion arose from our confidence in our scattered numbers, and the parsimony of our people, who, from an error in politics, would not expend five pounds to save twenty." — *MS Letter — Johnson to the Board of Trade, November 13,* 1763.

those of France, it was far otherwise; and this difference between the rival powers was naturally incident to their different forms of government, and different conditions of development. France labored with eager diligence to conciliate the Indians and win them to espouse her cause. Her agents were busy in every village, studying the language of the inmates, complying with their usages, flattering their prejudices, caressing them, cajoling them, and whispering friendly warnings in their ears against the wicked designs of the English. When a party of Indian chiefs visited a French fort, they were greeted with the firing of cannon and rolling of drums; they were regaled at the tables of the officers, and bribed with medals and decorations, scarlet uniforms and French flags. Far wiser than their rivals, the French never ruffled the self-complacent dignity of their guests, never insulted their religious notions, nor ridiculed their ancient customs. They met the savage half way, and showed an abundant readiness to mould their own features after his likeness.[1] Count Frontenac himself plumed and painted like an Indian chief, danced the war-dance and yelled the war-song at the camp fires of his delighted allies. It would have been well had the French been less exact in their imitations, for at times they copied their model with infamous fidelity, and fell into excesses scarcely credible but for the concurrent testimony of their own writers. Frontenac caused an Iroquois prisoner to

[1] Adair, *Post's Journals,* Croghan's *Journal,* MSS. of Sir W. Johnson, etc., etc.

be burnt alive to strike terror into his countrymen; and Louvigny, French commandant at Michillimackinac, in 1695, tortured an Iroquois ambassador to death, that he might break off a negotiation between that people and the Wyandots.[1]   Nor are these the only well-attested instances of such execrable inhumanity.   But if the French were guilty of these cruelties against their Indian enemies, they were no less guilty of unworthy compliance with the demands of their Indian friends, in cases where Christianity and civilization would have dictated a prompt refusal.   Even Montcalm stained his bright name by abandoning the hapless defenders of Oswego and William Henry to the tender mercies of an Indian mob.

In general, however, the Indian policy of the French cannot be charged with obsequiousness. Complaisance was tempered with dignity.   At an early period, they discerned the peculiarities of the native character, and clearly saw that while on the one hand it was necessary to avoid giving offence, it was not less necessary on the other to assume a bold demeanor and a show of power; to caress with one hand, and grasp a drawn sword with the other.[2]   Every crime against a Frenchman was promptly chastised by the sharp agency of military law; while among the English, the offender

---

[1] La Hontan, I. 177.   Potherie, *Hist. Am. Sept.* II. 298 (Paris, 1722).

These facts afford no ground for national reflections, when it is recollected that while Iroquois prisoners were tortured in the wilds of Canada, Elizabeth Gaunt was burned to death at Tyburn for yielding to the dictates of compassion, and giving shelter to a political offender.

[2] Le Jeune, *Rel. de la N. F.* 1636, 193.

could only be reached through the medium of the civil courts, whose delays, uncertainties and evasions excited the wonder and provoked the contempt of the Indians.

It was by observance of the course indicated above, that the French were enabled to maintain themselves in small detached posts, far aloof from the parent colony, and environed by barbarous tribes where an English garrison would have been cut off in a twelvemonth. They professed to hold these posts, not in their own right, but purely through the grace and condescension of the surrounding savages ; 'and by this conciliating assurance they sought to make good their position, until, with their growing strength, conciliation should no more be needed.

In its efforts to win the friendship and alliance of the Indian tribes, the French government found every advantage in the peculiar character of its subjects — that pliant and plastic temper which forms so marked a contrast to the stubborn spirit of the Englishman. From the beginning, the French showed a tendency to amalgamate with the forest tribes. "The manners of the savages," writes the Baron La Hontan, " are perfectly agreeable to my palate ; " and many a restless adventurer of high or low degree might have echoed the words of the erratic soldier. At first, great hopes were entertained that, by the mingling of French and Indians, the latter would be won over to civilization and the church ; but the effect was precisely the reverse ; for, as Charlevoix observes, the savages did not become French, but the French became savages. Hundreds betook themselves to the forest, never more to return. These outflowings of French civilization were merged in the waste of barbarism, as a river is lost in the sands of the desert. The wandering Frenchman chose a wife or a concubine among his Indian friends; and, in a few generations, scarcely a tribe of the west was free from an infusion of Celtic blood. The French empire in America could exhibit among its subjects every shade of color from white to red. every gradation of culture from the highest civilization of Paris to the rudest barbarism of the wigwam.

The fur-trade engendered a peculiar class of men, known by the appropriate name of bush-rangers, or *coureurs de bois*, half-civilized vagrants, whose chief vocation was conducting the canoes of the traders along the lakes and rivers of the interior; many of them, however, shaking loose every tie of blood and kindred, identified themselves with the Indians, and sank into utter barbarism. In many a squalid camp among the plains and forests of the west, the traveller would have encountered men owning the blood and speaking the language of France, yet, in their swarthy visages and barbarous costume, seeming more akin to those with whom they had cast their lot. The renegade of civilization caught the habits and imbibed the prejudices of his chosen associates. He loved to decorate his long hair with eagle feathers, to make his face hideous with vermilion, ochre, and soot, and to adorn his greasy hunting frock with horsehair fringes. His dwelling, if he had one, was a wigwam. He lounged on a bear-skin while his squaw boiled his venison and lighted his pipe. In hunting, in dancing, in singing, in taking a scalp, he rivalled the genuine Indian. His mind was tinctured with the superstitions of the forest. He had faith in the magic drum of the conjuror; he was not sure that a thunder cloud could not be frightened away by whistling at it through the wing bone of an eagle; he carried the tail of a rattlesnake in his bullet pouch by way of amulet; and he placed implicit trust in his dreams. This class of men is not yet extinct. In the cheerless wilds beyond the northern lakes, or among the mountain solitudes of the distant west, they may still be found, unchanged in life and character since the day when Louis the Great claimed sovereignty over this desert empire.

The borders of the English colonies displayed no such phenomena of mingling races; for here a thorny and impracticable barrier divided the white man from the red. The English fur-traders, and the rude men in their employ, showed it is true an ample alacrity to fling off the restraints of civilization; but though they became barbarians, they did not become Indians; and scorn on the one side and hatred on the other still marked the intercourse of the hostile races. With the settlers of the frontier it was much the same. Rude, fierce and contemptuous, they daily encroached upon the hunting-grounds of the Indians, and then paid them for the injury with curses and threats. Thus the native population shrank back from before the English, as from before an advancing pestilence; while, on the other hand, in the very heart of Canada, Indian communities sprang up, cherished by the government, and favored by the easy-tempered people. At Lorette, at Caughnawaga, at St. Francis, and elsewhere within the province, large bands were gathered together, consisting in part of fugitives from the borders of the hated English, and aiding in time of war to swell the forces of the French in repeated forays against the settlements of New York and New England.

There was one of the English provinces marked out from among the rest by the peculiar character of its founders, and by the course of conduct which was there pursued towards the Indian tribes. William Penn, his mind warmed with a broad philanthropy, and enlightened by liberal views of human government and human rights, planted on the banks of the Delaware the colony which, vivified by the principles it embodied, grew into the great commonwealth of Pennsylvania. Penn's treatment of the Indians was equally prudent and humane, and its results were of high advantage to the colony; but these results have been exaggerated, and the treatment which produced them made the theme of inordinate praise. It required no great benevolence to urge the Quakers to deal kindly with their savage neighbors. They were bound in common sense to propitiate them; since, by incurring their resentment, they would involve themselves in the dilemma of submitting their necks to the tomahawk, or wielding the carnal weapon, in glaring defiance of their pacific principles. In paying the Indians for the lands which his colonists occupied, — a piece of justice which has been greeted with a general clamor of applause, — Penn, as he himself confesses, acted on the prudent counsel of Compton, Bishop of London.[1] Nor is there any truth in the representations of Raynal and other eulogists of the Quaker legislator, who hold him up to the world as the only European who ever acquired Indian lands by purchase, instead of seizing them by fraud or violence. The example of purchase had been set fifty years before by the Puritans of New England ; and several of the other colonies had more recently pursued the same just and prudent course.[2]

With regard to the alleged results of the pacific conduct of the Quakers, our admiration will diminish on closely viewing the circumstances of the case. The position of the colony was a most fortunate one. Had the Quakers planted their colony on the banks of the St. Lawrence, or among the warlike tribes of New England, their shaking of hands and assurances of tender regard would not

---

[1] "I have exactly followed the Bishop of London's counsel, by buying, and not taking away, the natives' land " — Penn's Letter to the Ministry, Aug 14, 1683. See Chalmer's Polit Ann. 666.

[2] "If any of the salvages pretend right of inheritance to all or any part of the lands granted in our patent, we pray you endeavor to purchase their tytle, that we may avoid the least scruple of intrusion." — Instructions to Endicot, 1629   See Hazard, State Papers, I. 263.

" The inhabitants of New England had never, except in the territory of the Pequods, taken possession of a foot of land without first obtaining a title from the Indians." — Bancroft, Hist. U. S. II. 98.

long have availed to save them from the visitations of the scalping-knife. But the Delawares, the people on whose territory they had settled, were like themselves debarred the use of arms. The Iroquois had conquered them, disarmed them, and forced them to adopt the opprobrious name of *women*. The humble Delawares were but too happy to receive the hand extended to them, and dwell in friendship with their pacific neighbors; since to have lifted the hatchet would have brought upon their heads the vengeance of their conquerors, whose good will Penn had taken pains to secure.[1]

The sons of Penn, his successors in the proprietorship of the province, did not evince the same kindly feeling towards the Indians which had distinguished their father. Earnest to acquire new lands, they commenced through their agents a series of unjust measures, which gradually alienated the Indians; and, after a peace of seventy years, produced a disastrous rupture. The Quaker population of the colony sympathized in the kindness which its founder had cherished towards the benighted race. This feeling was strengthened by years of friendly intercourse; and except where private interest was concerned, the Quakers made good their reiterated professions of attachment. Kindness to the Indian was the glory of their sect. As years wore on, this feeling was wonderfully reënforced by the influence of party spirit. The time arrived when, alienated by English encroach-

---

[1] He paid twice for his lands; once to the Iroquois, who claimed them by right of conquest, and once to their occupants, the Delawares.

ment on the one hand and French seduction on the other, the Indians began to assume a threatening attitude towards the province; and many voices urged the necessity of a resort to arms. This measure, repugnant alike to their pacific principles and to their love of the Indians, was strenuously opposed by the Quakers. Their affection for the injured race was now inflamed into a sort of benevolent fanaticism. The more rabid of the sect would scarcely confess that an Indian could ever do wrong. In their view, he was always sinned against, always the innocent victim of injury and abuse; and in the days of the final rupture, when the woods were full of furious war-parties, and the German and Irish settlers on the frontier were butchered by hundreds; when the western sky was darkened with the smoke of burning settlements, and the wretched fugitives were flying in crowds across the Susquehanna, a large party among the Quakers, secure by their Philadelphia firesides, could not see the necessity of waging even a defensive war against their favorite people.[1]

The encroachments on the part of the proprietors, which have been alluded to above, and which many of the Quakers viewed with disapproval,

---

[1] 1755–1763. The feelings of the Quakers at this time may be gathered from the following sources : MS *Account of the Rise and Progress of the Friendly Association for gaining and preserving Peace with the Indians by pacific Measures Address of the Friendly Association to Governor Denny* See Proud, *Hist Pa*, *appendix*. Haz., *Pa. Reg* VIII 273, 293, 323. But a much livelier picture of the prevailing excitement will be found in a series of party pamphlets, published at Philadelphia in the year 1764.

consisted in the fraudulent interpretation of Indian deeds of conveyance, and in the granting out of lands without any conveyance at all. The most notorious of these transactions, and the one most lamentable in its results, was commenced in the year 1737, and was known by the name of the *walking purchase.* An old, forgotten deed was raked out of the dust of the previous century; a deed which was in itself of doubtful validity, and which had been virtually cancelled by a subsequent agreement. On this rotten title the proprietors laid claim to a valuable tract of land on the right bank of the Delaware. Its western boundary was to be defined by a line drawn from a certain point on Neshaminey Creek, in a north-westerly direction, as far as a man could walk in a day and a half. From the end of the walk, a line drawn eastward to the river Delaware was to form the northern limit of the purchase. The proprietors sought out the most active men who could be heard of, and put them in training for the walk; at the same time laying out a smooth road along the intended course, that no obstructions might mar their speed. By this means an incredible distance was accomplished within the limited time. And now it only remained to adjust the northern boundary. Instead of running the line directly to the Delaware, according to the evident meaning of the deed, the proprietors inclined it so far to the north as to form an acute angle with the river, and enclose many hundred thousand acres of valuable land, which would otherwise have remained in the hands of the Indians.[1]   The land thus obtained lay in the Forks of the Delaware, above Easton, and was then occupied by a powerful branch of the Delawares, who, to their amazement, now heard the summons to quit for ever their populous village and fields of half-grown maize.   In rage and distress they refused to obey, and the proprietors were in a perplexing dilemma.   Force was necessary; but a Quaker legislature would never consent to fight, and especially to fight against Indians.   An expedient was hit upon, at once safe and effectual.   The Iroquois were sent for.   A deputation of their chiefs appeared at Philadelphia, and having been well bribed. and deceived by false accounts of the transaction, they consented to remove the refractory Delawares.   The delinquents were summoned before their conquerors, and the Iroquois orator, Canassatego, a man of tall stature and imposing presence,[2] looking with a grim countenance on his cowering auditors, addressed them in the following words : —

" You ought to be taken by the hair of the head and shaken soundly till you recover your senses. You don't know what you are doing.   Our brother

---

[1] *Causes of the Alienation of the Delaware and Shawnoe Indians from the British Interest*, 33, 68, (Lond 1759).   This work is a pamphlet written by Charles Thompson, afterwards secretary of Congress, and designed to explain the causes of the rupture which took place at the outbreak of the French war   The text is supported by copious references to treaties and documents.   I have seen a copy in the possession of Francis Fisher, Esq , of Philadelphia, containing marginal notes in the handwriting of James Hamilton, who was twice governor of the province under the proprietary instructions   In these notes, though he cavils at several unimportant points of the relation, he suffers the essential matter to pass unchallenged

[2] *William Marshe's Journal.*

Onas's[1] cause is very just. On the other hand, your cause is bad, and you are bent to break the chain of friendship. How came you to take upon you to sell land at all? We conquered you; we made women of you; you know you are women, and can no more sell land than women. This land you claim is gone down your throats; you have been furnished with clothes, meat, and drink, by the goods paid you for it, and now you want it again, like children as you are. What makes you sell land in the dark? Did you ever tell us you had sold this land? Did we ever receive any part, even the value of a pipe-shank, from you for it? We charge you to remove instantly; we don't give you the liberty to think about it. You are women. Take the advice of a wise man and remove immediately. You may return to the other side of Delaware, where you came from; but we do not know whether, considering how you have demeaned yourselves, you will be permitted to live there; or whether you have not swallowed that land down your throats as well as the land on this side. We therefore assign you two places to go, either to Wyoming or Shamokin. We shall then have you more under our eye, and shall see how you behave. Don't deliberate, but take this belt of wampum, and go at once."[2]

The unhappy Delawares dared not disobey. They left their ancient homes, and removed, as they had

[1] Onas was the name given by the Indians to William Penn and his successors.
[2] *Minutes of Indian council held at Philadelphia,* 1742.

been ordered, to the Susquehanna, where some
settled at Shamokin, and some at Wyoming.[1] From
an early period, the Indians had been annoyed by
the unlicensed intrusion of settlers upon their lands,
and, in 1728, they had bitterly complained of the
wrong[2] The evil continued to increase. Many
families, chiefly German and Irish, began to cross
the Susquehanna and build their cabins along the
valleys of the Juniata and its tributary waters. The
Delawares sent frequent remonstrances from their
new abodes, and the Iroquois themselves made
angry complaints, declaring that the lands of the
Juniata were theirs by right of conquest, and that
they had given them to their cousins, the Delawares,
for hunting-grounds. Some efforts at redress were
made ; but the remedy proved ineffectual, and the
discontent of the Indians increased with every year.
The Shawanoes, with many of the Delawares,
removed westward, where for a time they would
be safe from intrusion ; and by the middle of the
century, the Delaware tribe was separated into two
divisions, one of which remained upon the Susquehanna, while the other, in conjunction with the
Shawanoes, dwelt on the waters of the Alleghany
and the Muskingum.

But now the French began to push their advanced
posts into the valley of the Ohio. Unhappily for
the English interest, they found the irritated minds
of the Indians in a state which favored their efforts
at seduction, and held forth a flattering promise

---

[1] Chapman, *Hist. Wyoming*, 19.
[2] *Colonial Records*, III 340.

that tribes so long faithful to the English might soon be won over to the cause of France.

While the English interests wore so inauspicious an aspect in this quarter, their prospects were not much better among the Iroquois. Since the peace of Utrecht, in 1713, these powerful tribes had so far forgotten their old malevolence against the French, that the latter were enabled to bring all their machinery of conciliation to bear upon them. They turned the opportunity to such good account, as not only to smooth away the asperity of the ancient grudge, but also to rouse in the minds of their former foes a growing jealousy against the English. Several accidental circumstances did much to aggravate this feeling. The Iroquois were in the habit of sending out frequent war-parties against their enemies, the Cherokees and Catawbas, who dwelt near the borders of Carolina and Virginia; and in these forays the invaders often became so seriously embroiled with the white settlers, that sharp frays took place, and an open war seemed likely to ensue.[1]

It was with great difficulty that the irritation caused by these untoward accidents was allayed; and even then enough remained in the neglect of governments, the insults of traders, and the haughty bearing of officials, to disgust the proud confederates with their English allies. In the war of 1745, they yielded but cold and doubtful aid; and fears were entertained of their final estrange-

[1] Letter of Governor Spotswood, of Virginia, Jan. 25, 1720. See *Colonial Records of Pa.* III 75.

ment.[1]   This result became still more imminent,
when, in the year 1749, the French priest Picquet
established his mission of La Présentation on the
St. Lawrence, at the site of Ogdensburg.[2]   This
pious father, like the martial churchmen of an
earlier day, deemed it no scandal to gird on earthly
armor against the enemies of the faith.   He built
a fort and founded a settlement; he mustered the
Indians about him from far and near, organized
their governments, and marshalled their war-parties.
From the crenelled walls of his mission-house the
warlike apostle could look forth upon a military
colony of his own creating, upon farms and clearings, white Canadian cabins, and the bark lodges
of Indian hordes which he had gathered under his
protecting wing.   A chief object of the settlement
was to form a barrier against the English; but the
purpose dearest to the missionary's heart was to
gain over the Iroquois to the side of France; and
in this he succeeded so well, that, as a writer of
good authority declares, the number of their war
riors within the circle of his influence surpassed
the whole remaining force of the confederacy.[3]

Thoughtful men in the English colonies saw with
anxiety the growing defection of the Iroquois, and
dreaded lest, in the event of a war with France, her
ancient foes might now be found her friends.   But
in this ominous conjuncture, one strong influence
was at work to bind the confederates to their old

[1] *Minutes of Indian Council*, 1746.
[2] *Doc. Hist. N. Y.* I. 423.
[3] MS. Letter — *Colden to Lord Halifax*, no date.

alliance ; and this influence was wielded by a man so remarkable in his character, and so conspicuous an actor in the scenes of the ensuing history, as to demand at least some passing notice.

About the year 1734, in consequence it is said of the hapless issue of a love affair, William Johnson, a young Irishman, came over to America at the age of nineteen, where he assumed the charge of an extensive tract of wild land in the province of New York, belonging to his uncle, Admiral Sir Peter Warren. Settling in the valley of the Mohawk, he carried on a prosperous traffic with the Indians ; and while he rapidly rose to wealth, he gained, at the same time, an extraordinary influence over the neighboring Iroquois. As his resources increased, he built two mansions in the valley, known respectively by the names of Johnson Castle and Johnson Hall, the latter of which,. a well-constructed building of wood and stone, is still standing in the village of Johnstown. Johnson Castle was situated at some distance higher up the river. Both were fortified against attack, and the latter was surrounded with cabins built for the reception of the Indians, who often came in crowds to visit the proprietor, invading his dwelling at all unseasonable hours, loitering in the doorways, spreading their blankets in the passages, and infecting the air with the fumes of stale tobacco.

Johnson supplied the place of his former love by a young Dutch damsel, who bore him several children ; and, in justice to them, he married her upon her death-bed. Soon afterwards he

found another favorite in the person of Molly
Brant, sister of the celebrated Mohawk war-chief,
whose black eyes and laughing face caught his
fancy, as, fluttering with ribbons, she galloped past
him at a muster of the Tryon county militia.

Johnson's importance became so conspicuous,
that when the French war broke out in 1755, he
was made a major general; and, soon after, the
colonial troops under his command gained the
battle of Lake George against the French forces
of Baron Dieskau. For this success, for which
however he was entitled to little credit, he was
raised to the rank of baronet, and rewarded with a
gift of five thousand pounds from the king. About
this time, he was appointed superintendent of Indian affairs for the northern tribes, a station in
which he did signal service to the country. In
1759, when General Prideaux was killed by the
bursting of a cohorn in the trenches before Niagara, Johnson succeeded to his command, routed the
French in another pitched battle, and soon raised
the red cross of England on the ramparts of the
fort. After the peace of 1763, he lived for many
years at Johnson Hall, constantly enriched by the
increasing value of his vast estate, and surrounded
by a hardy Highland tenantry, devoted to his interests; but when the tempest which had long
been brewing seemed at length about to break, and
signs of a speedy rupture with the mother country
thickened with every day, he stood wavering in
an agony of indecision, divided between his loy-
alty to the sovereign who was the source of all his

honors, and his reluctance to become the agent of
a murderous Indian warfare against his countrymen and friends. His final resolution was never
taken. In the summer of 1774, he was attacked
with a sudden illness, and died within a few hours,
in the sixtieth year of his age, hurried to his
grave by mental distress, or, as many believed, by
the act of his own hand.

Nature had well fitted him for the position in
which his propitious stars had cast his lot. His
person was tall, erect, and strong; his features
grave and manly. His direct and upright dealings,
his courage, eloquence, and address, were sure passports to favor in Indian eyes. He had a singular
facility of adaptation. In the camp, or at the
council-board, in spite of his defective education,
he bore himself as became his station; but at
home he was seen drinking flip and smoking tobacco with the Dutch boors, his neighbors, and
talking of improvements or the price of beaver-
skins; while in the Indian villages he would feast
on dog's flesh, dance with the warriors, and harangue his attentive auditors with all the dignity of
an Iroquois sachem. His temper was genial; he
encouraged rustic sports, and was respected and
beloved alike by whites and Indians.

His good qualities, however, were alloyed with
serious defects. His mind was as coarse as it was
vigorous; he was vain of his rank and influence,
and being quite free from any scruple of delicacy,
he lost no opportunity of proclaiming them. His
nature was eager and ambitious; and in pushing

his own way, he was never distinguished by an anxious solicitude for the rights of others.[1]

At the time of which we speak, his fortunes had not reached their zenith; yet his influence was great; and during the war of 1745, when he held the chief control of Indian affairs in New York, it was exercised in a manner most beneficial to the province. After the peace of Aix la Chapelle, in 1748, finding his measures ill supported, he threw up his office in disgust. Still his mere personal influence sufficed to embarrass the intrigues of the busy priest at La Présentation; and a few years later, when the public exigency demanded his utmost efforts, he resumed, under better auspices, the official management of Indian affairs.

And now, when the blindest could see that between the rival claimants to the soil of America nothing was left but the arbitration of the sword, no man friendly to the cause of England could observe without alarm how France had strengthened herself in Indian alliances. The Iroquois, it is true, had not quite gone over to her side; nor had the Delawares wholly forgotten their ancient league with William Penn. The Miamis, too, in the valley of the Ohio, had lately taken umbrage at the conduct of the French, and betrayed a leaning to the side of England, while several tribes of the south showed a similar disposition. But, with few and slight exceptions, the numerous tribes of the great lakes

[1] Allen, *Am. Biog. Dict.* and authorities there referred to. Campbell, *Annals of Tryon County, appendix.* Sabine, *Am. Loyalists*, 398. *Papers relating to Sir W. Johnson.* See *Doc. Hist. New York*, II. *MS. Papers of Sir W. Johnson*, etc., etc.

and the Mississippi, besides a host of domiciliated
savages in Canada itself, stood ready at the bidding
of France to grind their tomahawks and turn loose
their ravenous war-parties; while the British colonists had too much reason to fear that even those
tribes which seemed most friendly to their cause,
and which formed the sole barrier of their unprotected borders, might, at the first sound of the
war-whoop, be found in arms against them.

CHAPTER IV.

1700–1755.

COLLISION OF THE RIVAL COLONIES.

THE people of the northern English colonies had learned to regard their Canadian neighbors with the bitterest enmity. With them, the very name of Canada called up horrible recollections and ghastly images: the midnight massacre of Schenectady, and the desolation of many a New England hamlet; blazing dwellings and reeking scalps; and children snatched from their mothers' arms, to be immured in convents and trained up in the abominations of Popery. To the sons of the Puritans, their enemy was doubly odious. They hated him as a Frenchman, and they hated him as a Papist. Hitherto he had waged his murderous warfare from a distance, wasting their settlements with rapid onsets, fierce and transient as a summer storm; but now, with enterprising audacity, he was intrenching himself on their very borders. The English hunter, in the lonely wilderness of Vermont, as by the warm glow of sunset he piled the spruce boughs for his woodland bed, started as a deep, low sound struck faintly on his ear, the evening gun of Fort Frederic, booming over lake and forest. The erection of this fort, better known among the English as Crown Point, was a piece of daring encroachment which justly kindled resentment in the northern colonies. But it was not here that the immediate occasion of a final rupture was to arise. By an article of the treaty of Utrecht, confirmed by that of Aix la Chapelle, Acadia had been ceded to England ; but scarcely was the latter treaty signed, when debates sprang up touching the limits of the ceded province. Commissioners were named on either side to adjust the disputed boundary; but the claims of the rival powers proved utterly irreconcilable, and all nogotiation was fruitless.[1] Meantime, the French and English forces in Acadia began to assume a belligerent attitude, and indulge their ill blood in mutual aggression and reprisal.[2] But while this game was played on the coasts of the Atlantic, interests of far greater moment were at stake in the west.

The people of the middle colonies, placed by their local position beyond reach of the French, had heard with great composure of the sufferings of their New England brethren, and felt little concern at a danger so doubtful and remote. There were those among them, however, who with greater foresight had been quick to perceive the ambitious projects of the rival nation ; and, as early as 1716, Spotswood, governor of Virginia, had urged the expediency of securing the valley of the Ohio by

[1] Garneau, Book VIII. Chap. III.

[2] Holmes, *Annals*, II. 183. *Mémoire contenant Le Précis des Faits, Pièces Justificatives*, Part I.

a series of forts and settlements.[1] His proposal was coldly received, and his plan fell to the ground. The time at length was come when the danger was approaching too near to be slighted longer. In 1748, an association, called the Ohio Company, was formed with the view of making settlements in the region beyond the Alleghanies; and two years later, Gist, the company's surveyor, to the great disgust of the Indians, carried chain and compass down the Ohio as far as the falls at Louisville.[2] But so dilatory were the English, that before any effectual steps were taken, their agile enemies appeared upon the scene.

In the spring of 1753, the middle provinces were startled at the tidings that French troops had crossed Lake Erie, fortified themselves at the point of Presqu'-Isle, and pushed forward to the northern branches of the Ohio.[3] Upon this, Governor Dinwiddie, of Virginia, resolved to despatch a message requiring their removal from territories which he claimed as belonging to the British crown; and looking about him for the person best qualified to act as messenger, he made choice of George Washington, a young man twenty-one years of age, adjutant general of the Virginian militia.

Washington departed on his mission, crossed the mountains, descended to the bleak and leafless valley of the Ohio, and thence continued his jour-

---

[1] Smollett, III 370 (Edinburgh, 1805).

[2] Sparks's *Life and Writings of Washington*, II 478. *Gist's Journal*

[3] *Olden Time*, II 9, 10 This excellent antiquarian publication contains documents relating to this period which are not to be found elsewhere.

ney up the banks of the Alleghany until the fourth of December. On that day he reached Venango, an Indian town on the Alleghany, at the mouth of French Creek. Here was the advanced post of the French ; and here, among the Indian log-cabins and huts of bark, he saw their flag flying above the house of an English trader, whom the military intruders had unceremoniously ejected. They gave the young envoy a hospitable reception,[1] and referred him to the commanding officer, whose headquarters were at Le Bœuf, a fort which they had just built on French Creek, some distance above Venango. Thither Washington repaired, and on his arrival was received with stately courtesy by the officer, Legardeur de St. Pierre, whom he describes as an elderly gentleman of very soldier-like appearance. To the message of Dinwiddie, St. Pierre replied that he would forward it to the governor general of Canada ; but that, in the mean time, his orders were to hold possession of the country, and this he should do to the best of his ability. With this answer Washington, through all the rigors of the

---

[1] " He invited us to sup with them, and treated us with the greatest complaisance The wine, as they dosed themselves pretty plentifully with it, soon banished the restraint which at first appeared in their conversation, and gave a license to their tongues to reveal their sentiments more freely. They told me that it was their absolute design to take possession of the Ohio, and by G—d they would do it ; for that, although they were sensible the English could raise two men for their one, yet they knew their motions were too slow and dilatory to prevent any undertaking of theirs. They pretend to have an undoubted right to the river from a discovery made by one La Salle, sixty years ago ; and the rise of this expedition is, to prevent our settling on the river or waters of it, as they heard of some families moving out in order thereto." — Washington, *Journal.*

midwinter forest, retraced his steps, with one attendant, to the English borders.

With the first opening of spring, a newly raised
company of Virginian backwoodsmen, under Captain Trent, hastened across the mountains, and
began to build a fort at the confluence of the
Monongahela and Alleghany, where Pittsburg now
stands; when suddenly they found themselves
invested by a host of French and Indians, who,
with sixty bateaux and three hundred canoes, had
descended from Le Bœuf and Venango.[1] The
English were ordered to evacuate the spot; and,
being quite unable to resist, they obeyed the summons, and withdrew in great discomfiture towards
Virginia. Meanwhile Washington, with another
party of backwoodsmen, was advancing from the
borders; and, hearing of Trent's disaster, he
resolved to fortify himself on the Monongahela,
and hold his ground, if possible, until fresh troops
could arrive to support him. The French sent out
a scouting party under M. Jumonville, with the
design, probably, of watching his movements; but,
on a dark and stormy night, Washington surprised
them, as they lay lurking in a rocky glen not far
from his camp, killed the officer, and captured the
whole detachment.[2] Learning that the French,
enraged by this reverse, were about to attack him
in great force, he thought it prudent to fall back,
and retired accordingly to a spot called the Great

[1] Sparks, *Life and Writings of Washington*, II. 6.
[2] Sparks, II 447. The conduct of Washington in this affair is
regarded by French writers as a stain on his memory.

Meadows, where he had before thrown up a slight intrenchment. Here he found himself assailed by nine hundred French and Indians, commanded by a brother of the slain Jumonville. From eleven in the morning till eight at night, the backwoodsmen, who were half famished from the failure of their stores, maintained a stubborn defence, some fighting within the intrenchment, and some on the plain without. In the evening, the French sounded a parley, and offered terms. They were accepted, and on the following day Washington and his men retired across the mountains, leaving the disputed territory in the hands of the French.[1]

While the rival nations were beginning to quarrel for a prize which belonged to neither of them, the unhappy Indians saw, with alarm and amazement, their lands becoming a bone of contention between rapacious strangers. The first appearance of the French on the Ohio excited the wildest fears in the tribes of that quarter, among whom were those who, disgusted by the encroachments of the Pennsylvanians, had fled to these remote retreats to escape the intrusions of the white men. Scarcely was their fancied asylum gained, when they saw themselves invaded by a host of armed men from Canada. Thus placed between two fires, they knew not which way to turn. There was no union in their counsels, and they seemed like a mob of bewil-

[1] For the French account of these operations, see *Mémoire contenant le Précis des Faits*. This volume, an official publication of the French court, contains numerous documents, among which are the papers of the unfortunate Braddock, left on the field of battle by his defeated army.

dered children. Their native jealousy was roused to its utmost pitch. Many of them thought that the two white nations had conspired to destroy them, and then divide their lands. "You and the French," said one of them, a few years afterwards, to an English emissary, "are like the two edges of a pair of shears, and we are the cloth which is cut to pieces between them." [1]

The French labored hard to conciliate them, plying them with gifts and flatteries, [2] and proclaiming themselves their champions against the English. At first, these arts seemed in vain, but their effect soon began to declare itself; and this effect was greatly increased by a singular piece of infatuation on the part of the proprietors of Pennsylvania. During the summer of 1754, delegates of the several provinces met at Albany, to concert measures of defence in the war which now seemed inevitable. It was at this meeting that the memorable plan of a union of the colonies was brought forward; a plan, the fate of which was curious and significant, for the crown rejected it as giving too much power to the people, and the people as giving too much

[1] *First Journal* of C. F. Post.

[2] Letters of Robert Stobo, an English hostage at Fort du Quesne.

"Shamokin Daniel, who came with me, went over to the fort [du Quesne] by himself, and counselled with the governor, who presented him with a laced coat and hat, a blanket, shirts, ribbons, a new gun, powder, lead, &c. When he returned he was quite changed, and said, 'See here, you fools, what the French have given me. I was in Philadelphia, and never received a farthing;' and (directing himself to me) said, 'The English are fools, and so are you'" — Post, *First Journal.*

Washington, while at Fort Le Bœuf, was much annoyed by the conduct of the French, who did their utmost to seduce his Indian escort by bribes and promises.

power to the crown.[1]   A council was also held with
the Iroquois, and though they were found but lukewarm in their attachment to the English, a treaty
of friendship and alliance was concluded with their
deputies.[2]   It would have been well if the matter
had ended here; but, with ill-timed rapacity, the
proprietary agents of Pennsylvania took advantage
of this great assemblage of sachems to procure
from them the grant of extensive tracts, including
the lands inhabited by the very tribes whom the
French were at that moment striving to seduce.[3]
When they heard that, without their consent, their
conquerors and tyrants, the Iroquois, had sold the
soil from beneath their feet, their indignation was
extreme; and, convinced that there was no limit to
English encroachment, many of them from that
hour became fast allies of the French.

The courts of London and Versailles still maintained a diplomatic intercourse, both protesting
their earnest wish that their conflicting claims might
be adjusted by friendly negotiation; but while each
disclaimed the intention of hostility, both were
hastening to prepare for war.   Early in 1755, an
English fleet sailed from Cork, having on board
two regiments destined for Virginia, and commanded
by General Braddock; and soon after, a French

---

[1] Trumbull, *Hist. Conn.* II. 355.   Holmes, *Annals*, II 201.

[2] At this council an Iroquois sachem upbraided the English, with great
boldness, for their neglect of the Indians, their invasion of their lands, and
their dilatory conduct with regard to the French, who, as the speaker
averred, had behaved like men and warriors. — *Minutes of Conferences at
Albany*, 1754.

[3] *Causes of the Alienation of the Delaware and Shawanoe Indians from the
British Interest*, 77.

fleet put to sea from the port of Brest, freighted
with munitions of war and a strong body of troops
under Baron Dieskau, an officer who had distinguished himself in the campaigns of Marshal Saxe.
The English fleet gained its destination, and landed
its troops in safety.   The French were less fortunate.   Two of their ships, the Lys and the Alcide,
became involved in the fogs of the banks of New-
foundland ;   and when the weather cleared, they
found themselves under the guns of a superior British force, belonging to the squadron of Admiral
Boscawen, sent out for the express purpose of
intercepting them.   "Are we at peace or war?"
demanded the French commander.   A broadside
from the Englishman soon solved his doubts, and
after a stout resistance the French struck their
colors.[1]   News of the capture caused great excitement in England, but the conduct of the aggres-
sors was generally approved ; and under pretence
that the French had begun the war by their alleged
encroachments in America, orders were issued for
a general attack upon their marine.   So successful
were the British cruisers, that, before the end of
the year, three hundred French vessels and nearly
eight thousand sailors were captured and brought
into port.[2]   The French, unable to retort in kind,

[1] Garneau, II. 551.   *Gent. Mag.* XXV. 330.
[2] Smollett, III 436.
 "The French inveighed against the capture of their ships, before any
declaration of war, as flagrant acts of piracy ; and some neutral powers of
Europe seemed to consider them in the same point of view.   It was certainly high time to check the insolence of the French by force of arms ;
and surely this might have been as effectually and expeditiously exerted

. raised an outcry of indignation, and Mirepoix their ambassador withdrew from the court of London.

Thus began that memorable war which, kindling among the forests of America, scattered its fires over the kingdoms of Europe, and the sultry empire of the Great Mogul ; the war made glorious by the heroic death of Wolfe, the victories of Frederic, and the exploits of Clive ; the war which controlled the destinies of America, and was first in the chain of events which led on to her Revolution with all its vast and undeveloped consequences. On the old battle-ground of Europe, the contest bore the same familiar features of violence and horror which had marked the strife of former generations — fields ploughed by the cannon ball, and walls shattered by the exploding mine, sacked towns and blazing suburbs, the lamentations of women, and the license of a maddened soldiery. But in America, war assumed a new and striking aspect. A wilderness was its sublime arena. Army met army under the shadows of primeval woods ; their cannon resounded over wastes unknown to civilized man. And before the hostile powers could join in battle, endless forests must be traversed, and morasses passed, and everywhere the axe of the pioneer must hew a path for the bayonet of the soldier.

Before the declaration of war, and before the breaking off of negotiations between the courts of

under the usual sanction of a formal declaration, the omission of which exposed the administration to the censure of our neighbors, and fixed the imputation of fraud and freebooting on the beginning of the war " — Smollett, III 481 See also Mahon, *Hist England*, IV. 72.

France and England, the English ministry formed
the plan of assailing the French in America on all
sides at once, and repelling them, by one bold push,
from all their encroachments.[1]   A provincial army
was to advance upon Acadia, a second was to
attack Crown Point, and a third Niagara; while
the two regiments which had lately arrived in Virginia under General Braddock, aided by a strong
body of provincials, were to dislodge the French
from their newly-built fort of Du Quesne.   To
Braddock was assigned the chief command of all
the British forces in America; and a person worse
fitted for the office could scarcely have been found.
His experience had been ample, and none could
doubt his courage; but he was profligate, arrogant, perverse, and a bigot to military rules.[2]   On

[1] Instructions of General Braddock.   See *Précis des Faits*, 160, 168

[2] The following is Horace Walpole's testimony, and writers of better
authority have expressed themselves, with less liveliness and piquancy,
to the same effect. —

"Braddock is a very Iroquois in disposition He had a sister, who,
having gamed away all her little fortune at Bath, hanged herself with a
truly English deliberation, leaving only a note upon the table with those
lines, 'To die is landing on some silent shore,' &c When Braddock was
told of it, he only said, 'Poor Fanny ! I always thought she would play
till she would be forced *to tuck herself up.*' "

Here follows a curious anecdote of Braddock's meanness and profligacy,
which I omit The next is more to his credit "He once had a duel with
Colonel Gumley, Lady Bath's brother, who had been his great friend As
they were going to engage, Gumley, who had good humor and wit (Braddock had the latter), said, 'Braddock, you are a poor dog ! Here, take my
purse. If you kill me, you will be forced to run away, and then you will
not have a shilling to support you ' Braddock refused the purse, insisted
on the duel, was disarmed, and would not even ask his life However,
with all his brutality, he has lately been governor of Gibraltar, where
he made himself adored, and where scarce any governor was endured
before." — *Letters to Sir H Mann*, CCLXV. CCLXVI

Washington's opinion of Braddock may be gathered from his Writings,
II. 77.

his first arrival in Virginia, he called together the governors of the several provinces, in order to explain his instructions and adjust the details of the projected operations. These arrangements complete, Braddock advanced to the borders of Virginia, and formed his camp at Fort Cumberland, where he spent several weeks in training the raw backwoodsmen, who joined him, into such discipline as they seemed capable of; in collecting horses and wagons, which could only be had with the utmost difficulty; in railing at the contractors, who scandalously cheated him; and in venting his spleen by copious abuse of the country and the people. All at length was ready, and early in June, 1755, the army left civilization behind, and struck into the broad wilderness as a squadron puts out to sea.

It was no easy task to force their way over that rugged ground, covered with an unbroken growth of forest; and the difficulty was increased by the needless load of baggage which encumbered their march. The crash of falling trees resounded in the front, where a hundred axemen labored with ceaseless toil to hew a passage for the army.[1] The horses strained their utmost strength to drag the ponderous wagons over roots and stumps, through gullies and quagmires; and the regular troops were daunted by the depth and gloom of the forest which hedged them in on either hand, and closed its leafy arches above their heads. So tedious was their progress, that, by the advice of

---

[1] MS. *Diary of the Expedition*, in the British Museum.

Washington, twelve hundred chosen men moved on in advance with the lighter baggage and artillery, leaving the rest of the army to follow, by slower stages, with the heavy wagons. On the eighth of July, the advanced body reached the Monongahela, at a point not far distant from Fort du Quesne. The rocky and impracticable ground on the eastern side debarred their passage, and the general resolved to cross the river in search of a smoother path, and recross it a few miles lower down, in order to gain the fort. The first passage was easily made, and the troops moved, in glittering array, down the western margin of the water, rejoicing that their goal was well nigh reached, and the hour of their expected triumph close at hand.

Scouts and Indian runners had brought the tidings of Braddock's approach to the French at Fort du Quesne. Their dismay was great, and Contrecœur, the commander, thought only of retreat; when Beaujeu, a captain in the garrison, made the bold proposal of leading out a party of French and Indians to waylay the English in the woods, and harass or interrupt their march. The offer was accepted, and Beaujeu hastened to the Indian camps.

Around the fort and beneath the adjacent forest were the bark lodges of savage hordes, whom the French had mustered from far and near; Ojibwas and Ottawas, Hurons and Caughnawagas, Abenakis and Delawares. Beaujeu called the warriors together, flung a hatchet on the ground before them, and invited them to follow him out to battle; but the boldest stood aghast at the peril, and none would accept the challenge. A second interview took place with no better success; but the Frenchman was resolved to carry his point. "I am determined to go," he exclaimed. "What, will you suffer your father to go alone?"[1] His daring proved contagious. The warriors hesitated no longer; and when, on the morning of the ninth of July, a scout ran in with the news that ·the English army was but a few miles distant, the Indian camps were at once astir with the turmoil of preparation. Chiefs harangued their yelling followers, braves bedaubed themselves with war-paint, smeared themselves with grease, hung feathers in their scalp-locks, and whooped and stamped till they had wrought themselves into a delirium of valor.

That morning, James Smith, an English prisoner recently captured on the frontier of Pennsylvania, stood on the rampart, and saw the half-frenzied multitude thronging about the gateway, where kegs of bullets and gunpowder were broken open, that each might help himself at will.[2] Then band after band hastened away towards the forest, followed and supported by nearly two hundred and fifty French and Canadians, commanded by Beaujeu.

---

[1] Sparks's *Life and Writings of Washington*, II. 473. I am indebted to the kindness of President Sparks for copies of several French manuscripts, which throw much light on the incidents of the battle These manuscripts are alluded to in the Life and Writings of Washington.

[2] *Smith's Narrative* This interesting account has been several times published It may be found in Drake's *Tragedies of the Wilderness*

There were the Ottawas, led on, it is said, by the
remarkable man whose name stands on the title-
page of this history; there were the Hurons of
Lorette under their chief, whom the French called
Athanase,[1] and many more, all keen as hounds on
the scent of blood.   At about nine miles from the
fort, they reached a spot where the narrow road
descended to the river through deep and gloomy
woods, and where two ravines, concealed by trees
and· bushes, seemed formed by nature for an ambuscade.   Beaujeau well knew the ground; and it
was here that he had resolved to fight; but he and
his followers were well nigh too late; for as they
neared the ravines, the woods were resounding
with the roll of the British drums.

It was past noon of a day brightened with the
clear sunlight of an American midsummer, when
the forces of Braddock began, for a second time,
to cross the Monongahela, at the fording-place,
which to this day bears the name of their ill-fated
leader.   The scarlet columns of the British regu
lars, complete in martial appointment, the rude
backwoodsmen with shouldered rifles, the trains of
artillery and the white-topped wagons, moved on
in long procession through the shallow current,
and slowly mounted the opposing bank.[1]   Men

---

[1] "Went to Lorette, an Indian village about eight miles from Quebec.
Saw the Indians at mass, and heard them sing psalms tolerably well — a
dance.   Got well acquainted with Athanase, who was commander of the
Indians who defeated General Braddock, in 1755 — a very sensible fellow." — *MS Journal of an English Gentleman on a Tour through Canada, in*
1765.

[2] "My feelings were heightened by the warm and glowing narration
of that day's events, by Dr. Walker, who was an eye-witness.   He pointed

were there whose names have become historic:
Gage, who, twenty years later, saw his routed
battalions recoil in disorder from before the breastwork on Bunker Hill; Gates, the future conqueror
of Burgoyne; and one destined to a higher fame,
— George Washington, a boy in years, a man in
calm thought and self-ruling wisdom.

With steady and well ordered march, the troops
advanced into the great labyrinth of woods which
shadowed the eastern borders of the river. Rank
after rank vanished from sight. The forest swallowed them up, and the silence of the wilderness
sank down once more on the shores and waters of
the Monongahela.

Several engineers and guides and six light horsemen led the way; a body of grenadiers under Gage
was close behind, and the army followed in such
order as the rough ground would permit, along a
narrow road, twelve feet wide, tunnelled through
the dense and matted foliage. There were flank-
ing parties on either side, but no scouts to scour
the woods in front, and with an insane confidence
Braddock pressed on to meet his fate. The van
had passed the low grounds that bordered the river,
and were now ascending a gently rising ground,
where, on either hand, hidden by thick trees, by

out the ford where the army crossed the Monongahela (below Turtle
Creek, 800 yards). A finer sight could not have been beheld, — the
shining barrels of the muskets, the excellent order of the men, the clean-
liness of their appearance, the joy depicted on every face at being so near
Fort du Quesne — the highest object of their wishes. The music re-
echoed through the hills. How brilliant the morning — how melancholy
the evening ' " — *Letter of Judge Yeates, dated August,* 1776. See Haz.,
Pa. Reg , VI. 104.

tangled undergrowth and rank grasses, lay the two
fatal ravines.   Suddenly, Gordon, an engineer in
advance, saw the French and Indians bounding
forward through the forest and along the narrow
track, Beaujeau leading them on, dressed in a fringed
hunting-shirt, and wearing a silver gorget on his
breast.   He stopped, turned, and waved his hat,
and his French followers, crowding across the road,
opened a murderous fire upon the head of the
British column, while, screeching their war-cries,
the Indians thronged into the ravines, or crouched
behind rocks and trees on both flanks of the advancing troops.   The astonished grenadiers returned
the fire, and returned it with good effect; for a
random shot struck down the brave Beaujeau, and
the courage of the assailants was staggered by his
fall.   Dumas, second in command, rallied them to
the attack; and while he, with the French and
Canadians, made good the pass in front, the Indians
from their lurking places opened a deadly fire on
the right and left.   In a few moments, all was
confusion.   The advance guard fell back on the
main body, and every trace of subordination vanished.   The fire soon extended along the whole
length of the army, from front to rear.   Scarce
an enemy could be seen, though the forest resounded with their yells; though every bush and
tree was alive with incessant flashes; though the
lead flew like a hailstorm, and the men went down
by scores.   The regular troops seemed bereft of
their senses.   They huddled together in the road
like flocks of sheep; and happy did he think him

self who could wedge his way into the midst of the crowd, and place a barrier of human flesh between his life and the shot of the ambushed marksmen. Many were seen eagerly loading their muskets, and then firing them into the air, or shooting their own comrades in the insanity of their terror. The officers, for the most part, displayed a conspicuous gallantry; but threats and commands were wasted alike on the panic-stricken multitude. It is said that at the outset Braddock showed signs of fear; but he soon recovered his wonted intrepidity. Five horses were shot under him, and five times he mounted afresh.[1] He stormed and shouted, and, while the Virginians were fighting to good purpose, each man behind a tree, like the Indians themselves, he ordered them with furious menace to form in platoons, where the fire of the enemy mowed them down like grass. At length, a mortal shot silenced him, and two provincials bore him off the field. Washington rode through the tumult calm and undaunted. Two horses were killed under him, and four bullets pierced his clothes;[2] but his hour was not come, and he escaped without a wound. Gates was shot through the body, and Gage also was severely wounded. Of eighty-six officers, only twenty-three remained unhurt; and of twelve hundred soldiers who crossed the Monongahela, more than seven hundred were killed and wounded. None suffered more severely than the Virginians, who had displayed throughout a

[1] Letter — *Captain Orme, his aide-de-camp, to* ——, July 18.
[2] Sparks, I. 67.

degree of courage and steadiness which put the cowardice of the regulars to shame. The havoc among them was terrible. for of their whole number scarcely one-fifth left the field alive.[1]

The slaughter lasted three hours; when, at length, the survivors, as if impelled by a general impulse, rushed tumultously from the place of carnage, and with dastardly precipitation fled across the Monongahela. The enemy did not pursue beyond the river, flocking back to the field to collect the plunder, and gather a rich harvest of scalps. The routed troops pursued their flight until they met the rear division of the army, under Colonel Dunbar ; and even then their senseless terrors did not abate. Dunbar's soldier's caught the infection. Cannon, baggage, provisions and wagons were destroyed, and all fled together, eager to escape from the shadows of those awful woods, whose horrors haunted their imagination. They passed the defenceless settlements of the border, and hurried on to Philadelphia, leaving the unhappy people to defend themselves as they might against the tomahawk and scalping-knife.

The calamities of this disgraceful rout did not

---

[1] " The Virginia troops showed a good deal of bravery, and were nearly all killed; for I believe, out of three companies that were there, scarcely thirty men are left alive Captain Peyrouny, and all his officers, down to a corporal, were killed Captain Polson had nearly as hard a fate, for only one of his was left. In short, the dastardly behavior of those they call regulars exposed all others, that were inclined to do their duty, to almost certain death, and at last, in despite of all the efforts of the officers to the contrary, they ran, as sheep pursued by dogs, and it was impossible to rally them " — *Writings of Washington*, II. 87

The English themselves bore reluctant testimony to the good conduct of the Virginians. — See Entick, *Hist. Late War*, 147.

cease with the loss of a few hundred soldiers on the field of battle; for it brought upon the provinces all the miseries of an Indian war. Those among the tribes who had thus far stood neutral, wavering between the French and English, now hesitated no longer. Many of them had been disgusted by the contemptuous behavior of Braddock. All had learned to despise the courage of the English, and to regard their own prowess with unbounded complacency. It is not in Indian nature to stand quiet in the midst of war; and the defeat of Braddock was a signal for the western savages to snatch their tomahawks and assail the English settlements with one accord, murdering and pillaging with ruthless fury, and turning the frontier of Pennsylvania and Virginia into one wide scene of havoc and desolation.

The three remaining expeditions which the British ministry had planned for that year's campaign were attended with various results. Acadia was quickly reduced by the forces of Colonel Monkton; but the glories of this easy victory were tarnished by an act of cruelty. Seven thousand of the unfortunate people, refusing to take the prescribed oath of allegiance, were seized by the conquerors, torn from their homes, placed on shipboard like cargoes of negro slaves, and transported to the British provinces.[1] The expedition against Niagara was a total failure, for the troops did not even reach their destination. The movement against Crown Point met with no better

---

[1] Haliburton, *Hist. Nova Scotia*, I. Chap. IV.

success, as regards the main object of the enterprise. Owing to the lateness of the season, and other causes, the troops proceeded no farther than Lake George; but the attempt was marked by a feat of arms, which, in that day of failures, was greeted, both in England and America, as a signal victory.

General Johnson, afterwards Sir William Johnson, had been charged with the conduct of the Crown Point expedition; and his little army, a rude assemblage of hunters and farmers from New York and New England, officers and men alike ignorant of war, lay encamped at the southern extremity of Lake George. Here, while they languidly pursued their preparations, their active enemy anticipated them. Baron Dieskau, who, with a body of troops, had reached Quebec in the squadron which sailed from Brest in the spring, had intended to take forcible possession of the English fort of Oswego, erected upon ground claimed by the French as a part of Canada. Learning Johnson's movements, he changed his plan, crossed Lake Champlain, made a circuit by way of Wood Creek, and gained the rear of the English army, with a force of about two thousand French and Indians. At midnight, on the seventh of September, the tidings reached Johnson that the army of the French baron was but a few miles distant from his camp. A council of war was called, and the resolution formed of detaching a thousand men to reconnoitre. " If they are to be killed," said Hendrick, the Mohawk chief, " they are too many; if they are to fight, they are too few." His remonstrance was unheeded; and the brave old savage, unable from age and corpulence to fight on foot, mounted his horse, and joined the English detachment with two hundred of his warriors. At sunrise, the party defiled from the camp, and entering the forest disappeared from the eyes of their comrades.

Those who remained behind labored with all the energy of alarm to fortify their unprotected camp. An hour elapsed, when from the distance was heard a sudden explosion of musketry. The excited soldiers suspended their work to listen. A rattling fire succeeded, deadened among the woods, but growing louder and nearer, till none could doubt that their comrades had met the French, and were defeated.

This was indeed the case. Marching through thick woods, by the narrow and newly-cut road which led along the valley southward from Lake George, Williams, the English commander, had led his men full into an ambuscade, where all Dieskau's army lay in wait to receive them. From the woods on both sides rose an appalling shout, followed by a storm of bullets. Williams was soon shot down; Hendrick shared his fate; many officers fell, and the road was strewn with dead and wounded soldiers. The English gave way at once. Had they been regular troops, the result would have been worse; but every man was a woodsman and a hunter. Some retired in bodies along the road; while the greater part spread

themselves through the forest, opposing a wide
front to the enemy, fighting stubbornly as they
retreated, and shooting back at the French from
behind every tree or bush that could afford a cover.
The Canadians and Indians pressed them closely,
darting, with shrill cries, from tree to tree, while
Dieskau's regulars, with steadier advance, bore all
before them. Far and wide through the forest rang
shout and shriek and Indian whoop, mingled with
the deadly rattle of guns. Retreating and pursuing, the combatants passed northward towards
the English camp, leaving the ground behind them
strewn with dead and dying..

A fresh detachment from the camp came in aid
of the English, and the pursuit was checked. Yet
the retreating men were not the less rejoiced when
they could discern, between the brown columns
of the woods, the mountains and waters of Lake
George, with the white tents of their encampments
on its shore. The French followed no farther.
The blast of their trumpets was heard recalling
their scattered men for a final attack.

During the absence of Williams's detachment,
the main body of the army had covered the front
of their camp with a breastwork, — if that name
can be applied to a row of logs, — behind which the
marksmen lay flat on their faces. This preparation
was not yet complete, when the defeated troops
appeared issuing from the woods. Breathless and
perturbed, they entered the camp, and lay down
with the rest; and the army waited the attack in
a frame of mind which boded ill for the result.

Soon, at the edge of the woods which bordered the open space in front, painted Indians were seen, and bayonets glittered among the foliage, shining, in the homely comparison of a New-England soldier, like a row of icicles on a January morning. The French regulars marched in column to the edge of the clearing, and formed in line, confronting the English at the distance of a hundred and fifty yards. Their complete order, their white uniforms and bristling bayonets, were a new and startling sight to the eyes of Johnson's rustic soldiers, who raised but a feeble cheer in answer to the shouts of their enemies. Happily, Dieskau made no assault. The regulars opened a distant fire of musketry, throwing volley after volley against the English, while the Canadians and Indians, dispersing through the morasses on each flank of the camp, fired sharply, under cover of the trees and bushes. In the rear, the English were protected by the lake; but on the three remaining sides, they were hedged in by the flash and smoke of musketry.   ·

The fire of the French had little effect. The English recovered from their first surprise, and every moment their confidence rose higher and their shouts grew louder. Levelling their long hunting guns with cool precision, they returned a fire which thinned the ranks of the French, and galled them beyond endurance. Two cannon were soon brought to bear upon the morasses which sheltered the Canadians and Indians; and though the pieces were served with little skill, the assailants were so terrified by the crashing of the balls among the trunks and branches, that they gave way at once. Dieskau still persisted in the attack. From noon until past four o'clock, the firing was scarcely abated, when at length the French, who had suffered extremely, showed signs of wavering. At this, with a general shout, the English broke from their camp, and rushed upon their enemies, striking them down with the buts of their guns, and driving them through the woods like deer. Dieskau was taken prisoner, dangerously wounded, and leaning for support against the stump of a tree. The slaughter would have been great, had not the English general recalled the pursuers, and suffered the French to continue their flight unmolested. Fresh disasters still awaited the fugitives; for, as they approached the scene of that morning's ambuscade, they were greeted by a volley of musketry. Two companies of New York and New Hampshire rangers, who had come out from Fort Edward as a scouting party, had lain in wait to receive them. Favored by the darkness of the woods, — for night was now approaching, — they made so sudden and vigorous an attack, that the French, though far superior in number, were totally routed and dispersed.[1]

---

[1] Holmes, II. 210. Trumbull, *Hist. Conn.* II. 368. Dwight, *Travels,* III 361 Hoyt, *Indian Wars,* 279. Entick, *Hist. Late War,* I. 153 *Review of Military Operations in North America.* Johnson's *Letter to the Provincial Governors.* Blodgett's *Prospective View of the Battle near Lake George.*

Blodgett's pamphlet is accompanied by a curious engraving, giving a bird's eye view of the battle, including the surprise of Williams' detachment, and the subsequent attack on the camp of Johnson. In the first

This memorable conflict has cast its dark associations over one of the most beautiful spots in America. Near the scene of the evening fight, a pool, half overgrown by weeds and water lilies, and darkened by the surrounding forest, is pointed out to the tourist, and he is told that beneath its stagnant waters lie the bones of three hundred Frenchmen, deep buried in mud and slime.

The war thus begun was prosecuted for five succeeding years with the full energy of both nations. The period was one of suffering and anxiety to the colonists, who, knowing the full extent of their danger, spared no exertion to avert it. In the year 1758, Lord Abercrombie, who then commanded in America, had at his disposal a force amounting to fifty thousand men, of whom the greater part were provincials.[1] The operations of the war embraced a wide extent of country, from Cape Breton and Nova Scotia to the sources of the

half of the engraving, the French army is represented lying in ambuscade in the form of a horseshoe. Hendrick is conspicuous among the English, from being mounted on horseback, while all the others are on foot. In the view of the battle at the lake, the English are represented lying flat on their faces, behind their breastwork, and busily firing at the French and Indians, who are seen skulking among the woods and thickets.

I am again indebted to President Sparks for the opportunity of examining several curious manuscripts relating to the battle of Lake George. Among them is Dieskau's official account of the affair, and a curious paper, also written by the defeated general, and containing the story of his disaster, as related by himself in an imaginary conversation with his old commander, Marshal Saxe, in the Elysian Fields. Several writers have stated that Dieskau died of his wounds. This, however, was not the case. He was carried prisoner to England, where he lived for several years, but returned to France after the peace of 1763.

[1] Holmes, II. 226.

Ohio; but nowhere was the contest so actively carried on as in the neighborhood of Lake George,
the waters of which, joined with those of Lake
Champlain, formed the main avenue of communication between Canada and the British provinces.
Lake George is more than thirty miles long, but of
width so slight that it seems like some broad and
placid river, enclosed between ranges of lofty mountains; now contracting into narrows, dotted with
islands and shadowed by cliffs and crags, now
spreading into a clear and open expanse. It had
long been known to the French. The Jesuit Isaac
Jogues, bound on a fatal mission to the ferocious
Mohawks, had reached its banks on the eve of
Corpus Christi Day, and named it Lac St. Sac
rement. Its solitude was now rudely invaded.
Armies passed and repassed upon its tranquil
bosom. At its northern point the French planted
their stronghold of Ticonderoga; at its southern
stood the English fort William Henry, while the
mountains and waters between were a scene of
ceaseless ambuscades, surprises, and forest skirmishing. Through summer and winter, the crack
of rifles and the cries of men gave no rest to their
echoes; and at this day, on the field of many a forgotten fight, are dug up rusty tomahawks, corroded
bullets, and human bones, to attest the struggles of
the past.

The earlier years of the war were unpropitious
to the English, whose commanders displayed no
great degree of vigor or ability. In the summer of
1756, the French general Montcalm advanced upon

Oswego, took it, and levelled it to the ground. In August of the following year, he struck a heavier blow. Passing Lake George with a force of eight thousand men, including about two thousand Indians, gathered from the farthest parts of Canada, he laid siege to Fort William Henry, close to the spot where Dieskau had been defeated two years before. Planting his batteries against it, he beat down its ramparts and dismounted its guns, until the garrison, after a brave defence, were forced to capitulate. They marched out with the honors of war; but scarcely had they done so, when Montcalm's Indians assailed them, cutting down and scalping them without mercy. Those who escaped came in to Fort Edward with exaggerated accounts of the horrors from which they had fled, and a general terror was spread through the country. The inhabitants were mustered from all parts to repel the advance of Montcalm; but the French general, satisfied with what he had done, repassed Lake George, and retired behind the walls of Ticonderoga.

In the year 1758, the war began to assume a different aspect, for Pitt was at the head of the government. Sir Jeffrey Amherst laid siege to the strong fortress of Louisburg, and at length reduced it; while in the south, General Forbes marched against Fort du Quesne, and, more fortunate than his predecessor, Braddock, drove the French from that important point. Another successful stroke was the destruction of Fort Frontenac, which was taken by a provincial army under Colonel Bradstreet. These achievements were counterbalanced by a great disaster. Lord Abercrombie, with an army of sixteen thousand men, advanced to the head of Lake George, the place made memorable by Dieskau's defeat and the loss of Fort William Henry. On a brilliant July morning, he embarked his whole force for an attack on Ticonderoga. Many of those present have recorded with admiration the beauty of the spectacle, the lines of boats filled with troops stretching far down the lake, the flashing of oars, the glitter of weapons, and the music ringing back from crags and rocks, or dying in mellowed strains among the distant mountains. At night, the army landed, and, driving in the French outposts, marched through the woods towards Ticonderoga. One of their columns, losing its way in the forest, fell in with a body of the retreating French ; and in the conflict that ensued, Lord Howe, the favorite of the army, was shot dead. On the eighth of July, they prepared to storm the lines which Montcalm had drawn across the peninsula in front of the fortress. Advancing to the attack, they saw before them a breastwork of uncommon height and thickness. The French army were drawn up behind it, their heads alone visible, as they levelled their muskets against the assailants, while, for a hundred yards in front of the work, the ground was covered with felled trees, with sharpened branches pointing outward. The signal of assault was given. In vain the Highlanders, screaming with rage, hewed with their broadswords among the branches, struggling to get at the enemy. In vain the English, with their deep-toned shout, rushed on in heavy columns. A tempest of musket balls met them, and Montcalm's cannon swept the whole ground with terrible carnage. A few officers and men forced their way through the branches, passed the ditch, climbed the breastwork, and, leaping among the enemy, were instantly bayonetted. The English fought four hours with determined valor, but the position of the French was impregnable; and at length, having lost two thousand of their number, the army drew off, leaving many of their dead scattered upon the field. A sudden panic seized the defeated troops. They rushed in haste to their boats, and, though no pursuit was attempted, they did not regain their composure until Lake George was between them and the enemy. The fatal lines of Ticonderoga were not soon forgotten in the provinces; and marbles in Westminster Abbey preserve the memory of those who fell on that disastrous day.

This repulse, far from depressing the energies of the British commanders, seemed to stimulate them to new exertion; and the campaign of the next year, 1759, had for its object the immediate and total reduction of Canada. This unhappy country was full of misery and disorder. Peculation and every kind of corruption prevailed among its civil and military chiefs, a reckless licentiousness was increasing among the people, and a general famine seemed impending, for the population had of late years been drained away for military service, and the fields were left untilled. In spite of their suf-

feiings, the Canadians, strong in rooted antipathy
to the English, and highly excited by their priests,
resolved on fighting to the last. Prayers were
offered up in the churches, masses said, and pen-
ances enjoined, to avert the wrath of God from the
colony, while every thing was done for its defence
which the energies of a great and patriotic leader
could effect.

By the plan of this summer's campaign, Canada
was to be assailed on three sides at once. Upon
the west, General Prideaux was to attack Niagara;
upon the south, General Amherst was to advance
upon Ticonderoga and Crown Point; while upon
the east, General Wolfe was to besiege Quebec;
and each of these armies, having accomplished its
particular object, was directed to push forward, if
possible, until all three had united in the heart of
Canada. In pursuance of the plan, General Prideaux moved up Lake Ontario and invested Niagara.
This post was one of the greatest importance. Its
capture would cut off the French from the whole
interior country, and they therefore made every
effort to raise the siege. An army of seventeen
hundred French and Indians, collected at the distant garrisons of Detroit, Presqu' Isle, Le Bœuf,
and Venango, suddenly appeared before Niagara.[1]
Sir William Johnson was now in command of the
English, Prideaux having been killed by the bursting of a cohorn. Advancing in order of battle, he
met the French, charged, routed, and pursued them

---

[1] *Annual Register*, 1759, p. 33.

for five miles through the woods. This success was soon followed by the surrender of the fort.

In the mean time, Sir Jeffrey Amherst had crossed Lake George, and appeared before Ticonderoga ; upon which the French blew up their works, and retired down Lake Champlain to Crown Point. Retreating from this position also, on the approach of the English army, they collected all their forces, amounting to little more than three thousand men, at Isle Aux Noix, where they intrenched themselves, and prepared to resist the farther progress of the invaders. The lateness of the season prevented Amherst from carrying out the plan of advancing into Canada, and compelled him to go into winter-quarters at Crown Point. The same cause had withheld Prideaux's army from descending the St. Lawrence.

While the outposts of Canada were thus successfully attacked, a blow was struck at a more vital part. Early in June, General Wolfe sailed up the St. Lawrence with a force of eight thousand men, and formed his camp immediately below Quebec, on the Island of Orleans.[1] From thence he could discern, at a single glance, how arduous was the task before him. Piles of lofty cliffs rose with sheer ascent on the northern border of the river ; and from their summits the boasted citadel of Canada looked down in proud security, with its churches and convents of stone, its ramparts, bastions, and batteries ; while over them all, from the brink of

[1] Mante, *Hist. Late War*, 238

the precipice, towered the massive walls of the
Castle of St. Louis.   Above, for many a league, the
bank was guarded by an unbroken range of steep
acclivities.   Below, the River St. Charles, flowing
into the St. Lawrence, washed the base of the
rocky promontory on which the city stood.   Lower
yet lay an army of fourteen thousand men, under
an able and renowned commander, the Marquis of
Montcalm.   His front was covered by intrenchments and batteries, which lined the bank of the
St. Lawrence; his right wing rested on the city
and the St. Charles; his left, on the cascade
and deep gulf of Montmorenci; and thick forests
extended along his rear.   Opposite Quebec rose
the high promontory of Point Levi; and the St.
Lawrence, contracted to less than a mile in width,
flowed between, with deep and powerful current.
To a chief of less resolute temper, it might well
have seemed that art and nature were in league to
thwart his enterprise; but a mind like that of
Wolfe could only have seen in this majestic combi-
nation of forest and cataract, mountain and river, a
fitting theatre for the great drama about to be
enacted there.

Yet nature did not seem to have formed the
young English general for the conduct of a doubtful and almost desperate enterprise.   His person
was slight, and his features by no means of a martial cast.   His feeble constitution had been under-
mined by years of protracted and painful disease.[1]

[1] " I have this day signified to Mr Pitt that he may dispose of my
slight carcass as he pleases, and that I am ready for any undertaking

His kind and genial disposition seemed better fitted for the quiet of domestic life than for the stern duties of military command; but to these gentler traits he joined a high enthusiasm, and an unconquerable spirit of daring and endurance, which made him the idol of his soldiers, and bore his slender frame through every hardship and exposure.

The work before him demanded all his courage. How to invest the city, or even bring the army of Montcalm to action, was a problem which might have perplexed a Hannibal. A French fleet lay in the river above, and the precipices along the northern bank were guarded at every accessible point by sentinels and outposts. Wolfe would have crossed the Montmorenci by its upper ford, and attacked the French army on its left and rear; but the plan was thwarted by the nature of the ground and the vigilance of his adversaries. Thus baffled at every other point, he formed the bold design of storming Montcalm's position in front; and on the afternoon of the thirty-first of July, a strong body of troops was embarked in boats, and, covered by a furious cannonade from the English ships and batteries, landed on the beach just above the mouth of the Montmorenci. The grenadiers and Royal Americans were the first on shore, and their ill-timed

within the reach and compass of my skill and cunning. I am in a very bad condition, both with the gravel and rheumatism; but I had much rather die than decline any kind of service that offers : if I followed my own taste, it would lead me into Germany; and if my poor talent was consulted, they should place me to the cavalry, because nature has given me good eyes, and a warmth of temper to follow the first impressions. However, it is not our part to choose, but to obey." — *Letter — Wolfe to William Rickson Salisbury, December* 1, 1758.

impetuosity proved the ruin of the plan. Without
waiting to receive their orders or form their ranks,
they ran, pell-mell, across the level ground, and
with loud shouts began, each man for himself, to
scale the heights which rose in front, crested with
intrenchments and bristling with hostile arms. The
French at the top threw volley after volley among
the hot-headed assailants. The slopes were soon
covered with the fallen; and at that instant a
storm, which had long been threatening, burst with
sudden fury, drenched the combatants on both sides
with a deluge of rain, extinguished for a moment
the fire of the French, and at the same time made
the steeps so slippery that the grenadiers fell repeatedly in their vain attempts to climb. Night was
coming on with double darkness. The retreat was
sounded, and, as the English re-embarked, troops of
Indians came whooping down the heights, and hov-
ered about their rear, to murder the stragglers and
the wounded; while exulting cries of *Vive le roi*,
from the crowded summits, proclaimed the triumph
of the enemy.

With bitter agony of mind, Wolfe beheld the
headlong folly of his men, and saw more than four
hundred of the flower of his army fall a useless
sacrifice.[1] The anxieties of the siege had told
severely upon his slender constitution; and not
long after this disaster, he felt the first symptoms
of a fever, which soon confined him to his couch.
Still his mind never wavered from its purpose;
and it was while lying helpless in the chamber of a

---

[1] Knox, *Journals*, I. 358.

Canadian house, where he had fixed his head-quarters, that he embraced the plan of the enterprise which robbed him of life, and gave him immortal fame.

This plan had been first proposed during the height of Wolfe's illness, at a council of his subordinate generals, Monkton, Townshend, and Murray. It was resolved to divide the little army; and, while one portion remained before Quebec to alarm the enemy by false attacks, and distract their attention from the scene of actual operation, the other was to pass above the town, land under cover of darkness on the northern shore, climb the guarded heights, gain the plains above, and force Montcalm to quit his vantage-ground, and perhaps to offer battle. The scheme was daring even to rashness; but its audacity was the secret of its success.

Early in September, a crowd of ships and transports, under Admiral Holmes, passed the city under the hot fire of its batteries; while the troops designed for the expedition, amounting to scarcely five thousand, marched upward along the southern bank, beyond reach of the cannonade. All were then embarked; and on the evening of the twelfth, Holmes's fleet, with the troops on board, lay safe at anchor in the river, several leagues above the town. These operations had not failed to awaken the suspicions of Montcalm; and he had detached M. Bougainville to watch the movements of the English, and prevent their landing on the northern shore.

The eventful night of the twelfth was clear and

calm, with no light but that of the stars. Within
two hours before daybreak, thirty boats, crowded
with sixteen hundred soldiers, cast off from the
vessels, and floated downward, in perfect order,
with the current of the ebb tide. To the boundless
joy of the army, Wolfe's malady had abated, and
he was able to command in person. His ruined
health, the gloomy prospects of the siege, and the
disaster at Montmorenci, had oppressed him with
the deepest melancholy, but never impaired for a
moment the promptness of his decisions, or the
impetuous energy of his action.[1] He sat in the
stern of one of the boats, pale and weak, but borne
up to a calm height of resolution. Every order
had been given, every arrangement made, and it
only remained to face the issue. The ebbing tide
sufficed to bear the boats along, and nothing broke
the silence of the night but the gurgling of the
river, and the low voice of Wolfe, as he repeated
to the officers about him the stanzas of Gray's
" Elegy in a Country Churchyard," which had

---

[1] Entick, IV. 111.

In his letter to the Ministry, dated Sept. 2, Wolfe writes in these
desponding words : —

" By the nature of the river, the most formidable part of this arma-
ment is deprived of the power of acting , yet we have almost the whole
force of Canada to oppose In this situation there is such a choice of
difficulties, that I own myself at a loss how to determine The affairs of
Great Britain I know require the most vigorous measures, but then the
courage of a handful of brave troops should be exerted only where there
is some hope of a favorable event However, you may be assured, that
the small part of the campaign which remains shall be employed (as far
as I am able) for the honor of his Majesty, and the interest of the nation ;
in which I am sure of being well seconded by the admiral and by the
generals : happy if our efforts here can contribute to the success of his
Majesty's arms in any other part of America."

ıecently appeared and which he had just received from England.   Perhaps, as he uttered those strangely appropriate words, —

"The paths of glory lead but to the grave,"

the shadows of his own approaching fate stole with mournful prophecy across his mind. "Gentlemen," he said, as he closed his recital, "I would rather have written those lines than take Quebec to-morrow."[1]

As they approached the landing-place, the boats edged closer in towards the northern shore, and the woody precipices rose high on their left, like a wall of undistinguished blackness.

"*Qui vive?*" shouted a French sentinel, from out the impervious gloom.

"*La France!*" answered a captain of Fraser's Highlanders, from the foremost boat.

"*A quel régiment?*" demanded the soldier.

"*De la Reine!*" promptly replied the Highland captain, who chanced to know that the regiment so designated formed part of Bougainville's command.   As boats were frequently passing down the river with supplies for the garrison, and as a

---

[1] "This anecdote was related by the late celebrated John Robison, Professor of Natural Philosophy in the University of Edinburgh, who, in his youth, was a midshipman in the British navy, and was in the same boat with Wolfe.   His son, my kinsman, Sir John Robison, communicated it to me, and it has since been recorded in the Transactions of the Royal Society of Edinburgh.

'The paths of glory lead but to the grave'

is one of the lines which Wolfe must have recited as he strikingly exemplified its application" — Grahame, *Hist. U.S.* IV. 50.   See also *Playfair's Works*, IV. 126.

convoy from Bougainville was expected that very night, the sentinel was deceived, and allowed the English to proceed.

A few moments after, they were challenged again, and this time they could discern the soldier running close down to the water's edge, as if all his suspicions were aroused; but the skilful replies of the Highlander once more saved the party from discovery.[1]

They reached the landing-place in safety, — an indentation in the shore, about a league above the city, and now bearing the name of Wolfe's Cove. Here a narrow path led up the face of the heights, and a French guard was posted at the top to defend the pass. By the force of the current, the foremost boats, including that which carried Wolfe himself, were borne a little below the spot. The general was one of the first on shore. He looked upward at the rugged heights which towered above him in the gloom. "You can try it," he coolly observed to an officer near him; "but I don't think you'll get up."[2]

At the point where the Highlanders landed, one of their captains, Donald Macdonald, apparently the same whose presence of mind had just saved the enterprise from ruin, was climbing in advance of his men, when he was challenged by a sentinel.

---

[1] Smollett, V. 56, *note* (Edinburgh, 1805). Mante simply mentions that the English were challenged by the sentinels, and escaped discovery by replying in French.

[2] This incident is mentioned in a manuscript journal of the siege of Quebec, by John Johnson, clerk and quartermaster in the 58th regiment. The journal is written with great care, and abounds in curious details.

He replied in French, by declaring that he had been sent to relieve the guard, and ordering the soldier to withdraw.[1]   Before the latter was undeceived, a crowd of Highlanders were close at hand, while the steeps below were thronged with eager climbers, dragging themselves up by trees, roots, and bushes.[2] The guard turned out, and made a brief though brave resistance.   In a moment, they were cut to pieces, dispersed, or made prisoners; while men after men came swarming up the height, and quickly formed upon the plains above.   Meanwhile, the vessels had dropped downward with the current, and anchored opposite the landing-place. The remaining troops were disembarked, and, with the dawn of day, the whole were brought in safety to the shore.

The sun rose, and, from the ramparts of Quebec, the astonished people saw the Plains of Abraham glittering with arms, and the dark-red lines of the English forming in array of battle.   Breathless messengers had borne the evil tidings to Montcalm, and far and near his wide-extended camp resounded with the rolling of alarm drums and the din of startled preparation.   He, too, had had his struggles and his sorrows.   The civil power had thwarted him; famine, discontent, and disaffection were rife among his soldiers; and no small portion of the Canadian militia had dispersed from sheer starvation.   In spite of all, he had trusted to hold out till the winter frosts should drive the invaders from

---

[1] Knox, *Journal*, II. 68, note.
[2] Despatch of Admiral Saunders, Sept. 20, 1759.

ʼ before the town ; when, on that disastrous morning, the news of their successful temerity fell like a cannon shot upon his ear. Still he asssumed a tone of confidence. "They have got to the weak side of us at last," he is reported to have said, "and we must crush them with our numbers." With headlong haste, his troops were pouring over the bridge of the St. Charles, and gathering in heavy masses under the western ramparts of the town. Could numbers give assurance of success, their triumph would have been secure ; for five French battalions and the armed colonial peasantry amounted in all to more than seven thousand five hundred men. Full in sight before them stretched the long, thin lines of the British forces, — the half-wild Highlanders, the steady soldiery of England, and the hardy levies of the provinces, — less than five thousand in number, but all inured to battle, and strong in the full assurance of success. Yet, could the chiefs of that gallant army have pierced the secrets of the future, could they have foreseen that the victory which they burned to achieve would have robbed England of her proudest boast, that the conquest of Canada would pave the way for the independence of America, their swords would have dropped from their hands, and the heroic fire have gone out within their hearts.

It was nine o'clock, and the adverse armies stood motionless, each gazing on the other. The clouds hung low, and, at intervals, warm light showers descended, besprinkling both alike. The coppice and cornfields in front of the British troops were filled with French sharpshooters, who kept up a distant, spattering fire. Here and there a soldier fell in the ranks, and the gap was filled in silence.

At a little before ten, the British could see that Montcalm was preparing to advance, and, in a few moments, all his troops appeared in rapid motion. They came on in three divisions, shouting after the manner of their nation, and firing heavily as soon as they came within range. In the British ranks, not a trigger was pulled, not a soldier stirred; and their ominous composure seemed to damp the spirits of the assailants. It was not till the French were within forty yards that the fatal word was given, and the British muskets blazed forth at once in one crashing explosion. Like a ship at full career, arrested with sudden ruin on a sunken rock, the ranks of Montcalm staggered, shivered, and broke before that wasting storm of lead. The smoke, rolling along the field, for a moment shut out the view; but when the white wreaths were scattered on the wind, a wretched spectacle was disclosed; men and officers tumbled in heaps, battalions resolved into a mob, order and obedience gone; and when the British muskets were levelled for a second volley, the masses of the militia were seen to cower and shrink with uncontrollable panic. For a few minutes, the French regulars stood their ground, returning a sharp and not ineffectual fire. But now, echoing cheer on cheer, redoubling volley on volley, trampling the dying and the dead and driving the fugitives in crowds, the British troops advanced and swept the field before them.

The ardor of the men burst all restraint. They broke into a run, and with unsparing slaughter chased the flying multitude to the gates of Quebec. Foremost of all, the light-footed Highlanders dashed along in furious pursuit, hewing down the Frenchmen with their broadswords, and slaying many in the very ditch of the fortifications. Never was victory more quick or more decisive.[1]

In the short action and pursuit, the French lost fifteen hundred men, killed, wounded, and taken. Of the remainder, some escaped within the city, and others fled across the St. Charles to rejoin their comrades who had been left to guard the camp. The pursuers were recalled by sound of trumpet; the broken ranks were formed afresh, and the English troops withdrawn beyond reach of the cannon of Quebec. Bougainville, with his corps, arrived from the upper country, and, hovering about their rear, threatened an attack; but when he saw what greeting was prepared for him, he abandoned his purpose and withdrew. Townshend and Murray, the only general officers who remained unhurt, passed to the head of every regiment in turn, and thanked the soldiers for the bravery they had shown; yet the triumph of the victors was mingled with sadness, as the tidings went from rank to rank that Wolfe had fallen.

In the heat of the action, as he advanced at the head of the grenadiers of Louisburg, a bullet shat-

---

[1] Despatch of General Townshend, Sept. 20. Gardiner, *Memoirs of the Siege of Quebec*, 28. *Journal of the Siege of Quebec, by a Gentleman in an Eminent Station on the Spot*, 40. *Letter to a Right Honorable Patriot on the Glorious Success of Quebec Annual Register for 1759*, 40.

tered his wrist; but he wrapped his handkerchief about the wound, and showed no sign of pain.   A moment more, and a ball pierced his side.   Still he pressed forward, waving his sword and cheering his soldiers to the attack, when a third shot lodged deep within his breast.   He paused, reeled, and, staggering to one side, fell to the earth. Brown, a lieutenant of the grenadiers, Henderson, a volunteer, an officer of artillery, and a private soldier, raised him together in their arms, and, bearing him to the rear, laid him softly on the grass.   They asked if he would have a surgeon; but he shook his head, and answered that all was over with him.   His eyes closed with the torpor of approaching death, and those around sustained his fainting form.   Yet they could not withhold their gaze from the wild turmoil before them, and the charging ranks of their companions rushing through fire and smoke.   "See how they run," one of the officers exclaimed, as the French fled in confusion before the levelled bayonets. "Who run?" demanded Wolfe, opening his eyes like a man aroused from sleep.   "The enemy, sir," was the reply; "they give way everywhere." "Then," said the dying general, "tell Colonel Burton to march Webb's regiment down to Charles River, to cut off their retreat from the bridge. Now, God be praised, I will die in peace," he murmured; and, turning on his side, he calmly breathed his last.[1]

---

[1] Knox, II 78.   Knox derived his information from the person who supported Wolfe in his dying moments.

Almost at the same moment fell his great adversary, Montcalm, as he strove, with vain bravery, to rally his shattered ranks. Struck down with a mortal wound, he was placed upon a litter and borne to the General Hospital on the banks of the St. Charles. The surgeons told him that he could not recover. "I am glad of it," was his calm reply. He then asked how long he might survive, and was told that he had not many hours remaining. "So much the better," he said; "I am happy that I shall not live to see the surrender of Quebec." Officers from the garrison came to his bedside to ask his orders and instructions. "I will give no more orders," replied the defeated soldier; "I have much business that must be attended to, of greater moment than your ruined garrison and this wretched country. My time is very short; therefore, pray leave me." The officers withdrew, and none remained in the chamber but his confessor and the Bishop of Quebec. To the last, he expressed his contempt for his own mutinous and half-famished troops, and his admiration for the disciplined valor of his opponents.[1] He died before midnight, and was buried at his own desire in a cavity of the earth formed by the bursting of a bombshell.

The victorious army encamped before Quebec, and pushed their preparations for the siege with zealous energy; but before a single gun was brought to bear, the white flag was hung out, and

---

[1] Knox, II. 77.

the garrison surrendered. On the eighteenth of September, 1759, the rock-built citadel of Canada passed forever from the hands of its ancient masters.

The victory on the Plains of Abraham and the downfall of Quebec filled all England with pride and exultation. From north to south, the land blazed with illuminations, and resounded with the ringing of bells, the firing of guns, and the shouts of the multitude. In one village alone all was dark and silent amid the general joy; for here dwelt the widowed mother of Wolfe. The populace, with unwonted delicacy, respected her lonely sorrow, and forbore to obtrude the sound of their rejoicings upon her grief for one who had been through life her pride and solace, and repaid her love with a tender and constant devotion.[1]

Canada, crippled and dismembered by the disasters of this year's campaign, lay waiting, as it were, the final stroke which was to extinguish her last remains of life, and close the eventful story of French dominion in America. Her limbs and her head were lopped away, but life still fluttered at her heart. Quebec, Niagara, Frontenac, and Crown Point had fallen; but Montreal and the adjacent country still held out, and thither, with the opening season of 1760, the British commanders turned all their energies. Three armies were to enter Canada at three several points, and, conquering as they advanced, converge towards Mon-

---

[1] *Annual Register for* 1759, 43.

treal as a common centre. In accordance with this plan, Sir Jeffrey Amherst embarked at Oswego, crossed Lake Ontario, and descended the St. Lawrence with ten thousand men ; while Colonel Haviland advanced by way of Lake Champlain and the River Sorel, and General Murray ascended from Quebec, with a body of the veterans who had fought on the Plains of Abraham.

By a singular concurrence of fortune and skill, the three armies reached the neighborhood of Montreal on the same day. The feeble and disheartened garrison could offer no resistance, and on the eighth of September, 1760, the Marquis de Vaudreuil surrendered Canada, with all its dependencies, to the British crown.

CHAPTER V.

1755–1763.

THE WILDERNESS AND ITS TENANTS AT THE CLOSE OF THE FRENCH WAR.

WE have already seen how, after the defeat of Braddock, the western tribes rose with one accord against the English. Then, for the first time, Pennsylvania felt the scourge of Indian war; and her neighbors, Maryland and Virginia, shared her misery. Through the autumn of 1755, the storm raged with devastating fury; but the following year brought some abatement of its violence. This may be ascribed partly to the interference of the Iroquois, who, at the instances of Sir William Johnson, urged the Delawares to lay down the hatchet, and partly to the persuasions of several prominent men among the Quakers, who, by kind and friendly treatment, had gained the confidence of the Indians.[1] By these means, that portion of the Delawares and their kindred tribes who dwelt upon the Susquehanna, were induced to send a deputation of chiefs to Easton, in the summer of

---

[1] Gordon, *Hist Penn.* 321. *Causes of the Alienation of the Delaware and Shawanese Indians from the British Interest. MS. Johnson Papers.*

1757, to meet the provincial delegates; and here, after much delay and difficulty, a treaty of peace was concluded.

This treaty, however, did not embrace the Indians of the Ohio, who comprised the most formidable part of the Delawares and Shawanoes, and who still continued their murderous attacks. It was not till the summer of 1758, when General Forbes, with a considerable army, was advancing against Fort du Quesne, that these exasperated savages could be brought to reason. Well knowing that, should Forbes prove successful, they might expect a summary chastisement for their misdeeds, they began to waver in their attachment to the French; and the latter, in the hour of peril, found themselves threatened with desertion by allies who had shown an ample alacrity in the season of prosperity. This new tendency of the Ohio Indians was fostered by a wise step on the part of the English. A man was found bold and hardy enough to venture into the midst of their villages, bearing the news of the treaty at Easton, and the approach of Forbes, coupled with proposals of peace from the governor of Pennsylvania.

This stout-hearted emissary was Christian Frederic Post, a Moravian missionary, who had long lived with the Indians, had twice married·among them, and, by his upright dealings and plain good sense, had gained their confidence and esteem. His devout and conscientious spirit, his fidelity to what he deemed his duty, his imperturbable courage, his prudence and his address, well fitted him for the critical mission. His journals, written in a style of quaint simplicity, are full of lively details, and afford a curious picture of forest life and character. He left Philadelphia in July, attended by a party of friendly Indians, on whom he relied for protection. Reaching the Ohio, he found himself beset with perils from the jealousy and malevolence of the savage warriors, and the machinations of the French, who would gladly have destroyed him.[1]   Yet he found friends where-

---

[1] The following are extracts from his journals : —

" We set out from Kushkushkee for Sankonk ; my company consisted of twenty-five horsemen and fifteen foot. We arrived at Sankonk in the afternoon. The people of the town were much disturbed at my coming, and received me in a very rough manner. They surrounded me with drawn knives in their hands, in such a manner that I could hardly get along ; running up against me with their breasts open, as if they wanted some pretence to kill me. I saw by their countenances they sought my death. Their faces were quite distorted with rage, and they went so far as to say, I should not live long ; but some Indians, with whom I was formerly acquainted, coming up and saluting me in a friendly manner, their behavior to me was quickly changed." . . . "Some of my party desired me not to stir from the fire, for that the French had offered a great reward for my scalp, and that there were several parties out on that purpose. Accordingly I stuck constantly as close to the fire as if I had been chained there. . . .

"In the afternoon, all the captains gathered together in the middle town ; they sent for us, and desired we should give them information of our message. Accordingly we did. We read the message with great satisfaction to them. It was a great pleasure both to them and us. The number of captains and counsellors were sixteen. In the evening, messengers arrived from Fort Duquesne, with a string of wampum from the commander ; upon which they all came together in the house where we lodged. The messengers delivered their string, with these words from their father, the French king. —

" ' My children, come to me, and hear what I have to say. The English are coming with an army to destroy both you and me. I therefore desire you immediately, my children, to hasten with all the young men ; we will drive the English and destroy them. I, as a father, will tell you always what is best.' He laid the string before one of the captains. After a little conversation, the captain stood up, and said, ' I have just

ever he went, and finally succeeded in convincing the Indians that their true interest lay in a strict neutrality. When, therefore, Forbes appeared before Fort du Quesne, the French found themselves abandoned to their own resources; and, unable to hold their ground, they retreated down the Ohio, leaving the fort an easy conquest to the invaders. During the autumn, the Ohio Indians sent their deputies to Easton, where a great council was held, and a formal peace concluded with the provinces.[1]

While the friendship of these tribes was thus lost and regained, their ancient tyrants, the Iroquois, remained in a state of very doubtful attachment. At the outbreak of the war, they had shown, it is true, many signs of friendship;[2] but the disasters of the first campaign had given them

heard something of our brethren, the English, which pleaseth me much better. I will not go Give it to the others; maybe they will go.' The messenger took up again the string, and said, 'He won't go; he has heard of the English.' Then all cried out, 'Yes, yes, we have heard from the English.' He then threw the string to the other fireplace, where the other captains were; but they kicked it from one to another, as if it was a snake. Captain Peter took a stick, and with it flung the string from one end of the room to the other, and said, 'Give it to the French captain, and let him go with his young men; he boasted much of his fighting; now let us see his fighting. We have often ventured our lives for him; and had hardly a loaf of bread when we came to him; and now he thinks we should jump to serve him.' Then we saw the French captain mortified to the uttermost; he looked as pale as death. The Indians discoursed and joked till midnight; and the French captain sent messengers at midnight to Fort Duquesne."

The kicking about of the wampum belt is the usual indication of contempt for the message of which the belt is the token. The uses of wampum will be described hereafter.

[1] *Minutes of Council at Easton*, 1758.

[2] *Account of Conferences between Major-General Sir W. Johnson and the Chief Suchems and Warriors of the Six Nations* (Lond. 1756).

a contemptible idea of British prowess. This impression was deèpened, when, in the following year, they saw Oswego taken by the French, and the British general, Webb, retreat with dastardly haste from an enemy who did not dream of pursuing him. At this time, some of the confederates actually took up the hatchet on the side of France, and there was danger that the rest might follow their example.[1] But now a new element was infused into the British counsels. The fortunes of the conflict began to change. Du Quesne and Louisburg were taken, and the Iroquois conceived a better opinion of the British arms. Their friendship was no longer a matter of doubt; and in 1760, when Amherst was preparing to advance on Montreal, the warriors flocked to his camp like vultures to the carcass. Yet there is little doubt, that, had their sachems and orators followed the dictates of their cooler judgment, they would not have aided in destroying Canada; for they could see that in the colonies of France lay the only barrier against the growing power and ambition of the English provinces.

The Hurons of Lorette, the Abenakis, and other domiciliated tribes of Canada, ranged themselves on the side of France throughout the war; and at its conclusion, they, in common with the Canadians, may be regarded in the light of a conquered people.

The numerous tribes of the remote west had, with few exceptions, played the part of active

---

[1] MS. *Johnson Papers.*

allies of the French; and warriors might be found on the farthest shores of Lake Superior who garnished their war-dress with the scalp-locks of murdered Englishmen. With the conquest of Canada, these tribes subsided into a state of inaction, which was not long to continue.

And now, before launching into the story of the sanguinary war which forms our proper and immediate theme, it will be well to survey the grand arena of the strife, the goodly heritage which the wretched tribes of the forest struggled to retrieve from the hands of the spoiler.

One vast. continuous forest shadowed the fertile soil, covering the land as the grass covers a garden lawn, sweeping over hill and hollow in endless undulation, burying mountains in verdure, and mantling brooks and rivers from the light of day. Green intervals dotted with browsing deer, and broad plains alive with buffalo, broke the sameness of the woodland scenery. Unnumbered rivers seamed the forest with their devious windings. Vast lakes washed its boundaries, where the Indian voyager, in his birch canoe, could descry no land beyond the world of waters. Yet this prolific wilderness, teeming with waste fertility, was but a hunting-ground and a battle-field to a few fierce hordes of savages. Here and there, in some rich meadow opened to the sun, the Indian squaws turned the black mould with their rude implements of bone or iron, and sowed their scanty stores of maize and beans. Human labor drew no other tribute from that exhaustless soil.

So thin and scattered was the native population, that, even in those parts which were thought well peopled, one might sometimes journey for days together through the twilight forest, and meet no human form. Broad tracts were left in solitude. All Kentucky was a vacant waste, a mere skirmishing ground for the hostile war-parties of the north and south. A great part of Upper Canada, of Michigan, and of Illinois, besides other portions of the west, were tenanted by wild beasts alone. To form a close estimate of the numbers of the erratic bands who roamed this wilderness would be impossible; but it may be affirmed that, between the Mississippi on the west and the ocean on the east, between the Ohio on the south and Lake Superior on the north, the whole Indian population, at the close of the French war, did not greatly exceed ten thousand fighting men. Of these, following the statement of Sir William Johnson, in 1763, the Iroquois had nineteen hundred and fifty, the Delawares about six hundred, the Shawanoes about three hundred, the Wyandots about four hundred and fifty, and the Miami tribes, with their neighbors the Kickapoos, eight hundred; while the Ottawas, the Ojibwas, and other wandering tribes of the north, defy all efforts at enumeration.[1]

A close survey of the condition of the tribes at this period will detect some signs of improvement,

[1] The estimates given by Croghan, Bouquet, and Hutchins, do not quite accord with that of Johnson. But the discrepancy is no greater than might have been expected from the difficulties of the case.

but many more of degeneracy and decay. To
commence with the Iroquois, for to them with justice the priority belongs: Onondaga, the ancient
capital of their confederacy, where their council-
fire had burned from immemorial time, was now
no longer what it had been in the days of its greatness, when Count Frontenac had mustered all
Canada to assail it. The thickly clustered dwellings, with their triple rows of palisades, had vanished. A little stream, twisting along the valley,
choked up with logs and driftwood, and half hidden by woods and thickets, some forty houses of
bark, scattered along its banks, amid rank grass,
neglected clumps of bushes, and ragged patches
of corn and peas, — such was Onondaga when
Bartram saw it, and such, no doubt, it remained at
the time of which I write.[1] Conspicuous among
the other structures, and distinguished only by its
superior size, stood the great council-house, whose
bark walls had often sheltered the congregated
wisdom of the confederacy, and heard the highest
efforts of forest eloquence. The other villages of
the Iroquois resembled Onondaga; for though several were of larger size, yet none retained those
defensive stockades which had once protected them.[2]
From their European neighbors the Iroquois had
borrowed many appliances of comfort and subsistence. Horses, swine, and in some instances cattle,

[1] Bartram, *Observations*, 41.

[2] I am indebted to the kindness of Rev. S. K. Lothrop for a copy of
the journal of Mr Kirkland on his missionary tour among the Iroquois
in 1765. The journal contains much information respecting their man
ners and condition at this period.

were to be found among them. Guns and gunpowder aided them in the chase. Knives, hatchets, kettles, and hoes of iron, had supplanted their rude household utensils and implements of tillage; but with all this, English whiskey had more than cancelled every benefit which English civilization had conferred.

High up the Susquehanna were seated the Nanticokes, Conoys, and Mohicans, with a portion of the Delawares. Detached bands of the western Iroquois dwelt upon the head waters of the Alleghany, mingled with their neighbors, the Delawares, who had several villages upon this stream. The great body of the latter nation, however, lived upon the Beaver Creeks and the Muskingum, in numerous scattered towns and hamlets, whose barbarous names it is useless to record. Squalid log cabins and conical wigwams of bark were clustered at random, or ranged to form rude streets and squares. Starveling horses grazed on the neighboring meadows; girls and children bathed and laughed in the adjacent river; warriors smoked their pipes in haughty indolence; squaws labored in the cornfields, or brought fagots from the forest, and shrivelled hags screamed from lodge to lodge. In each village one large building stood prominent among the rest, devoted to purposes of public meeting, dances, festivals, and the entertainment of strangers. Thither the traveller would be conducted, seated on a bear-skin, and plentifully regaled with hominy and venison.

The Shawanoes had sixteen small villages upon

the Scioto and its branches. Farther towards the
west, on the waters of the Wabash and the
Maumee, dwelt the Miamis, who, less exposed,
from their position, to the poison of the whiskey-
keg, and the example of debauched traders, retained their ancient character and customs in
greater purity than their eastern neighbors. This
cannot be said of the Illinois, who dwelt near the
borders of the Mississippi, and who, having lived
for more than half a century in close contact with
the French, had become a corrupt and degenerate
race. The Wyandots of Sandusky and Detroit far
surpassed the surrounding tribes in energy of
character and in social progress. Their log dwellings were strong and commodious, their agriculture
was very considerable, their name stood high in
war and policy, and they were regarded with
deference by all the adjacent Indians. It is needless to pursue farther this catalogue of tribes,
since the position of each will appear hereafter as
they advance in turn upon the stage of action.

The English settlements lay like a narrow strip
between the wilderness and the sea, and, as the sea
had its ports, so also the forest had its places of
rendezvous and outfit. Of these, by far the most
important in the northern provinces was the frontier
city of Albany. From thence it was that traders
and soldiers, bound to the country of the Iroquois,
or the more distant wilds of the interior, set out
upon their arduous journey. Embarking in a
bateau or a canoe, rowed by the hardy men who
earned their livelihood in this service, the traveller

would ascend the Mohawk, passing the old Dutch town of Schenectady, the two seats of Sir William Johnson, Fort Hunter at the mouth of the Scoharie, and Fort Herkimer at the German Flats, until he reached Fort Stanwix at the head of the river navigation.   Then crossing over land to Wood Creek, he would follow its tortuous course, over-shadowed by the dense forest on its banks, until he arrived at the little fortification called the Royal Blockhouse, and the waters of the Oneida Lake spread before him.   Crossing to its western ex-tremity, and passing under the wooden ramparts of Fort Brewerton, he would descend the River Oswego to Oswego,[1] on the banks of Lake Ontario. Here the vast navigation of the Great Lakes would

---

[1] MS *Journal of Lieutenant Gorell*, 1763.   Anonymous MS. *Journal of a Tour to Niagara in* 1765.   The following is an extract from the latter : —

"July 2d.   Dined with Sir Wm. at Johnson Hall.   The office of Superintendent very troublesome   Sir Wm. continually plagued with Indians about him — generally from 300 to 900 in number — spoil his garden, and keep his house always dirty . . .

"10th.   Punted and rowed up the Mohawk River against the stream, which, on account of the rapidity of the current, is very hard work for the poor soldiers   Encamped on the banks of the river, about 9 miles from Harkimer's.

" The inconveniences attending a married Subaltern strongly appear in this tour.   What with the sickness of their wives, the squealing of their children, and the smallness of their pay, I think the gentlemen discover no common share of philosophy in keeping themselves from running mad. Officers and soldiers, with their wives and children, legitimate and ille-gitimate, make altogether a pretty compound oglio, which does not tend towards showing military matrimony off to any great advantage, . .

"Monday, 14th   Went on horseback by the side of Wood Creek, 20 miles, to the Royal Blockhouse, a kind of wooden castle, proof against any Indian attacks   It is now abandoned by the troops, and a sutler lives there, who keeps rum, milk, rackoons, etc , which, though none of the most elegant, is comfortable to strangers passing that way.   The Blockhouse is situated on the east end of the Oneida Lake, and is sur rounded by the Oneida Indians, one of the Six Nations."

be open before him, interrupted only by the difficult portage at the Cataract of Niagara.

The chief thoroughfare from the middle colonies to the Indian country was from Philadelphia westward, across the Alleghanies, to the valley of the Ohio. Peace was no sooner concluded with the hostile tribes, than the adventurous fur-traders, careless of risk to life and property, hastened over the mountains, each eager to be foremost in the wilderness market. Their merchandise was sometimes carried in wagons as far as the site of Fort du Quesne, which the English rebuilt after its capture, changing its name to Fort Pitt. From this point the goods were packed on the backs of horses, and thus distributed among the various Indian villages. More commonly, however, the whole journey was performed by means of trains, or, as they were called, brigades of packhorses, which, leaving the frontier settlements, climbed the shadowy heights of the Alleghanies, and threaded the forests of the Ohio, diving through thickets, and wading over streams. The men employed in this perilous calling were a rough, bold, and intractable class, often as fierce and truculent as the Indians themselves. A blanket coat, or a frock of smoked deer-skin, a rifle on the shoulder, and a knife and tomahawk in the belt, formed their ordinary equipment. The principal trader, the owner of the merchandise, would fix his headquarters at some large Indian town, whence he would despatch his subordinates to the surrounding villages, with a suitable supply of blankets and red cloth, guns and hatchets, liquor, tobacco, paint, beads, and hawks' bells. This wild traffic was liable to every species of disorder; and it is not to be wondered at that, in a region where law was unknown, the jealousies of rival traders should become a fruitful source of broils, robberies, and murders.

In the backwoods, all land travelling was on foot, or on horseback. It was no easy matter for a novice, embarrassed with his cumbrous gun, to urge his horse through the thick trunks and under-growth, or even to ride at speed along the narrow Indian trails, where at every yard the impending branches switched him across the face. At night, the camp would be formed by the side of some rivulet or spring; and, if the traveller was skilful in the use of his rifle, a haunch of venison would often form his evening meal. If it rained, a shed of elm or bass-wood bark was the ready work of an hour, a pile of evergreen boughs formed a bed, and the saddle or the knapsack a pillow. A party of Indian wayfarers would often be met journeying through the forest, a chief, or a warrior, perhaps, with his squaws and family. The Indians would usually make their camp in the neighborhood of the white men; and at meal-time the warrior would seldom fail to seat himself by the traveller's fire, and gaze with solemn gravity at the viands before him. If, when the repast was over, a frag-ment of bread or a cup of coffee should be handed to him, he would receive these highly prized rarities with an ejaculation of gratitude; for nothing is more remarkable in the character of this people than the union of inordinate pride and a generous love of glory with the mendicity of a beggar or a child.

He who wished to visit the remoter tribes of the Mississippi valley — an attempt, however, which, until several years after the conquest of Canada, no Englishman could have made without great risk of losing his scalp — would find no easier course than to descend the Ohio in a canoe or bateau. He might float for more than eleven hundred miles down this liquid highway of the wilderness, and, except the deserted cabins of Logstown, a little below Fort Pitt, the remnant of a Shawanoe village at the mouth of the Scioto, and an occasional hamlet or solitary wigwam along the deeply wooded banks, he would discern no trace of human habitation through all this vast extent. The body of the Indian population lay to the northward, about the waters of the tributary streams. It behooved the voyager to observe a sleepless caution and a hawk-eyed vigilance. Sometimes his anxious scrutiny would detect a faint blue smoke stealing upward above the green bosom of the forest, and betraying the encamping place of some lurking war-party. Then the canoe would be drawn in haste beneath the overhanging bushes which skirted the shore ; nor would the voyage be resumed until darkness closed, when the little vessel would drift swiftly and safely by the point of danger.[1]

[1] Mitchell, *Contest in America.* Pouchot, *Guerre de l'Amérique.* *Expedition against the Ohio Indians, appendix.* Hutchins, *Topographical Descrip-*

Within the nominal limits of the Illinois Indians, and towards the southern extremity of the present state of Illinois, were those isolated Canadian settlements, which had subsisted here since the latter part of the preceding century. Kaskaskia, Cahokia, and Vincennes were the centres of this scattered population. From Vincennes one might paddle his canoe northward up the Wabash. until he reached the little wooden fort of Ouatanon. Thence a path through the woods led to the banks of the Maumee. Two or three Canadians, or half-breeds, of whom there were numbers about the fort, would carry the canoe on their shoulders, or, for a bottle of whiskey, a few Miami Indians might be bribed to undertake the task. On the Maumee, at the end of the path, stood Fort Miami, near the spot where Fort Wayne was afterwards built. From this point one might descend the Maumee to Lake Erie, and visit the neighboring fort of Sandusky, or, if he chose, steer through the Strait of Detroit, and explore the watery wastes of the northern lakes, finding occasional harborage at the little military posts which commanded their important points. Most of these western posts were transferred to the English, during the autumn of 1760; but the settlements of the Illinois remained several years longer under French control.

Eastward, on the waters of Lake Erie, and the Alleghany, stood three small forts, Presqu' Isle, Le

tion of Virginia, etc. Pownall, *Topographical Description of North America.* Evans, *Analysis of a Map of the Middle British Colonies.* Beatty, *Journal of a Tour in America.* Smith, *Narrative.* M'Cullough, *Narrative* Jemmison, *Narrative* Post, *Journals.* Washington, *Journals,* 1753–1770 Gist, *Journal,* 1750 Croghan. *Journal,* 1765, etc., etc.

Bœuf, and Venango, which had passed into the
hands of the English soon after the capture of
Fort du Quesne.   The feeble garrisons of all these
western posts, exiled from civilization, lived in the
solitude of military hermits.   Through the long,
hot days of summer, and the protracted cold of
winter, time hung heavy on their hands.   Their
resources of employment and recreation were few
and meagre.   They found partners in their loneli-
ness among the young beauties of the Indian camps.
They hunted and fished, shot at targets, and played
at games of chance; and when, by good fortune, a
traveller found his way among them, he was greeted
with a hearty and open-handed welcome, and plied
with eager questions touching the great world from
which they were banished men.   Yet, tedious as it
was, their secluded life was seasoned with stirring
danger.   The surrounding forests were peopled
with a race dark and subtle as their own sunless
mazes.   At any hour, those jealous tribes might
raise the war-cry.   No human foresight could pre-
dict the sallies of their fierce caprice, and in ceaseless watching lay the only safety.

When the European and the savage are brought
in contact, both are gainers, and both are losers.
The former loses the refinements of civilization,
but he gains, in the rough schooling of the wilderness, a rugged independence, a self-sustaining
energy, and powers of action and perception before
unthought of.   The savage gains new means of
comfort and support, cloth, iron, and gunpowder:
yet these apparent benefits have often proved but

instruments of ruin. They soon become necessities, and the unhappy hunter, forgetting the weapons of his fathers, must thenceforth depend on the white man for ease, happiness, and life itself.

Those rude and hardy men, hunters and traders, scouts and guides, who ranged the woods beyond the English borders, and formed a connecting link between barbarism and civilization, have been touched upon already. They were a distinct, peculiar class, marked with striking contrasts of good and evil. Many, though by no means all, were coarse, audacious, and unscrupulous; yet, even in the worst, one might often have found a vigorous growth of warlike virtues, an iron endurance, an undespairing courage, a wondrous sagacity, and singular fertility of resource. In them was renewed, with all its ancient energy, that wild and daring spirit, that force and hardihood of mind, which marked our barbarous ancestors of Germany and Norway. These sons of the wilderness still survive. We may find them to this day, not in the valley of the Ohio, nor on the shores of the lakes, but far westward on the desert range of the buffalo, and among the solitudes of Oregon. Even now, while I write, some lonely trapper is climbing the perilous defiles of the Rocky Mountains, his strong frame cased in time-worn buck-skin, his rifle griped in his sinewy hand. Keenly he peers from side to side, lest Blackfoot or Arapahoe should ambuscade his path. The rough earth is his bed, a morsel of dried meat and a draught of water are his food and drink, and death and danger his companions. No anchorite could fare worse, no hero could dare more ; yet his wild, hard life has resistless charms ; and, while he can wield a rifle, he will never leave it. Go with him to the rendezvous, and he is a stoic no more. Here, rioting among his comrades, his native appetites break loose in mad excess, in deep carouse, and desperate gaming. Then follow close the quarrel, the challenge, the fight, — two rusty rifles and fifty yards of prairie.

The nursling of civilization, placed in the midst of the forest, and abandoned to his own resources, is helpless as an infant. There is no clew to the labyrinth. Bewildered and amazed, he circles round and round in hopeless wanderings. Despair and famine make him their prey, and unless the birds of heaven minister to his wants, he dies in misery. Not so the practised woodsman. To him, the forest is a home. It yields him food, shelter, and raiment, and he threads its trackless depths with undeviating foot. To lure the game, to circumvent the lurking foe, to guide his course by the stars, the wind, the streams, or the trees, — such are the arts which the white man has learned from the red. Often, indeed, the pupil has outstripped his master. He can hunt as well ; he can fight better ; and yet there are niceties of the woodsman's craft in which the white man must yield the palm to his savage rival. Seldom can he boast, in equal measure, that subtlety of sense, more akin to the instinct of brutes than to human reason, which reads the signs of the forest as the scholar reads the printed page, to which the whistle of a bird

can speak clearly as the tongue of man, and the
rustle of a leaf give knowledge of life or death.[1]
With us the name of the savage is a byword of
reproach. The Indian would look with equal scorn
on those who, buried in useless lore, are blind and
deaf to the great world of nature.

A striking example of Indian acuteness once came under my observation   Travelling in company with a Canadian named Raymond, and
an Ogillallah Indian, we came at nightfall to a small stream called Chug-
water, a branch of Laramie Creek   As we prepared to encamp, we observed the ashes of a fire, the footprints of men and horses, and other
indications that a party had been upon the spot not many days before.
Having secured our horses for the night, Raymond and I sat down and
lighted our pipes, my companion, who had spent his whole life in the
Indian country, hazarding various conjectures as to the numbers and
character of our predecessors   Soon after, we were joined by the Indian,
who, meantime, had been prowling about the place. Raymond asked
what discovery he had made.   He answered, that the party were friendly,
and that they consisted of eight men, both whites and Indians, several of
whom he named, affirming that he knew them well   To an inquiry how
he gained his information, he would make no intelligible reply.   On the
next day, reaching Fort Laramie, a post of the American Fur Company,
we found that he was correct in every particular, — a circumstance the
more remarkable, as he had been with us for three weeks, and could have
had no other means of knowledge than we ourselves.

CHAPTER VI.

1760.

THE ENGLISH TAKE POSSESSION OF THE WESTERN POSTS.

THE war was over. The plains around Montreal were dotted with the white tents of three victorious armies, and the work of conquest was complete. Canada, with all her dependencies, had yielded to the British crown; but it still remained to carry into full effect the terms of the surrender, and take possession of those western outposts, where the lilies of France had not as yet descended from the flagstaff. The execution of this task, neither an easy nor a safe one, was assigned to a provincial officer, Major Robert Rogers.

Rogers was a native of New Hampshire. He commanded a body of provincial rangers, and stood in high repute as a partisan officer. Putnam and Stark were his associates; and it was in this woodland warfare that the former achieved many of those startling adventures and hair-breadth escapes which have made his name familiar at every New-England fireside. Rogers's Rangers, half hunters, half woodsmen, trained in a discipline of their

11

own, and armed, like Indians, with hatchet, knife, and gun, were employed in a service of peculiar hardship. Their chief theatre of action was the mountainous region of Lake George, the debatable ground between the hostile forts of Ticonderoga and William Henry. The deepest recesses of these romantic solitudes had heard the French and Indian yell, and the answering shout of the hardy New-England men. In summer, they passed down the lake in whale boats or canoes, or threaded the pathways of the woods in single file, like the savages themselves. In winter, they journeyed through the swamps on snowshoes, skated along the frozen surface of the lake, and bivouacked at night among the snow-drifts. They intercepted French messengers, encountered French scouting parties, and carried off prisoners from under the very walls of Ticonderoga. Their hardships and adventures, their marches and countermarches, their frequent skirmishes and midwinter battles, had made them famous throughout America; and though it was the fashion of the day to sneer at the efforts of provincial troops, the name of Rogers's Rangers was never mentioned but with honor.

Their commander was a man tall and strong in person, and rough in feature. He was versed in all the arts of woodcraft, sagacious, prompt, and resolute, yet so cautious withal that he sometimes incurred the unjust charge of cowardice. His mind, naturally active, was by no means uncultivated; and his books and unpublished letters bear witness that his style as a writer was not contemptible. But his vain, restless, and grasping spirit, and more than doubtful honesty, proved the ruin of an enviable reputation. Six years after the expedition of which I am about to speak, he was tried by a court-martial for a meditated act of treason, the surrender of Fort Michillimackinac into the hands of the Spaniards, who were at that time masters of Upper Louisiana.[1] Not long after, if we may trust his own account, he passed over to the Barbary States, entered the service of the Dey of Algiers, and fought two battles under his banners. At the opening of the war of independence, he returned to his native country, where he made professions of patriotism, but was strongly suspected by many, including Washington himself, of acting the part of a spy. In fact, he soon openly espoused the British cause, and received a colonel's commission from the crown. His services, however, proved of little consequence. In 1778, he was proscribed and banished, under the act of New Hampshire, and the remainder of his life was passed in such obscurity that it is difficult to determine when and where he died.[2]

[1] MS. *Gage Papers*

[2] Sabine, *American Loyalists*, 576. Sparks, *Writings of Washington*, III 208, 244, 439 ; IV. 128, 520, 524.

Although Rogers, especially where his pecuniary interest was concerned, was far from scrupulous, I have no hesitation in following his account of the expedition up the lakes. The incidents of each day are minuted down in a dry, unambitious style, bearing the clear impress of truth. Extracts from the orderly books and other official papers are given, while portions of the narrative, verified by contemporary documents, may stand as earnests for the truth of the whole.

Rogers's published works consist of the *Journals* of his ranging service

On the twelfth of September, 1760, Rogers, then at the height of his reputation, received orders from Sir Jeffrey Amherst to ascend the lakes with a detachment of rangers, and take possession, in the name of his Britannic Majesty, of Detroit, Michillimackinac, and other western posts included in the late capitulation. He left Montreal, on the following day, with two hundred rangers, in fifteen whale boats. Stemming the surges of La Chine and the Cedars, they left behind them the straggling hamlet which bore the latter name, and formed at that day the western limit of Canadian settlement.[1] They gained Lake Ontario, skirted its northern shore, amid rough and boisterous weather, and crossing at its western extremity, reached Fort Niagara on the first of October. Carrying their

and his *Concise Account of North America*, a small volume containing much valuable information. Both appeared in London in 1765. To these may be added a curious drama, called *Ponteach, or the Savages of America*, which appears to have been written, in part, at least, by him. It is very rare, and besides the copy in my possession, I know of but one other, which may be found in the library of the British Museum. For an account of this curious production, see Appendix, B. An engraved full-length portrait of Rogers was published in London in 1776. He is represented as a tall, strong man, dressed in the costume of a ranger, with a powder-horn slung at his side, a gun resting in the hollow of his arm, and a countenance by no means prepossessing. Behind him, at a little distance, stand his Indian followers.

The steep mountain called Rogers' Slide, near the northern end of Lake George, derives its name from the tradition that, during the French war, being pursued by a party of Indians, he slid on snowshoes down its precipitous front, for more than a thousand feet, to the frozen lake below. On beholding the achievement, the Indians, as well they might, believed him under the protection of the Great Spirit, and gave over the chase. The story seems unfounded ; yet it was not far from this mountain that the rangers fought one of their most desperate winter battles, against a force of many times their number.

[1] Henry, *Travels and Adventures*, 9.

boats over the portage, they launched them once
more above the cataract, and slowly pursued their
voyage; while Rogers, with a few attendants,
hastened on in advance to Fort Pitt, to deliver
despatches, with which he was charged, to General
Monkton. This errand accomplished, he rejoined
his command at Presqu' Isle, about the end of the
month, and the whole proceeded together along
the southern margin of Lake Erie. The season
was far advanced. The wind was chill, the lake
was stormy, and the woods on shore were tinged
with the fading hues of autumn. On the seventh
of November, they reached the mouth of a river
called by Rogers the Chogage. No body of troops
under the British flag had ever before penetrated
so far. The day was dull and rainy, and, resolving
to rest until the weather should improve, Rogers
ordered his men to prepare their encampment in
the neighboring forest.

Soon after the arrival of the rangers, a party
of Indian chiefs and warriors entered the camp.
They proclaimed themselves an embassy from
Pontiac, ruler of all that country, and directed,
in his name, that the English should advance no
farther until they had had an interview with the
great chief, who was already close at hand. In
truth, before the day closed, Pontiac himself
appeared; and it is here, for the first time, that
this remarkable man stands forth distinctly on
the page of history. He greeted Rogers with the
haughty demand, what was his business in that
country, and how he dared enter it without his

permission. Rogers informed him that the French were defeated, that Canada had surrendered, and that he was on his way to take possession of Detroit, and restore a general peace to white men and Indians alike. Pontiac listened with attention, but only replied that he should stand in the path of the English until morning. Having inquired if the strangers were in need of any thing which his country could afford, he withdrew, with his chiefs, at nightfall, to his own encampment; while the English, ill at ease, and suspecting treachery, stood well on their guard throughout the night.[1]

In the morning, Pontiac returned to the camp with his attendant chiefs, and made his reply to Rogers's speech of the previous day. He was willing, he said, to live at peace with the English, and suffer them to remain in his country as long as they treated him with due respect and deference. The Indian chiefs and provincial officers smoked the calumet together, and perfect harmony seemed established between them.[2]

Up to this time, Pontiac had been, in word and deed, the fast ally of the French; but it is easy to discern the motives that impelled him to renounce his old adherence. The American forest never produced a man more shrewd, politic, and ambitious. Ignorant as he was of what was passing in the world, he could clearly see that the French power

---

[1] There can be no reasonable doubt, that the interview with Pontiac, described by Rogers in his *Account of North America*, took place on the occasion indicated in his *Journals*, under date of the 7th of November. The Indians whom he afterwards met are stated to have been Hurons.

[2] Rogers, *Journals*, 214; *Account of North America*, 210, 243.

was on the wane, and he knew his own interest too well to prop a falling cause. By making friends of the English, he hoped to gain powerful allies, who would aid his ambitious projects, and give him an increased influence over the tribes; and he flattered himself that the new-comers would treat him with the same respect which the French had always observed. In this, and all his other expectations of advantage from the English, he was doomed to disappointment.

A cold storm of rain set in, and the rangers were detained several days in their encampment. During this time, Rogers had several interviews with Pontiac, and was constrained to admire the native vigor of his intellect, no less than the singular control which he exercised over those around him.

On the twelfth of November, the detachment was again in motion, and within a few days they had reached the western end of Lake Erie. Here they heard that the Indians of Detroit were in arms against them, and that four hundred warriors lay in ambush at the entrance of the river to cut them off. But the powerful influence of Pontiac was exerted in behalf of his new friends. The warriors abandoned their design, and the rangers continued their progress towards Detroit, now within a short distance.

In the mean time, Lieutenant Brehm had been sent forward with a letter to Captain Belêtre, the commandant at Detroit, informing him that Canada had capitulated, that his garrison was included in the capitulation, and that an English detachment was approaching to relieve it. The Frenchman, in great wrath at the tidings, disregarded the message as an informal communication, and resolved to keep a hostile attitude to the last. He did his best to rouse the fury of the Indians. Among other devices, he displayed upon a pole, before the yelling multitude, the effigy of a crow pecking a man's head; the crow representing himself, and the head, observes Rogers, " being meant for my own." All his efforts were unavailing, and his faithless allies showed unequivocal symptoms of defection in the hour of need.

Rogers had now entered the mouth of the River Detroit, whence he sent forward Captain Campbell with a copy of the capitulation, and a letter from the Marquis de Vaudreuil, directing that the place should be given up, in accordance with the terms agreed upon between him and General Amherst. Belêtre was forced to yield, and with a very ill grace declared himself and his garrison at the disposal of the English commander.

The whale boats of the rangers moved slowly upwards between the low banks of the Detroit, until at length the green uniformity of marsh and forest was relieved by the Canadian houses, which began to appear on either bank, the outskirts of the secluded and isolated settlement. Before them, on the right side, they could see the village of the Wyandots, and on the left the clustered lodges of the Pottawattamies; while, a little beyond, the flag of France was flying for the last time above

the bark roofs and weather-beaten palisades of the
little fortified town.

The rangers landed on the opposite bank, and
pitched their tents upon a meadow, while two
officers, with a small detachment, went across the
river to take possession of the place. In obedience
to their summons, the French garrison defiled upon
the plain, and laid down their arms. The *fleur de
lis* was lowered from the flagstaff, and the cross of
St. George rose aloft in its place, while seven hundred Indian warriors, lately the active allies of
France, greeted the sight with a burst of triumphant yells. The Canadian militia were next
called together and disarmed. The Indians looked
on with amazement at their obsequious behavior,
quite at a loss to understand why so many men
should humble themselves before so few. Nothing
is more effective in gaining the respect, or even
attachment, of Indians than a display of power.
The savage spectators conceived the loftiest idea
of English prowess, and were astonished at the
forbearance of the conquerors in not killing their
vanquished enemies on the spot.

It was on the twenty-ninth of November, 1760,
that Detroit fell into the hands of the English.
The garrison were sent as prisoners down the lake,
but the Canadian inhabitants were allowed to retain
their farms and houses, on condition of swearing
allegiance to the British crown. An officer was
sent southward to take possession of the forts
Miami and Ouatanon, which guarded the communication between Lake Erie and the Ohio; while

Rogers himself, with a small party, proceeded northward to relieve the French garrison of Michillimackinac. The storms and gathering ice of Lake Huron forced him back without accomplishing his object; and Michillimackinac, with the three remoter posts of St. Marie, Green Bay, and St. Joseph, remained for a time in the hands of the French. During the next season, however, a detachment of the 60th regiment, then called the Royal Americans, took possession of them; and nothing now remained within the power of the French, except the few posts and settlements on the Mississippi and the Wabash, not included in the capitulation of Montreal.

The work of conquest was finished. The fertile wilderness beyond the Alleghanies, over which France had claimed sovereignty, — that boundless forest, with its tracery of interlacing streams, which, like veins and arteries, gave it life and nourishment, — had passed into the hands of her rival. It was by a few insignificant forts, separated by oceans of fresh water and uncounted leagues of forest, that the two great European powers, France first, and now England, endeavored to enforce their claims to this vast domain. There is something ludicrous in the disparity between the importance of the possession and the slenderness of the force employed to maintain it. A region embracing so many thousand miles of surface was consigned to the keeping of some five or six hundred men. Yet the force, small as it was, appeared adequate to its object, for there seemed no enemy to contend with.   The hands of the French were tied by the capitulation, and little apprehension was felt from the red inhabitants of the woods.   The lapse of two years sufficed to show how complete and fatal was the mistake.

CHAPTER VII.

ANGER OF THE INDIANS.—THE CONSPIRACY.

THE country was scarcely transferred to the English, when smothered murmurs of discontent began to be audible among the Indian tribes. From the head of the Potomac to Lake Superior, and from the Alleghanies to the Mississippi, in every wigwam and hamlet of the forest, a deep-rooted hatred of the English increased with rapid growth. Nor is this to be wondered at. We have seen with what sagacious policy the French had labored to ingratiate themselves with the Indians; and the slaughter of the Monongahela, with the horrible devastation of the western frontier, the outrages perpetrated at Oswego, and the massacre at Fort William Henry, bore witness to the success of their efforts. Even the Delawares and Shawanoes, the faithful allies of William Penn, had at length been seduced by their blandishments; and the Iroquois, the ancient enemies of Canada, had half forgotten their former hostility, and well-nigh taken part against the British colonists. The remote nations of the west had also joined in the war, descending in their canoes for hundreds of miles, to fight against the enemies of France. All these tribes entertained towards the English that rancorous enmity which an Indian always feels against those to whom he has been opposed in war.

Under these circumstances, it behooved the English to use the utmost care in their conduct towards the tribes. But even when the conflict with France was impending, and the alliance with the Indians was of the last importance, they had treated them with indifference and neglect. They were not likely to adopt a different course now that their friendship seemed a matter of no consequence. In truth, the intentions of the English were soon apparent. In the zeal for retrenchment, which prevailed after the close of hostilities, the presents which it had always been customary to give the Indians, at stated intervals, were either withheld altogether, or doled out with a niggardly and reluctant hand; while, to make the matter worse, the agents and officers of government often appropriated the presents to themselves, and afterwards sold them at an exorbitant price to the Indians.[1] When the French had possession of the remote forts, they were accustomed, with a wise liberality, to supply the surrounding Indians with guns, ammunition, and clothing, until the latter had forgotten the weapons and garments of their forefathers, and depended on the white men for support. The sudden withholding of these supplies was, therefore, a grievous

---

[1] *MS. Johnson Papers.*

calamity. Want, suffering, and death, were the consequences; and this cause alone would have been enough to produce general discontent. But, unhappily, other grievances were superadded.[1]

The English fur-trade had never been well regulated, and it was now in a worse condition than ever. Many of the traders, and those in their

[1] Extract from a MS. letter — *Sir W. Johnson to Governor Colden,* Dec. 24, 1763.

"I shall not take upon me to point out the Originall Parsimony &c. to w^h the first defection of the Indians can with justice & certainty be attributed, but only observe, as I did in a former letter, that the Indians (whose friendship was never cultivated by the English with that attention, expense, & assiduity with w^h ye French obtained their favour) were for many years jealous of our growing power, were repeatedly assured by the French (who were at ye pains of having many proper emissaries among them) that so soon as we became masters of this country, we should immediately treat them with neglect, hem them in with Posts & Forts, encroach upon their Lands, and finally destroy them. All w^h after the reduction of Canada, seemed to appear too clearly to the Indians, who thereby lost the great advantages resulting from the possession w^h the French formerly had of Posts & Trade in their Country, neither of which they could have ever enjoyed but for the notice they took of the Indians, & the presents they bestowed so bountifully upon them, w^h however expensive, they wisely foresaw was infinitely cheaper, and much more effectual than the keeping of a large body of Regular Troops, in their several Countrys, . . . a Plan which has endeared their memory to most of the Indian Nations, who would I fear generally go over to them in case they ever got footing again in this Country, & who were repeatedly exhorted, & encouraged by the French (from motives of Interest & dislike w^h they will always possess) to fall upon us, by representing that their liberties & Country were in ye utmost danger." In January, 1763, Colonel Bouquet, commanding in Pennsylvania, writes to General Amherst, stating the discontent produced among the Indians by the suppression of presents. The commander-in-chief replies, "As to appropriating a particular sum to be laid out yearly to the warriors in presents, &c., that I can by no means agree to; nor can I think it necessary to give them any presents by way of *Bribes*, for if they do not behave properly they are to be punished." And again, in February, to the same officer, "As you are thoroughly acquainted with my sentiments regarding the treatment of the Indians in general, you will of course order Cap Ecuyer . . . not to give those who are able to provide for their families any encouragement to loiter away their time in idleness about the Fort."

employ, were ruffians of the coarsest stamp, who
vied with each other in rapacity, violence, and
profligacy.   They cheated, cursed, and plundered
the Indians, and outraged their families; offering,
when compared with the French traders, who were
under better regulation, a most unfavorable example
of the character of their nation.

The officers and soldiers of the garrisons did
their full part in exciting the general resentment.
Formerly, when the warriors came to the forts,
they had been welcomed by the French with attention and respect.   The inconvenience which their
presence occasioned had been disregarded, and
their peculiarities overlooked.   But now they were
received with cold looks and harsh words from the
officers, and with oaths, menaces, and sometimes
blows, from the reckless and brutal soldiers.
When, after their troublesome and intrusive fashion, they were lounging everywhere about the fort,
or lazily reclining in the shadow of the walls,
they were met with muttered ejaculations of impa
tience, or abrupt orders to be gone, enforced, perhaps, by a touch from the butt of a sentinel's
musket.   These marks of contempt were unspeak-
ably galling to their haughty spirit.[1]

---

[1] Some of the principal causes of the war are exhibited with spirit and
truth in the old tragedy of *Ponteach*, written probably by Major Rogers
The portion of the play referred to is given in Appendix, B

" The English treat us with much Disrespect, and we have the greatest
Reason to believe, by their Behavior, they intend to Cut us off entirely ; They have possessed themselves of our Country, it is now in our
power to Dispossess them and Recover it, if we will but Embrace the
opportunity before they have time to assemble together, and fortify
themselves, there is no time to be lost, let us Strike immediately." —
Speech of a Seneca chief to the Wyandots and Ottawas of Detroit. July, 1761.

But what most contributed to the growing dis-content of the tribes was the intrusion of settlers upon their lands, at all times a fruitful source of Indian hostility. Its effects, it is true, could only be felt by those whose country bordered upon the English settlements; but among these were the most powerful and influential of the tribes. The Delawares and Shawanoes, in particular, had by this time been roused to the highest pitch of exas-peration. Their best lands had been invaded, and all remonstrance had been fruitless. They viewed with wrath and fear the steady progress of the white man, whose settlements had passed the Sus-quehanna, and were fast extending to the Allegha-nies, eating away the forest like a spreading canker. The anger of the Delawares was abundantly shared by their ancient conquerors, the Six Nations. The threatened occupation of Wyoming by settlers from Connecticut gave great umbrage to the confederacy.[1] The Senecas were more especially incensed at Eng-lish intrusion, since, from their position, they were farthest removed from the soothing influence of Sir William Johnson, and most exposed to the seduc-tions of the French; while the Mohawks, another member of the confederacy, were justly alarmed at seeing the better part of their lands patented out without their consent. Some Christian Indians of the Oneida tribe, in the simplicity of their hearts, sent an earnest petition to Sir William Johnson, that the English forts within the limits of the Six

---

[1] *Minutes of Conference with the Six Nations at Hartford, 1763, MS. Letter — Hamilton to Amherst,* May 10, 1761.

Nations might be removed, or, as the petition expresses it, *kicked out of the way.*[1]

The discontent of the Indians gave great satisfaction to the French, who saw in it an assurance of safe and bloody vengeance on their conquerors. Canada, it is true, was gone beyond hope of recovery; but they still might hope to revenge its loss. Interest, moreover, as well as passion, prompted them to inflame the resentment of the Indians; for most of the inhabitants of the French settlements upon the lakes and the Mississippi were engaged in the fur-trade, and, fearing the English as formidable rivals, they would gladly have seen them driven out of the country. Traders, *habitans, coureurs de bois*, and all classes of this singular population, accordingly dispersed themselves among the villages of the Indians, or held councils with them in the secret places of the woods, urging them to take up arms against the English. They exhibited the conduct of the latter in its worst light, and spared neither misrepresentation nor falsehood. They told their excited hearers that the English had formed a deliberate scheme to root out the whole Indian race, and, with that design, had already begun to

---

[1] "We are now left in Peace, and have nothing to do but to plant our Corn, Hunt the wild Beasts, smoke our Pipes, and mind Religion. But as these Forts, which are built among us, disturb our Peace, & are a great hurt to Religion, because some of our Warriors are foolish, & some of our Brother Soldiers don't fear God, we therefore desire that these Forts may be pull'd down, & kick'd out of the way."

At a conference at Philadelphia, in August, 1761, an Iroquois sachem said, "We, your Brethren of the several Nations, are penned up like Hoggs There are Forts all around us, and therefore we are apprehensive that Death is coming upon us."

hem them in with settlements on the one hand, and a chain of forts on the other. Among other atrocious plans for their destruction, they had instigated the Cherokees to attack and destroy the tribes of the Ohio valley.[1] These groundless calumnies found ready belief. The French declared, in addition, that the King of France had of late years fallen asleep; that, during his slumbers, the English had seized upon Canada; but that he was now awake again, and that his armies were advancing up the St. Lawrence and the Mississippi, to drive out the intruders from the country of his red children. To these fabrications was added the more substantial encouragement of arms, ammunition, clothing, and provisions, which the French trading companies, if not the officers of the crown, distributed with a liberal hand.[2]

The fierce passions of the Indians, excited by their wrongs, real or imagined, and exasperated by

---

[1] Croghan, *Journal.* See Hildreth, *Pioneer History,* 68. Also Butler, *Hist. Kentucky,* Appendix.

[2] Examination of Gershom Hicks, a spy. See *Pennsylvania Gazette,* No. 1846.

Many passages from contemporary letters and documents might be cited in support of the above. The following extract from a letter of Lieut Edward Jenkins, commanding at Fort Ouatanon on the Wabash, to Major Gladwin commanding at Detroit, is a good example. The date is 28 March, 1763. "The Canadians here are eternally telling lies to the Indians . . One La Pointe told the Indians a few days ago that we should all be prisoners in a short time (showing when the corn was about a foot high), that there was a great army to come from the Mississippi, and that they were to have a great number of Indians with them; therefore advised them not to help us. That they would soon take Detroit and these small posts, and then they would take Quebec, Montreal, &c, and go into our country. This, I am informed, they tell them from one end of the year to the other." He adds that the Indians will rather give six beaver-skins for a blanket to a Frenchman than three to an Englishman.

the representations of the French, were yet farther wrought upon by influences of another kind. A prophet rose among the Delawares. This man may serve as a counterpart to the famous Shawanoe prophet, who figured so conspicuously in the Indian outbreak, under Tecumseh, immediately before the war with England in 1812. Many other parallel instances might be shown, as the great suscepti-bility of the Indians to superstitious impressions renders the advent of a prophet among them no very rare occurrence. In the present instance, the inspired Delaware seems to have been rather an enthusiast than an impostor; or perhaps he com-bined both characters. The objects of his mission were not wholly political. By means of certain external observances, most of them sufficiently friv olous and absurd, his disciples were to strengthen and purify their natures, and make themselves acceptable to the Great Spirit, whose messenger he proclaimed himself to be. He also enjoined them to lay aside the weapons and clothing which they received from the white men, and return to the primitive life of their ancestors. By so doing, and by strictly observing his other precepts, the tribes would soon be restored to their ancient great-ness and power, and be enabled to drive out the white men who infested their territory. The pro-phet had many followers. Indians came from far and near, and gathered together in large encamp-ments to listen to his exhortations. His fame spread even to the nations of the northern lakes; but though his disciples followed most of his injunctions, flinging away flint and steel, and making copious use of emetics, with other observances equally troublesome, yet the requisition to abandon the use of fire-arms was too inconvenient to be complied with.[1]

With so many causes to irritate their restless and warlike spirit, it could not be supposed that the Indians would long remain quiet. Accordingly, in the summer of the year 1761, Captain Campbell, then commanding at Detroit, received information that a deputation of Senecas had come to the neighboring village of the Wyandots for the purpose of instigating the latter to destroy him and his garrison.[2] On farther inquiry, the plot proved

---

[1] *M'Cullough's Narrative.* See *Incidents of Border Life,* 98. M'Cullough was a prisoner among the Delawares, at the time of the prophet's appearance.

[2] MS. *Minutes of a Council held by Deputies of the Six Nations, with the Wyandots, Ottawas, Ojibwas, and Pottawattamies, at the Wyandot town, near Detroit,* July 3, 1761.

Extract from a MS. Letter — *Captain Campbell, commanding at Detroit, to Major Walters, commanding at Niagara.*

{ "Detroit, June 17th, 1761,
{ two o'clock in the morning.

" Sir:

" I had the favor of Yours, with General Amherst's Dispatches.

" I have sent You an Express with a very Important piece of Intelligence I have had the good fortune to Discover. I have been Lately alarmed with Reports of the bad Designs of the Indian Nations against this place and the English in General; I can now Inform You for certain it Comes from the Six Nations; and that they have Sent Belts of Wampum & Deputys to all the Nations, from Nova Scotia to the Illinois, to take up the hatchet against the English, and have employed the Messagues to send Belts of Wampum to the Northern Nations . . .

" Their project is as follows: the Six Nations — at least the Senecas — are to Assemble at the head of French Creek, within five and twenty Leagues of Presqu' Isle, part of the Six Nations, the Delawares and Shanese, are to Assemble on the Ohio, and all at the same time, about the latter End of this Month, to surprise Niagara & Fort Pitt, and Cut off the Communication Every where; I hope this will Come time Enough to put

to be general; and Niagara, Fort Pitt, and other posts, were to share the fate of Detroit. Campbell instantly despatched messengers to Sir Jeffrey Amherst, and the commanding officers of the different forts; and, by this timely discovery, the conspiracy was nipped in the bud. During the following summer, 1762, another similar design was detected and suppressed. They proved to be the precursors of a tempest. When, early in 1763, it was announced to the tribes that the King of France had ceded all their country to the King of England, without even asking their leave, a ferment of indignation at once became apparent among them;[1] and, within a few weeks, a plot was matured, such as was never, before or since, conceived or executed by a North-American Indian. It was determined to attack all the English forts upon the same day; then, having destroyed their garrisons, to turn upon the defenceless frontier, and ravage and lay waste the settlements, until, as

You on Your Guard and to send to Oswego, and all the Posts on that communication, they Expect to be Joined by the Nations that are Come from the North by Toronto "

[1] Letter, *Geo. Croghan to Sir J. Amherst, Fort Pitt, April* 30, 1763, MS. Amherst replies characteristically, " Whatever idle notions they may entertain in regard to the cessions made by the French Crown can be of very little consequence "

Croghan, Sir William Johnson's deputy, and a man of experience, had for some time been anxious as to the results of the arrogant policy of Amherst On March 19th he wrote to Colonel Bouquet: "How they (*the Indians*) may behave I can't pretend to say, but I do not approve of Gen¹· Amherst's plan of distressing them too much, as in my opinion they will not consider consequences if too much distrest, tho' Sir Jeffrey thinks they will."

Croghan urges the same views, with emphasis, in other letters; but Amherst was deaf to all persuasion.

many of the Indians fondly believed, the English should all be driven into the sea, and the country restored to its primitive owners.

It is difficult to determine which tribe was first to raise the cry of war. There were many who' might have done so, for all the savages in the back-woods were ripe for an outbreak. and the movement seemed almost simultaneous. The Delawares and Senecas were the most incensed, and Kiashuta, a chief of the latter, was perhaps foremost to apply the torch; but, if this was the case, he touched fire to materials already on the point of igniting. It belonged to a greater chief than he to give method and order to what would else have been a wild burst of fury, and convert desultory attacks into a formidable and protracted war. But for Pontiac, the whole might have ended in a few troublesome inroads upon the frontier, and a little whooping and yelling under the walls of Fort Pitt.

Pontiac, as already mentioned, was principal chief of the Ottawas. The Ottawas, Ojibwas, and Pottawattamies, had long been united in a loose kind of confederacy, of which he was the virtual head. Over those around him his authority was almost despotic, and his power extended far beyond the limits of the three united tribes. His influence was great among all the nations of the Illinois country; while, from the sources of the Ohio to those of the Mississippi, and, indeed, to the farthest boundaries of the wide-spread Algonquin race, his name was known and respected.

The fact that Pontiac was born the son of a

chief would in no degree account for the extent of
his power; for, among Indians, many a chief's son
sinks back into insignificance, while the offspring
of a common warrior may succeed to his place.
Among all the wild tribes of the continent, personal merit is indispensable to gaining or preserving
dignity.   Courage, resolution, address, and eloquence are sure passports to distinction. With
all these Pontiac was pre-eminently endowed. and
·it was chiefly to them, urged to their highest
activity by a vehement ambition, that he owed
his greatness. He possessed a commanding energy
and force of mind, and in subtlety and craft could
match the best of his wily race.   But, though
capable of acts of magnanimity, he was a thorough
savage, with a wider range of intellect than those
around him, but sharing all their passions and
prejudices, their fierceness and treachery.   His
faults were the faults of his race ; and they cannot
eclipse his nobler qualities. His memory is still
cherished among the remnants of many Algonquin tribes, and the celebrated Tecumseh adopted
him for his model, proving himself no unworthy
imitator.[1]

[1] Drake, *Life of Tecumseh*, 188.
Several tribes, the Miamis, Sacs, and others, have claimed connection
with the great chief; but it is certain that he was, by adoption at least,
an Ottawa. Henry Conner, formerly government interpreter for the
northern tribes, declared, on the faith of Indian tradition, that he was
born among the Ottawas of an Ojibwa mother, a circumstance which
proved an advantage to him by increasing his influence over both tribes.
An Ojibwa Indian told the writer that some portion of his power was to
be ascribed to his being a chief of the *Metai*, a magical association among
the Indians of the lakes, in which character he exerted an influence on
the superstition of his followers.

Pontiac was now about fifty years old. Until Major Rogers came into the country, he had been, from motives probably both of interest and inclination, a firm friend of the French. Not long before the French war broke out, he had saved the garrison of Detroit from the imminent peril of an attack from some of the discontented tribes of the north. During the war, he had fought on the side of France. It is said that he commanded the Ottawas at the memorable defeat of Braddock; and it is certain that he was treated with much honor by the French officers, and received especial marks of esteem from the Marquis of Montcalm.[1]

We have seen how, when the tide of affairs changed, the subtle and ambitious chief trimmed his bark to the current, and gave the hand of friendship to the English. That he was disappointed in their treatment of him, and in all the hopes that he had formed from their alliance, is sufficiently evident from one of his speeches. A new light soon began to dawn upon his untaught but powerful mind, and he saw the altered posture of affairs under its true aspect.

It was a momentous and gloomy crisis for the Indian race, for never before had they been exposed to such imminent and pressing danger. With the downfall of Canada, the tribes had sunk at once from their position of importance. Hitherto the two rival European nations had kept each other

---

[1] The venerable Pierre Chouteau, of St. Louis, remembered to have seen Pontiac, a few days before his death, attired in the complete uniform of a French officer, which had been given him by the Marquis of Montcalm not long before the battle on the Plains of Abraham.

in check upon the American continent, and the
Indians had, in some measure, held the balance of
power between them. To conciliate their good
will and gain their alliance, to avoid offending
them by injustice and encroachment, was the
policy both of the French and English. But now
the face of affairs was changed. The English had
gained an undisputed ascendency, and the Indians,
no longer important as allies, were treated as mere
barbarians, who might be trampled upon with im-
punity. Abandoned to their own feeble resources
and divided strength, they must fast recede, and
dwindle away before the steady progress of the
colonial power. Already their best hunting-
grounds were invaded, and from the eastern
ridges of the Alleghanies they might see, from
far and near, the smoke of the settlers' clearings,
rising in tall columns from the dark-green bosom
of the forest. The doom of the race was sealed,
and no human power could avert it; but they, in
their ignorance, believed otherwise, and vainly
thought that, by a desperate effort, they might
yet uproot and overthrow the growing strength
of their destroyers.

It would be idle to suppose that the great mass
of the Indians understood, in its full extent, the
danger which threatened their race. With them,
the war was a mere outbreak of fury, and they
turned against their enemies with as little reason
or forecast as a panther when he leaps at the throat
of the hunter. Goaded by wrongs and indignities,
they struck for revenge, and for relief from the evil

of the moment. But the mind of Pontiac could embrace a wider and deeper view. The peril of the times was unfolded in its full extent before him, and he resolved to unite the tribes in one grand, effort to avert it. He did not, like many of his people, entertain the absurd idea that the Indians, by their unaided strength, could drive the English into the sea. He adopted the only plan consistent with reason, that of restoring the French ascendency in the west, and once more opposing a check to British encroachment. With views like these, he lent a greedy ear to the plausible falsehoods of the Canadians, who assured him that the armies of King Louis were already advancing to recover Canada, and that the French and their red brethren, fighting side by side, would drive the English dogs back within their own narrow limits.

Revolving these thoughts, and remembering that his own ambitious views might be advanced by the hostilities he meditated, Pontiac no longer hesitated. Revenge, ambition, and patriotism wrought upon him alike, and he resolved on war. At the close of the year 1762, he sent ambassadors to the different nations. They visited the country of the Ohio and its tributaries, passed northward to the region of the upper lakes, and the borders of the River Ottawa ; and far southward towards the mouth of the Mississippi.[1] Bearing with them the war-belt of wampum,[2] broad and long, as the

----

[1] MS. Letter — *M. D'Abbadie to M. Neyon,* 1764.

[2] Wampum was an article much in use among many tribes, not only for ornament, but for the graver purposes of councils, treaties, and embas-

importance of the message demanded, and the tomahawk stained red, in token of war, they went from
camp to camp, and village to village. Wherever
they appeared, the sachems and old men assembled,
to hear the words of the great Pontiac. Then the
chief of the embassy flung down the tomahawk on
the ground before them, and holding the war-belt
in his hand, delivered, with vehement gesture, word
for word, the speech with which he was charged.
It was heard everywhere with approval; the belt
was accepted, the hatchet snatched up, and the
assembled chiefs stood pledged to take part in
the war. The blow was to be struck at a certain
time in the month of May following, to be indicated
by the changes of the moon. The tribes were to
rise together, each destroying the English garrison
in its neighborhood, and then, with a general rush,
the whole were to turn against the settlements
of the frontier.

The tribes, thus banded together against the English, comprised, with a few unimportant exceptions,
the whole Algonquin stock, to whom were united
the Wyandots, the Senecas, and several tribes of
the lower Mississippi. The Senecas were the only
members of the Iroquois confederacy who joined
in the league, the rest being kept quiet by the
influence of Sir William Johnson, whose utmost

sies. In ancient times it consisted of small shells, or fragments of shells,
rudely perforated, and strung together; but more recently, it was manu-
factured by the white men, from the inner portions of certain marine and
fresh water shells. In shape, the grains or beads resembled small pieces of
broken pipe-stem, and were of various sizes and colors, black, purple, and
white. When used for ornament, they were arranged fancifully in neck-

exertions, however, were barely sufficient to allay their irritation.[1]

While thus on the very eve of an outbreak, the Indians concealed their designs with the dissimulation of their race. The warriors still lounged about the forts, with calm, impenetrable faces, begging, as usual, for tobacco, gunpowder, and whiskey. Now and then, some slight intimation of danger would startle the garrisons from their security. An English trader, coming in from the Indian villages, would report that, from their manner and behavior, he suspected them of brooding mischief; or some scoundrel half-breed would be heard boasting in his cups, that before next summer he would have English hair to fringe his hunt-

laces, collars, and embroidery; but when employed for public purposes, they were disposed in a great variety of patterns and devices, which, to the minds of the Indians, had all the significance of hieroglyphics. An Indian orator, at every clause of his speech, delivered a belt or string of wampum, varying in size, according to the importance of what he had said, and, by its figures and coloring, so arranged as to perpetuate the remembrance of his words. These belts were carefully stored up like written documents, and it was generally the office of some old man to interpret their meaning.

When a wampum belt was sent to summon the tribes to join in war, its color was always red or black, while the prevailing color of a peace-belt was white. Tobacco was sometimes used on such occasions as a substitute for wampum, since in their councils the Indians are in the habit of constantly smoking, and tobacco is therefore taken as the emblem of deliberation. With the tobacco or the belt of wampum, presents are not unfrequently sent to conciliate the good will of the tribe whose alliance is sought. In the summer of the year 1846, when the western bands of the Dahcotah were preparing to go in concert against their enemies the Crows, the chief who was at the head of the design, and of whose village the writer was an inmate, impoverished himself by sending most of his horses as presents to the chiefs of the surrounding villages. On this occasion, tobacco was the token borne by the messengers, as wampum is not in use among the tribes of that region.

[1] MS. *Johnson Papers.*

ing-frock. On one occasion, the plot was nearly
discovered. Early in March, 1763, Ensign Holmes,
commanding at Fort Miami, was told by a friendly
Indian that the warriors in the neighboring village
had lately received a war-belt, with a message urging them to destroy him and his garrison, and that
this they were preparing to do. Holmes called the
Indians together, and boldly charged them with
their design. They did as Indians on such occasions have often done, confessed their fault with
much apparent contrition, laid the blame on a
neighboring tribe, and professed eternal friendship
to their brethren, the English. Holmes writes to
report his discovery to Major Gladwyn, who, in his
turn, sends the information to Sir Jeffrey Amherst,
expressing his opinion that there has been a general
irritation among the Indians, but that the affair will
soon blow over, and that, in the neighborhood of
his own post, the savages were perfectly tranquil.[1]
Within cannon shot of the deluded officer's palisades, was the village of Pontiac himself, the arch

[1] MS *Speech of a Miami Chief to Ensign Holmes.* MS. Letter — *Holmes
to Gladwyn, March* 16, 1763. *Gladwyn to Amherst, March* 21, 1763

Extract from a MS. Letter — *Ensign Holmes commanding at Miamis, to
Major Gladwyn :* —

{ "Fort Miamis,
{ March 30th, 1763

"Since my Last Letter to You, wherein I Acquainted You of the
Bloody Belt being in this Village, I have made all the search I could
about it, and have found it out to be True ; Whereon I Assembled all
the Chiefs of this Nation, & after a long and troublesome Spell with them,
I Obtained the Belt, with a Speech, as You will Receive Enclosed ; This
Affair is very timely Stopt, and I hope the News of a Peace will put a
Stop to any further Troubles with these Indians, who are the Principal
Ones of Setting Mischief on Foot. I send you the Belt, with this Packet,
which I hope You will Forward to the General."

enemy of the English, and prime mover in the plot.

With the approach of spring, the Indians, coming in from their wintering grounds, began to appear in small parties about the various forts ; but now they seldom entered them, encamping at a little distance in the woods. They were fast pushing their preparations for the meditated blow, and waiting with stifled eagerness for the appointed hour.

CHAPTER VIII.

1763.

INDIAN PREPARATION.

I INTERRUPT the progress of the narrative to glance for a moment at the Indians in their military capacity, and observe how far they were qualified to prosecute the formidable war into which they were about to plunge.

A people living chiefly by the chase, and therefore, of necessity, thinly and widely scattered; divided into numerous tribes, held together by no strong principle of cohesion, and with no central government to combine their strength, could act with little efficiency against such an enemy as was now opposed to them. Loose and disjointed as a whole, the government even of individual tribes, and of their smallest separate communities, was too feeble to deserve the name. There were, it is true, chiefs whose office was in a manner hereditary; but their authority was wholly of a moral nature, and enforced by no compulsory law. Their province was to advise, and not to command. Their influence, such as it was, is chiefly to be ascribed to the principle of hero-worship, natural to the

Indian character, and to the reverence for age, which belongs to a state of society where a patriarchal element largely prevails. It was their office to declare war and make peace; but when war was declared, they had no power to carry the declaration into effect. The warriors fought if they chose to do so; but if, on the contrary, they preferred to remain quiet, no man could force them to raise the hatchet. The war-chief, whose part it was to lead them to battle, was a mere partisan, whom his bravery and exploits had led to distinction. If he thought proper, he sang his war-song and danced his war-dance; and as many of the young men as were disposed to follow him, gathered around and enlisted themselves under him. Over these volunteers he had no legal authority, and they could desert him at any moment, with no other penalty than disgrace. When several war parties, of different bands or tribes, were united in a common enterprise, their chiefs elected a leader, who was nominally to command the whole; but unless this leader was a man of uncommon reputation and ability, his commands were disregarded, and his authority was a cipher. Among his followers, every latent element of discord, pride, jealousy, and ancient half-smothered feuds, were ready at any moment to break out, and tear the whole asunder. His warriors would often desert in bodies; and many an Indian army, before reaching the enemy's country, has been known to dwindle away until it was reduced to a mere scalping party.

To twist a rope of sand would be as easy a task

as to form a permanent and effective army of such materials. The wild love of freedom, and impatience of all control, which mark the Indian race, render them utterly intolerant of military discipline. Partly from their individual character, and partly from this absence of subordination, spring results highly unfavorable to continued and extended military operations. Indian warriors, when acting in large masses, are to the last degree wayward, capricious, and unstable ; infirm of purpose as a mob of children, and devoid of providence and foresight. To provide supplies for a campaign forms no part of their system. Hence the blow must be struck at once, or not struck at all; and to postpone victory is to insure defeat. It is when acting in small, detached parties, that the Indian warrior puts forth his energies, and displays his admirable address, endurance, and intrepidity. It is then that he becomes a truly formidable enemy. Fired with the hope of winning scalps, he is stanch as a bloodhound. No hardship can divert him from his purpose, and no danger subdue his patient and cautious courage.

From their inveterate passion for war, the Indians are always prompt enough to engage in it ; and on the present occasion, the prevailing irritation gave ample assurance that they would not remain idle. While there was little risk that they would capture any strong and well-defended fort, or carry any important position, there was, on the other hand, every reason to apprehend wide-spread havoc, and a destructive war of detail. That the war might

be carried on with effect, it was the part of the
Indian leaders to work upon the passions of their
people, and keep alive their irritation ; to whet
their native appetite for blood and glory, and cheer
them on to the attack ; to guard against all that
might quench their ardor, or cool their fierceness ;
to avoid pitched battles ; never to fight except under
advantage ; and to avail themselves of all the aid
which craft and treachery could afford.   The very
circumstances which unfitted the Indians for continued and concentrated attack were, in another
view, highly advantageous, by preventing the enemy
from assailing them with vital effect.   It was no
easy task to penetrate tangled woods in search of
a foe, alert and active as a lynx, who would seldom
stand and fight, whose deadly shot and triumphant
whoop were the first and often the last tokens of
his presence, and who, at the approach of a hostile
force, would vanish into the black recesses of forests and pine swamps, only to renew his attacks
with unabated ardor.   There were no forts to capture, no magazines to destroy, and little property
to seize upon.   No warfare could be more perilous
and harassing in its prosecution, or less satisfactory
in its results.

The English colonies at this time were but ill
fitted to bear the brunt of the impending war.
The army which had conquered Canada was
broken up and dissolved; the provincials were
disbanded, and most of the regulars sent home.
A few fragments of regiments, miserably wasted
by war and sickness, had just arrived from the

West Indies; and of these, several were already ordered to England, to be disbanded. There remained barely troops enough to furnish feeble garrisons for the various forts on the frontier and in the Indian country.[1] At the head of this dilapidated army was Sir Jeffrey Amherst, who had achieved the reduction of Canada, and clinched the nail which Wolfe had driven. In some respects he was well fitted for the emergency; but, on the other hand, he held the Indians in supreme contempt, and his arbitrary treatment of them and total want of every quality of conciliation where they were concerned, had had no little share in exciting them to war.

While the war was on the eve of breaking out, an event occurred which had afterwards an important effect upon its progress, — the signing of the treaty of peace at Paris, on the tenth of February, 1763. By this treaty France resigned her claims to the territories east of the Mississippi, and that great river now became the western boundary of the British colonial possessions. In portioning out her new acquisitions into separate governments, England left the valley of the Ohio and the adjacent regions as an Indian domain, and by the proclamation of the seventh of October following, the intrusion of settlers upon these lands was strictly prohibited. Could these just and necessary measures have been sooner adopted, it is probable that the Indian war might have been

[1] Mante, 485

prevented, or, at all events, rendered less general and violent, for the treaty would have made it apparent that the French could never repossess themselves of Canada, and would have proved the futility of every hope which the Indians entertained of assistance from that quarter, while, at the same time, the royal proclamation would have tended to tranquillize their minds, by removing the chief cause of irritation. But the remedy came too late, and served only to inflame the evil. While the sovereigns of France, England, and Spain, were signing the treaty at Paris, countless Indian warriors in the American forests were singing the war-song, and whetting their scalping-knives.

Throughout the western wilderness, in a hundred camps and villages, were celebrated the savage rites of war. Warriors, women, and children were alike eager and excited; magicians consulted their oracles, and prepared charms to insure success; while the war-chief, his body painted black from head to foot, concealed himself in the solitude of rocks and caverns, or the dark recesses of the forest. Here, fasting and praying, he calls day and night upon the Great Spirit, consulting his dreams, to draw from them auguries of good or evil; and if, perchance, a vision of the great war-eagle seems to hover over him with expanded wings, he exults in the full conviction of triumph. When a few days have elapsed, he emerges from his retreat, and the people discover him descending from the woods, and approaching their camp, black as a demon of war, and shrunken with fasting and vigil. They

flock around and listen to his wild harangue. He
calls on them to avenge the blood of their slaughtered relatives; he assures them that the Great
Spirit is on their side, and that victory is certain
With exulting cries they disperse to their wigwams,
to array themselves in the savage decorations of
the war-dress. An old man now passes through
the camp, and invites the warriors to a feast in the
name of the chief. They gather from all quarters
to his wigwam, where they find him seated, no
longer covered with black, but adorned with the
startling and fantastic blazonry of the war-paint.
Those who join in the feast pledge themselves, by
so doing, to follow him against the enemy. The
guests seat themselves on the ground, in a circle
around the wigwam, and the flesh of dogs is placed
in wooden dishes before them, while the chief,
though goaded by the pangs of his long, unbroken
fast, sits smoking his pipe with unmoved countenance, and takes no part in the feast.

Night has now closed in; and the rough clearing is illumined by the blaze of fires and burning
pine-knots, casting their deep red glare upon the
dusky boughs of the surrounding forest, and upon
the wild multitude who, fluttering with feathers
and bedaubed with paint, have gathered for the
celebration of the war-dance. A painted post is
driven into the ground, and the crowd form a wide
circle around it. The chief leaps into the vacant
space, brandishing his hatchet as if rushing upon
an enemy, and, in a loud, vehement tone, chants
his own exploits and those of his ancestors, enact-

ing the deeds which he describes, yelling the war-
whoop, throwing himself into all the postures of
actual fight, striking the post as if it were an
enemy, and tearing the scalp from the head of the
imaginary victim. Warrior after warrior follows
his example, until the whole assembly, as if fired
with sudden frenzy, rush together into the ring,
leaping, stamping, and whooping, brandishing
knives and hatchets in the fire-light, hacking and
stabbing the air, and breaking at intervals into a
burst of ferocious yells, which sounds for miles
away over the lonely, midnight forest.

In the morning, the warriors prepare to depart.
They leave the camp in single file, still decorated
with all their finery of paint, feathers, and scalp-
locks; and, as they enter the woods, the chief fires
his gun, the warrior behind follows his example,
and the discharges pass in slow succession from
front to rear, the salute concluding with a general
whoop. They encamp at no great distance from
the village, and divest themselves of their much-
prized ornaments, which are carried back by the
women, who have followed them for this purpose.
The warriors pursue their journey, clad in the
rough attire of hard service, and move silently and
stealthily through the forest towards the hapless
garrison, or defenceless settlement, which they
have marked as their prey.   •

The woods were now filled with war-parties
such as this, and soon the first tokens of the
approaching tempest began to alarm the unhappy
settlers of the frontier. At first, some trader or

hunter, weak and emaciated, would come in from the forest, and relate that his companions had been butchered in the Indian villages, and that he alone had escaped. Next succeeded vague and uncertain rumors of forts attacked and garrisons slaughtered; and soon after, a report gained ground that every post throughout the Indian country had been taken, and every soldier killed. Close upon these tidings came the enemy himself. The Indian war-parties broke out of the woods like gangs of wolves, murdering, burning, and laying waste; while hundreds of terror-stricken families, abandoning their homes, fled for refuge towards the older settlements, and all was misery and ruin.

Passing over, for the present, this portion of the war, we will penetrate at once into the heart of the Indian country, and observe those passages of the conflict which took place under the auspices of Pontiac himself. — the siege of Detroit, and the capture of the interior posts and garrisons.

CHAPTER IX.

1763.

THE COUNCIL AT THE RIVER ECORCES.

To begin the war was reserved by Pontiac as his own peculiar privilege. With the first opening of spring his preparations were complete. His light-footed messengers, with their wampum belts and gifts of tobacco, visited many a lonely hunting camp in the gloom of the northern woods, and called chiefs and warriors to attend the general meeting. The appointed spot was on the banks of the little River Ecorces, not far from Detroit. Thither went Pontiac himself, with his squaws and his children. Band after band came straggling in from every side, until the meadow was thickly dotted with their frail wigwams.[1] Here were idle warriors smoking and laughing in groups, or beguiling the lazy hours with gambling, feasting, or doubtful stories of their own martial exploits. Here were youthful gallants, bedizened with all the foppery of beads, feathers, and hawks' bells, but held as yet in light esteem, since they had slain no enemy, and taken no scalp.

---

[1] *Pontiac*, MS. See Appendix, C.

Here too were young damsels, radiant with bears' oil, ruddy with vermilion, and versed in all the arts of forest coquetry; shrivelled hags, with limbs of wire, and the voices of screech-owls; and troops of naked children, with small, black, mischievous eyes, roaming along the outskirts of the woods.

The great Roman historian observes of the ancient Germans, that when summoned to a public meeting, they would lag behind the appointed time in order to show their independence. The remark holds true, and perhaps with greater emphasis, of the American Indians; and thus it happened, that several days elapsed before the assembly was complete. In such a motley concourse of barbarians, where different bands and different tribes were mustered on one common camp ground, it would need all the art of a prudent leader to prevent their dormant jealousies from starting into open strife. No people are more prompt to quarrel, and none more prone, in the fierce excitement of the present, to forget the purpose of the future; yet, through good fortune, or the wisdom of Pontiac, no rupture occurred; and at length the last loiterer appeared, and farther delay was needless.

The council took place on the twenty-seventh of April. On that morning, several old men, the heralds of the camp, passed to and fro among the lodges, calling the warriors, in a loud voice, to attend the meeting.

In accordance with the summons, they issued from their cabins: the tall, naked figures of the wild Ojibwas, with quivers slung at their backs, and light war-clubs resting in the hollow of their arms; Ottawas, wrapped close in their gaudy blankets; Wyandots, fluttering in painted shirts, their heads adorned with feathers, and their leggins garnished with bells. All were soon seated in a wide circle upon the grass, row within row, a grave and silent assembly. Each savage countenance seemed carved in wood, and none could have detected the ferocious passions hidden beneath that immovable mask. Pipes with ornamented stems were lighted, and passed from hand to hand.

Then Pontiac rose, and walked forward into the midst of the council. According to Canadian tradition, he was not above the middle height, though his muscular figure was cast in a mould of remarkable symmetry and vigor. His complexion was darker than is usual with his race, and his features, though by no means regular, had a bold and stern expression; while his habitual bearing was imperious and peremptory, like that of a man accustomed to sweep away all opposition by the force of his impetuous will. His ordinary attire was that of the primitive savage, — a scanty cincture girt about his loins, and his long, black hair flowing loosely at his back; but on occasions like this he was wont to appear as befitted his power and character, and he stood doubtless before the council plumed and painted in the full costume of war.

Looking round upon his wild auditors he began to speak, with fierce gesture, and a loud, impassioned voice; and at every pause, deep, guttural ejaculations of assent and approval responded to his words. He inveighed against the arrogance, rapacity, and injustice, of the English, and contrasted them with the French, whom they had driven from the soil. He declared that the British commandant had treated him with neglect and contempt; that the soldiers of the garrison had abused the Indians; and that one of them had struck a follower of his own. He represented the danger that would arise from the supremacy of the English. They had expelled the French, and now they only waited for a pretext to turn upon the Indians and destroy them. Then, holding out a broad belt of wampum, he told the council that he had received it from their great father the King of France, in token that he had heard the voice of his red children; that his sleep was at an end; and that his great war canoes would soon sail up the St. Lawrence, to win back Canada, and wreak vengeance on his enemies. The Indians and their French brethren would fight once more side by side, as they had always fought; they would strike the English as they had struck them many moons ago, when their great army marched down the Monongahela, and they had shot them from their ambush, like a flock of pigeons in the woods.

Having roused in his warlike listeners their native thirst for blood and vengeance, he next addressed himself to their superstition, and told the following tale. Its precise origin is not easy to determine.   It is possible that the Delaware prophet, mentioned in a former chapter, may have had some part in it; or it might have been the offspring of Pontiac's heated imagination, during his period of fasting and dreaming.   That he deliberately invented it for the sake of the effect it would produce, is the least probable conclusion of all; for it evidently proceeds from the superstitious mind of an Indian, brooding upon the evil days in which his lot was cast, and turning for relief to the mysterious Author of his being.   It is, at all events, a characteristic specimen of the Indian legendary tales, and, like many of them bears an allegoric significancy.   Yet he who endeavors to interpret an Indian allegory through all its erratic windings and puerile inconsistencies, has undertaken no enviable task.

" A Delaware Indian," said Pontiac, " conceived an eager desire to learn wisdom from the Master of Life ; but, being ignorant where to find him, he had recourse to fasting, dreaming, and magical incantations.   By these means it was revealed to him, that, by moving forward in a straight, undeviating course, he would reach the abode of the Great Spirit.   He told his purpose to no one, and having provided the equipments of a hunter,— gun, powder-horn, ammunition, and a kettle for preparing his food, — he set out on his errand. For some time he journeyed on in high hope and confidence.   On the evening of the eighth day, he stopped by the side of a brook at the edge of a meadow, where he began to make ready his

evening meal, when, looking up, he saw three
large openings in the woods before him, and three
well-beaten paths which entered them. He was
much surprised ; but his wonder increased, when,
after it had grown dark, the three paths were more
clearly visible than ever. Remembering the important object of his journey, he could neither rest nor
sleep ; and, leaving his fire, he crossed the meadow,
and entered the largest of the three openings. He
had advanced but a short distance into the forest,
when a bright flame sprang out of the ground
before him, and arrested his steps. In great amazement, he turned back, and entered the second path,
where the same wonderful phenomenon again
encountered him ; and now, in terror and bewilderment, yet still resolved to persevere, he took the
last of the three paths. On this he journeyed a
whole day without interruption, when at length,
emerging from the forest, he saw before him a vast
mountain, of dazzling whiteness. So precipitous
was the ascent, that the Indian thought it hopeless
to go farther, and looked around him in despair :
at that moment, he saw, seated at some distance
above, the figure of a beautiful woman arrayed in
white, who arose as he looked upon her, and thus
accosted him : 'How can you hope, encumbered
as you are, to succeed in your design? Go down
to the foot of the mountain, throw away your gun,
your ammunition, your provisions, and your clothing ; wash yourself in the stream which flows
there, and you will then be prepared to stand
before the Master of Life.' The Indian obeyed,

and again began to ascend among the rocks, while
the woman, seeing him still discouraged, laughed
at his faintness of heart, and told him that, if he
wished for success, he must climb by the aid of
one hand and one foot only.   After great toil and
suffering, he at length found himself at the summit.
The woman had disappeared, and he was left alone.
A rich and beautiful plain lay before him, and at
a little distance he saw three great villages, far
superior to the squalid wigwams of the Delawares.
As he approached the largest, and stood hesitating
whether he should enter, a man gorgeously attired
stepped forth, and, taking him by the hand, welcomed him to the celestial abode.   He then con
ducted him into the presence of the Great Spirit,
where the Indian stood confounded at the unspeakable splendor which surrounded him.   The Great
Spirit bade him be seated, and thus addressed
him : —

" ' I am the Maker of heaven and earth, the trees,
lakes, rivers, and all things else.   I am the Maker
of mankind ; and because I love you, you must do
my will.   The land on which you live I have made
for you, and not for others.   Why do you suffer
the white men to dwell among you ?   My children,
you have forgotten the customs and traditions of
your forefathers.   Why do you not clothe yourselves
in skins, as they did, and use the bows and arrows,
and the stone-pointed lances, which they used?
You have bought guns, knives, kettles, and blankets, from the white men, until you can no longer do
without them ; and, what is worse, you have drunk

the poison fire-water, which turns you into fools. Fling all these things away; live as your wise forefathers lived before you. And as for these English, — these dogs dressed in red, who have come to rob you of your hunting-grounds, and drive away the game, — you must lift the hatchet against them. Wipe them from the face of the earth, and then you will win my favor back again, and once more be happy and prosperous. The children of your great father, the King of France, are not like the English. Never forget that they are your brethren. They are very dear to me, for they love the red men, and understand the true mode of worshipping me.' "

The Great Spirit next gave his hearer various precepts of morality and religion, such as the prohibition to marry more than one wife; and a warning against the practice of magic, which is worshipping the devil. A prayer, embodying the substance of all that he had heard, was then presented to the Delaware. It was cut in hieroglyphics upon a wooden stick, after the custom of his people; and he was directed to send copies of it to all the Indian villages.[1]

The adventurer now departed, and, returning to the earth, reported all the wonders he had seen in the celestial regions.

Such was the tale told by Pontiac to the council;

---

[1] *Pontiac*, MS — *M'Dougal*, MSS. M'Dougal states that he derived his information from an Indian. The author of the *Pontiac* MS probably writes on the authority of Canadians, some of whom were present at the council.

and it is worthy of notice, that not he alone, but many of the most notable men who have arisen among the Indians, have been opponents of civilization, and stanch advocates of primitive barbarism. Red Jacket and Tecumseh would gladly have brought back their people to the rude simplicity of their original condition. There is nothing progressive in the rigid, inflexible nature of an Indian. He will not open his mind to the idea of improvement; and nearly every change that has been forced upon him has been a change for the worse.

Many other speeches were doubtless made in the council, but no record of them has been preserved. All present were eager to attack the British fort; and Pontiac told them, in conclusion, that on the second of May he would gain admittance, with a party of his warriors, on pretence of dancing the calumet dance before the garrison; that they would take note of the strength of the fortification; and that he would then summon another council to determine the mode of attack.

The assembly now dissolved, and all the evening the women were employed in loading the canoes, which were drawn up on the bank of the stream. The encampments broke up at so early an hour, that when the sun rose, the savage swarm had melted away; the secluded scene was restored to its wonted silence and solitude, and nothing remained but the slender frame-work of several hundred cabins, with fragments of broken utensils, pieces of cloth, and scraps of hide, scattered over the trampled grass; while the smouldering embers of numberless fires mingled their dark smoke with the white mist which rose from the little river.

Every spring, after the winter hunt was over, the Indians were accustomed to return to their villages, or permanent encampments, in the vicinity of Detroit; and, accordingly, after the council had broken up, they made their appearance as usual about the fort. On the first of May, Pontiac came to the gate with forty men of the Ottawa tribe, and asked permission to enter and dance the calumet dance, before the officers of the garrison. After some hesitation, he was admitted; and proceeding to the corner of the street, where stood the house of the commandant, Major Gladwyn, he and thirty of his warriors began their dance, each recounting his own exploits, and boasting himself the bravest of mankind. The officers and men gathered around them; while, in the mean time, the remaining ten of the Ottawas strolled about the fort, observing every thing it contained. When the dance was over, they all quietly withdrew, not a suspicion of their designs having arisen in the minds of the English.[1]

After a few days had elapsed, Pontiac's messengers again passed among the Indian cabins, calling the principal chiefs to another council, in the Pottawattamie village. Here there was a large structure of bark, erected for the public use on occasions like the present. A hundred chiefs were seated

---

[1] *Pontiac*, MS.

around this dusky council-house, the fire in the centre shedding its fitful light upon their dark, naked forms, while the pipe passed from hand to hand. To prevent interruption, Pontiac had stationed young men as sentinels, near the house. He once more addressed the chiefs; inciting them to hostility against the English, and concluding by the proposal of his plan for destroying Detroit. It was as follows: Pontiac would demand a council with the commandant concerning matters of great importance; and on this pretext he flattered himself that he and his principal chiefs would gain ready admittance within the fort. They were all to carry weapons concealed beneath their blankets. While in the act of addressing the commandant in the council-room, Pontiac was to make a certain signal, upon which the chiefs were to raise the war-whoop, rush upon the officers present, and strike them down. The other Indians, waiting meanwhile at the gate, or loitering among the houses, on hearing the yells and firing within the building, were to assail the astonished and half-armed soldiers; and thus Detroit would fall an easy prey.

In opening this plan of treachery, Pontiac spoke rather as a counsellor than as a commander. Haughty as he was, he had too much sagacity to wound the pride of a body of men over whom he had no other control than that derived from his personal character and influence. No one was hardy enough to venture opposition to the proposal of their great leader. His plan was eagerly adopted.   Hoarse ejaculations of applause echoed his speech ; and, gathering their blankets around them, the chiefs withdrew to their respective villages, to prepare for the destruction of the unsuspecting garrison.

CHAPTER X.

1763.

DETROIT.

To the credulity of mankind each great calamity has its dire prognostics. Signs and portents in the heavens, the vision of an Indian bow, and the figure of a scalp imprinted on the disk of the moon, warned the New England Puritans of impending war. The apparitions passed away, and Philip of Mount Hope burst from the forest with his Narragansett warriors. In October, 1762, thick clouds of inky blackness gathered above the fort and settlement of Detroit. The river darkened beneath the awful shadows. and the forest was wrapped in double gloom. Drops of rain began to fall, of strong, sulphurous odor, and so deeply colored that the people, it is said, collected them and used them for writing.[1] A literary and philosophical journal of the time seeks to explain this strange phenomenon on some principle of physical science; but the simple Canadians held a different faith. Throughout the winter, the shower of black rain was the foremost topic of their fireside talk; and

---

[1] Carver, *Travels*, 153. *Gent. Mag.* XXXIV. 408.

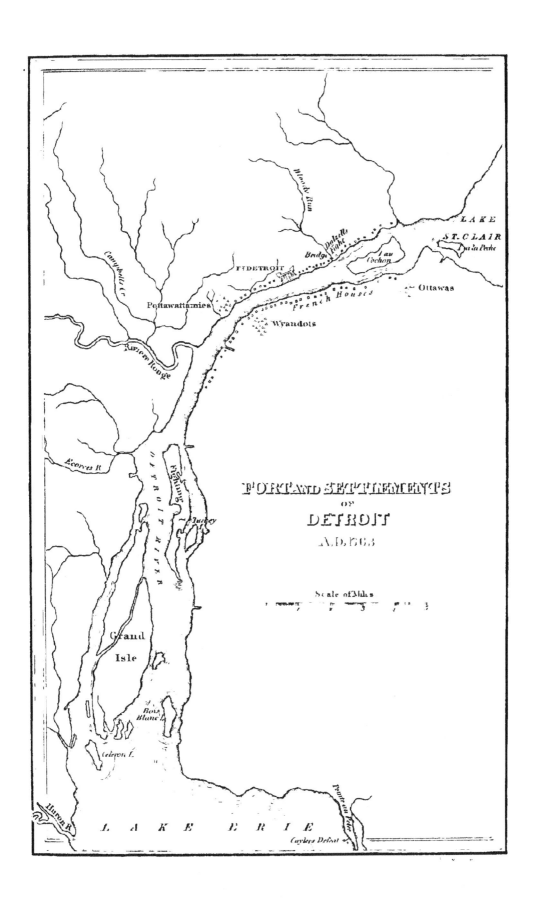

FORT AND SETTLEMENTS
OF
DETROIT
A.D. 1763

Scale of Miles

forebodings of impending evil disturbed the breast of many a timorous matron.

La Motte-Cadillac was the founder of Detroit. In the year 1701, he planted the little military colony, which time has transformed into a thriving American city.[1] At an earlier date, some feeble efforts had been made to secure the possession of this impor tant pass; and when La Hontan visited the lakes, a small post, called Fort St. Joseph, was standing near the present site of Fort Gratiot. The wandering Jesuits, too, made frequent sojourns upon the borders of the Detroit, and baptized the savage children whom they found there.

Fort St. Joseph was abandoned in the year 1688. The establishment of Cadillac was destined to a better fate, and soon rose to distinguished importance among the western outposts of Canada. Indeed, the site was formed by nature for prosperity; and a bad government and a thriftless people could not prevent the increase of the colony. At the close of the French war, as Major Rogers tells us, the place contained twenty-five hundred inhabitants.[2] The centre of the settlement was the fortified town, currently called the Fort, to distinguish it from the straggling dwellings along the river banks. It stood on the western margin of the river, covering a small part of the ground now occupied by the city of Detroit, and contained about a hundred houses, compactly pressed together, and surrounded by a palisade.

[1] *Memorial of La Motte Cadillac* See Schoolcraft, *Oneota*, 407.
[2] A high estimate Compare Rameau, *Colonie du Detroit*, 28.

Both above and below the fort, the banks of the stream were lined on both sides with small Canadian dwellings, extending at various intervals for nearly eight miles. Each had its garden and its orchard, and each was enclosed by a fence of rounded pickets. To the soldier or the trader, fresh from the harsh scenery and ambushed perils of the surrounding wilds, the secluded settlement was welcome as an oasis in the desert.

The Canadian is usually a happy man. Life sits lightly upon him; he laughs at its hardships, and soon forgets its sorrows. A lover of roving and adventure, of the frolic and the dance, he is little troubled with thoughts of the past or the future, and little plagued with avarice or ambition. At Detroit, all his propensities found ample scope. Aloof from the world, the simple colonists shared none of its pleasures and excitements, and were free from many of its cares. Nor were luxuries wanting which civilization might have envied them. The forests teemed with game, the marshes with wild fowl, and the rivers with fish. The apples and pears of the old Canadian orchards are even to this day held in esteem. The poorer inhabitants made wine from the fruit of the wild grape, which grew profusely in the woods, while the wealthier class procured a better quality from Montreal, in exchange for the canoe loads of furs which they sent down with every year. Here, as elsewhere in Canada, the long winter was a season of social enjoyment; and when, in summer and autumn, the traders and voyageurs, the *coureurs de bois*, and half-breeds, gathered from the distant forests of the north-west, the whole settlement was alive with dancing and feasting, drinking, gaming, and carousing.

Within the limits of the settlement were three large Indian villages. On the western shore, a little below the fort, were the lodges of the Potta-wattamies; nearly opposite, on the eastern side, was the village of the Wyandots; and on the same side, five miles higher up, Pontiac's band of Ottawas had fixed their abode. The settlers had always maintained the best terms with their savage neighbors. In truth, there was much congeniality between the red man and the Canadian. Their harmony was seldom broken; and among the woods and wilds of the northern lakes roamed many a lawless half-breed, the mongrel offspring of the colonists of Detroit and the Indian squaws.

We have already seen how, in an evil hour for the Canadians, a party of British troops took pos-session of Detroit, towards the close of the year 1760. The British garrison, consisting partly of regulars and partly of provincial rangers, was now quartered in a well-built range of barracks within the town or fort. The latter, as already mentioned, contained about a hundred small houses. Its form was nearly square, and the palisade which sur-rounded it was about twenty-five feet high. At each corner was a wooden bastion, and a block-house was erected over each gateway. The houses were small, chiefly built of wood, and roofed with bark or a thatch of straw. The streets also were extremely narrow, though a wide passage way, known as the *chemin du ronde*, surrounded the town, between the houses and the palisade. Besides the barracks, the only public buildings were a council-house and a rude little church.

The garrison consisted of a hundred and twenty soldiers, with about forty fur-traders and *engagés*; but the latter, as well as the Canadian inhabitants of the place, could little be trusted, in the event of an Indian outbreak. Two small, armed schooners, the Beaver and the Gladwyn, lay anchored in the stream, and several light pieces of artillery were mounted on the bastions.

Such was Detroit, — a place whose defences could have opposed no resistance to a civilized enemy; and yet, far removed as it was from the hope of speedy succor, it could only rely, in the terrible struggles that awaited it, upon its own slight strength and feeble resources.[1]

Standing on the water bastion of Detroit, a pleasant landscape spread before the eye. The river, about half a mile wide, almost washed the foot of the stockade; and either bank was lined with the white Canadian cottages. The joyous sparkling of the bright blue water; the green

---

[1] Croghan, *Journal.* Rogers, *Account of North America*, 168. Various MS Journals, Letters, and Plans have also been consulted. The most remarkable of these is the *Plan Topographique du Detroit*, made by or for General Collot, in 1796. It is accompanied by a drawing in water-colors of the town as it appeared in that year. A fac-simile of this drawing is in my possession The regular fortification, which, within the recollection of many now living, covered the ground in the rear of the old town of Detroit, was erected at a date subsequent to the period of this history.

luxuriance of the woods; the white dwellings, looking out from the foliage; and, in the distance, the Indian wigwams curling their smoke against the sky, — all were mingled in one broad scene of wild and rural beauty.

Pontiac, the Satan of this forest paradise, was accustomed to spend the early part of the summer upon a small island at the opening of the Lake St. Clair, hidden from view by the high woods that covered the intervening Isle au Cochon.[1] " The king and lord of all this country," as Rogers calls him, lived in no royal state. His cabin was a small, oven-shaped structure of bark and rushes. Here he dwelt, with his squaws and children; and here, doubtless, he might often have been seen, lounging, half-naked, on a rush mat, or a bear-skin, like any ordinary warrior. We may fancy the current of his thoughts, the turmoil of his uncurbed passions, as he revolved the treacheries which, to his savage mind, seemed fair and honorable. At one moment, his fierce heart would burn with the anticipation of vengeance on the detested English; at another, he would meditate how he best might turn the approaching tumults to the furtherance of his own ambitious schemes. Yet we may believe that Pontiac was not a stranger to the high emotion of the patriot hero, the champion not merely of his nation's rights, but of the very existence of his race. He did not dream how desperate a game he was about to play. He

---

[1] Tradition, communicated to H. R. Schoolcraft, Esq., by Henry Conner, formerly Indian interpreter at Detroit

hourly flattered himself with the futile hope of aid from France, and thought in his ignorance that the British colonies must give way before the rush of his savage warriors; when, in truth, all the combined tribes of the forest might have chafed in vain rage against the rock-like strength of the Anglo-Saxon.

Looking across an intervening arm of the river, Pontiac could see on its eastern bank the numerous lodges of his Ottawa tribesmen, half hidden among the ragged growth of trees and bushes. On the afternoon of the fifth of May, a Canadian woman, the wife of St. Aubin, one of the principal settlers, crossed over from the western side, and visited the Ottawa village, to obtain from the Indians a supply of maple sugar and venison. She was surprised at finding several of the warriors engaged in filing off the muzzles of their guns, so as to reduce them, stock and all, to the length of about a yard. Returning home in the evening, she mentioned what she had seen to several of her neighbors. Upon this, one of them, the blacksmith of the village, remarked that many of the Indians had lately visited his shop, and attempted to borrow files and saws for a purpose which they would not explain.[1] These circumstances excited the suspicion of the experienced Canadians. Doubtless there were many in the settlement who might, had they chosen, have revealed the plot; but it is no less certain that the more numerous and respectable

---

[1] *St. Aubin's Account*, MS. See Appendix, C.

class in the little community had too deep an inter-est in the preservation of peace, to countenance the designs of Pontiac.   M. Gouin, an old and wealthy settler, went to the commandant, and con-jured him to stand upon his guard; but Gladwyn, a man of fearless temper, gave no heed to the friendly advice.[1]

In the Pottawattamie village, if there be truth in tradition, lived an Ojibwa girl, who could boast a larger share of beauty than is common in the wig-wam.   She had attracted the eye of Gladwyn.   He had formed a connection with her, and she had be-come much attached to him.   On the afternoon of the sixth, Catharine — for so the officers called her — came to the fort, and repaired to Gladwyn's quar-ters, bringing with her a pair of elk-skin moccasons, ornamented with porcupine work, which he had requested her to make.   There was something unusual in her look and manner.   Her face was sad and downcast.   She said little, and soon left the room; but the sentinel at the door saw her still lingering at the street corner, though the hour for closing the gates was nearly come.   At length she attracted the notice of Gladwyn himself; and calling her to him, he pressed her to declare what was weighing upon her mind.   Still she remained for a long time silent, and it was only after much urgency and many promises not to betray her, that she revealed her momentous secret.

To-morrow, she said, Pontiac will come to the fort with sixty of his chiefs.   Each will be armed

---

[1] *Gouin's Account*, MS.

with a gun, cut short, and hidden under his blanket. Pontiac will demand to hold a council; and after he has delivered his speech, he will offer a peace-belt of wampum, holding it in a reversed position. This will be the signal of attack. The chiefs will spring up and fire upon the officers, and the Indians in the street will fall upon the garrison. Every Englishman will be killed, but not the scalp of a single Frenchman will be touched.[1]

[1] Letter to the writer from H. R. Schoolcraft, Esq, containing the traditional account from the lips of the interpreter, Henry Conner. See, also, Carver, *Travels*, 155 (Lond 1778)

Carver's account of the conspiracy and the siege is in several points inexact, which throws a shade of doubt on this story. Tradition, however, as related by the interpreter Conner, sustains him; with the addition that Catharine was the mistress of Gladwyn, and a few other points, including a very unromantic end of the heroine, who is said to have perished, by falling, when drunk, into a kettle of boiling maple-sap. This was many years after (see Appendix). Maxwell agrees in the main with Carver. There is another tradition, that the plot was disclosed by an old squaw. A third, current among the Ottawas, and sent to me in 1858 by Mr Hosmer, of Toledo, declares that a young squaw told the plot to the commanding officer, but that he would not believe her, as she had a bad name, being a "straggler among the private soldiers." An Indian chief, pursues the same story, afterwards warned the officer. The Pontiac MS says that Gladwyn was warned by an Ottawa warrior, though a woman was suspected by the Indians of having betrayed the secret. Peltier says that a woman named Catharine was accused of revealing the plot, and severely flogged by Pontiac in consequence. There is another story, that a soldier named Tucker, adopted by the Indians, was warned by his Indian sister. But the most distinct and satisfactory evidence is the following, from a letter written at Detroit on the twelfth of July, 1763, and signed James Macdonald. It is among the *Haldimand Papers* in the British Museum. There is also an imperfect copy, found among the papers of Colonel John Brodhead, in the library of the Historical Society of Pennsylvania: "About six o'clock that afternoon [May 7], six of their warriors returned and brought an old squaw prisoner, alleging that she had given us false information against them. The major declared she had never given us any kind of advice. They then insisted on naming the author of what he had heard with regard to the Indians, which he declined to do, but told them that it was one of themselves,

Such is the story told in 1768 to the traveller Carver at Detroit, and preserved in local tradition, but not sustained by contemporary letters or diaries. What is certain is, that Gladwyn received secret information, on the night of the sixth of May, that an attempt would be made on the morrow to capture the fort by treachery. He called some of his officers, and told them what he had heard. The defences of the place were feeble and extensive, and the garrison by far too weak to repel a general assault. The force of the Indians at this time is variously estimated at from six hundred to two thousand; and the commandant greatly feared that some wild impulse might precipitate their plan, and that they would storm the fort before the morning. Every preparation was made to meet the sudden emergency. Half the garrison were ordered under arms, and all the officers prepared to spend the night upon the ramparts.

The day closed, and the hues of sunset faded. Only a dusky redness lingered in the west, and the darkening earth seemed her dull self again. Then night descended, heavy and black, on the

whose name he promised never to reveal; whereupon they went off, and carried the old woman prisoner with them. When they arrived at their camp, Pontiac, their greatest chief, seized on the prisoner, and gave her three strokes with a stick on the head, which laid her flat on the ground, and the whole nation assembled round her, and called repeated times, 'Kill her! kill her!'"

Thus it is clear that the story told by Carver must be taken with many grains of allowance. The greater part of the evidence given above has been gathered since the first edition of this book was published It has been thought best to retain the original passage, with the necessary qualifications The story is not without interest, and those may believe it who will.

fierce Indians and the sleepless English. From sunset till dawn, an anxious watch was kept from the slender palisades of Detroit. The soldiers were still ignorant of the danger; and the sentinels did not know why their numbers were ·doubled, or why, with such unwonted vigilance, their officers repeatedly visited their posts. Again and again Gladwyn mounted his wooden ramparts, and looked forth into the gloom. There seemed nothing but repose and peace in the soft, moist air of the warm spring evening, with the piping of frogs along the river bank, just roused from their torpor by the genial influence of May. But, at intervals, as the night wind swept across the bastion, it bore sounds of fearful portent to the ear, the sullen booming of the Indian drum and the wild chorus of quavering yells, as the warriors, around their distant camp-fires, danced the war-dance, in preparation for the morrow's work.[1]

[1] *Maxwell's Account*, MS. See *Appendix*, C.

CHAPTER XI.

1763.

TREACHERY OF PONTIAC.

THE night passed without alarm. The sun rose upon fresh fields and newly budding woods, and scarcely had the morning mists dissolved, when the garrison could see a fleet of birch canoes crossing the river from the eastern shore, within range of cannon shot above the fort. Only two or three warriors appeared in each, but all moved slowly, and seemed deeply laden. In truth, they were full of savages, lying flat on their faces, that their numbers might not excite the suspicion of the English.[1]

At an early hour the open common behind the fort was thronged with squaws, children, and warriors, some naked, and others fantastically arrayed in their barbarous finery. All seemed restless and uneasy, moving hither and thither, in apparent preparation for a general game of ball. Many tall warriors, wrapped in their blankets, were seen stalking towards the fort, and casting malignant furtive glances upward at the palisades. Then

---

[1] *Meloche's Account,* MS.

with an air of assumed indifference, they would move towards the gate.   They were all admitted; for Gladwyn, who, in this instance at least, showed some knowledge of Indian character, chose to convince his crafty foe that, though their plot was detected, their hostility was despised.[1]

The whole garrison was ordered under arms. Sterling, and the other English fur-traders, closed their storehouses and armed their men, and all in cool confidence stood waiting the result.

Meanwhile, Pontiac, who had crossed with the canoes from the eastern shore, was approaching along the river road, at the head of his sixty chiefs, all gravely marching in Indian file.   A Canadian settler, named Beaufait, had been that morning to the fort.   He was now returning homewards, and as he reached the bridge which led over the stream then called Parent's Creek, he saw the chiefs in the act of crossing from the farther bank.   He stood aside to give them room.   As the last Indian passed, Beaufait recognized him as an old friend and associate.   The savage greeted him with the usual ejaculation, opened for an instant the folds of his blanket, disclosed the hidden gun, and, with an emphatic gesture towards the fort, indicated the purpose to which he meant to apply it.[2]

At ten o'clock, the great war-chief, with his treacherous followers, reached the fort, and the gateway was thronged with their savage faces.

---

[1] *Penn Gaz* No 1808.

[2] This incident was related, by the son of Beaufait, to General Cass. See Cass, *Discourse before the Michigan Historical Society*, 30.

All were wrapped to the throat in colored blankets. Some were crested with hawk, eagle, or raven plumes; others had shaved their heads, leaving only the fluttering scalp-lock on the crown; while others, again, wore their long, black hair flowing loosely at their backs, or wildly hanging about their brows like a lion's mane. Their bold yet crafty features, their cheeks besmeared with ochre and vermilion, white lead and soot, their keen, deep-set eyes gleaming in their sockets, like those of rattlesnakes, gave them an aspect grim, uncouth, and horrible. For the most part, they were tall, strong men, and all had a gait and bearing of peculiar stateliness.

As Pontiac entered, it is said that he started, and that a deep ejaculation half escaped from his breast. Well might his stoicism fail, for at a glance he read the ruin of his plot. On either hand, within the gateway, stood ranks of soldiers and hedges of glittering steel. The swarthy *engagés* of the fur-traders, armed to the teeth, stood in groups at the street corners, and the measured tap of a drum fell ominously on the ear. Soon regaining his composure, Pontiac strode forward into the narrow street; and his chiefs filed after him in silence, while the scared faces of women and children looked out from the windows as they passed. Their rigid muscles betrayed no sign of emotion; yet, looking closely, one might have seen their small eyes glance from side to side with restless scrutiny.

Traversing the entire width of the little town,

they reached the door of the council-house, a large building standing near the margin of the river. On entering, they saw Gladwyn, with several of his officers, seated in readiness to receive them, and the observant chiefs did not fail to remark that every Englishman wore a sword at his side, and a pair of pistols in his belt. The conspirators eyed each other with uneasy glances. " Why," demanded Pontiac, " do I see so many of my father's young men standing in the street with their guns?" Gladwyn replied through his interpreter, La Butte, that he had ordered the soldiers under arms for the sake of exercise and discipline. With much delay and many signs of distrust, the chiefs at length sat down on the mats prepared for them; and, after the customary pause, Pontiac rose to speak. Holding in his hand the wampum belt which was to have given the fatal signal, he addressed the commandant, professing strong attachment to the English, and declaring, in Indian phrase, that he had come to smoke the pipe of peace, and brighten the chain of friendship. The officers watched him keenly as he uttered these hollow words, fearing lest, though conscious that his designs were suspected, he might still attempt to accomplish them. And once, it is said, he raised the wampum belt as if about to give the signal of attack. But at that instant Gladwyn signed slightly with his hand. The sudden clash of arms sounded from the passage without, and a drum rolling the charge filled the council-room with its stunning din. At this, Pontiac stood like one confounded. Some writers will have it, that Gladwyn, rising from his seat, drew the chief's blanket aside, exposed the hidden gun, and sternly rebuked him for his treachery. But the commandant wished only to prevent the consummation of the plot, without bringing on an open rupture. His own letters affirm that he and his officers remained seated as before. Pontiac, seeing his unruffled brow and his calm eye fixed steadfastly upon him, knew not what to think, and soon sat down in amazement and perplexity. Another pause ensued, and Gladwyn commenced a brief reply. He assured the chiefs that friendship and protection should be extended towards them as long as they continued to deserve it, but threatened ample vengeance for the first act of aggression. The council then broke up; but, before leaving the room, Pontiac told the officers that he would return in a few days, with his squaws and children, for he wished that they should all shake hands with their fathers the English. To this new piece of treachery Gladwyn deigned no reply. The gates of the fort, which had been closed during the conference, were again flung open, and the baffled savages were suffered to depart, rejoiced, no doubt, to breathe once more the free air of the open fields.[1]

[1] Carver, *Travels*, 159 (London, 1778). M'Kenney, *Tour to the Lakes*, 130 Cass, *Discourse*, 32. *Penn. Gaz* Nos. 1807, 1808 *Pontiac* MS. *M'Dougal*, MSS. *Gouin's Account*, MS *Meloche's Account*, MS. *St. Aubin's Account*, MS.

Extract from a MS. Letter — *Major Gladwyn to Sir J. Amherst:*

"Detroit, May 14, 1763

" Sir.

" On the First Instant, Pontiac, the Chief of the Ottawa Nation, came here with about Fifty of his Men (forty, Pontiac MS.), and told me that in

Gladwyn has been censured, and perhaps with
justice, for not detaining the chiefs as hostages for
the good conduct of their followers. An entrapped
wolf meets no quarter from the huntsman; and a
savage, caught in his treachery, has no claim to
forbearance. Perhaps the commandant feared
lest, should he arrest the chiefs when gathered at
a public council, and guiltless as yet of open violence, the act might be interpreted as cowardly
and dishonorable. He was ignorant, moreover, of
the true nature of the plot. In his view, the
whole affair was one of those impulsive outbreaks
so common among Indians; and he trusted that,
could an immediate rupture be averted, the threatening clouds would soon blow over.

Here, and elsewhere, the conduct of Pontiac is
marked with the blackest treachery; and one cannot
but lament that a commanding and magnanimous
nature should be stained with the odious vice of
cowards and traitors. He could govern, with
almost despotic sway, a race unruly as the winds.
In generous thought and deed, he rivalled the
heroes of ancient story; and craft and cunning

a few days, when the rest of his Nation came in, he Intended to Pay me a
Formal Visit. The 7th he came, but I was luckily Informed, the Night
before, that he was coming with an Intention to Surprize Us; Upon
which I took such Precautions that when they Entered the Fort, tho'
they were, by the best Accounts, about Three Hundred, and Armed with
Knives, Tomyhawks, and a great many with Guns cut short, and hid
under their Blankets), they were so much surprized to see our Dispo-
sition, that they would scarcely sit down to Council: However in about
Half an hour, after they saw their Designs were Discovered, they sat
Down, and Pontiac made a speech which I Answered calmly, without
Intimating my suspicion of their Intentions, and after receiving some
Trifling Presents, they went away to their Camp."

might well seem alien to a mind like his. Yet Pontiac was a thorough savage, and in him stand forth, in strongest light and shadow, the native faults and virtues of the Indian race. All children, says Sir Walter Scott, are naturally liars; and truth and honor are developments of later education. Barbarism is to civilization what childhood is to maturity; and all savages, whatever may be their country, their color, or their lineage, are prone to treachery and deceit. The barbarous ancestors of our own frank and manly race are no less obnoxious to the charge than those of the cat-like Bengalee; for in this childhood of society brave men and cowards are treacherous alike.

The Indian differs widely from the European in his notion of military virtue. In his view, artifice is wisdom; and he honors the skill that can circumvent, no less than the valor that can subdue, an adversary. The object of war, he argues, is to destroy the enemy. To accomplish this end, all means are honorable; and it is folly, not bravery, to incur a needless risk. Had Pontiac ordered his followers to storm the palisades of Detroit, not one of them would have obeyed him. They might, indeed. after their strange superstition, have reverenced him as a madman; but, from that hour, his fame as a war-chief would have sunk forever.

Balked in his treachery, the great chief withdrew to his village, enraged and mortified, yet still resolved to persevere. That Gladwyn had suffered him to escape, was to his mind an ample proof either of cowardice or ignorance. The latter supposition seemed the more probable; and he resolved to visit the English once more, and convince them, if possible, that their suspicions against him were unfounded.   Early on the following morning, he repaired to the fort with three of his chiefs, bearing in his hand the sacred calumet, or pipe of peace, its bowl carved in stone, and its stem adorned with feathers.   Offering it to the commandant, he addressed him and his officers to the following effect: "My fathers, evil birds have sung lies in your ear.   We that stand before you are friends of the English. We love them as our brothers; and, to prove our love, we have come this day to smoke the pipe of peace."   At his departure, he gave the pipe to Captain Campbell, second in command, as a farther pledge of his sincerity.

That afternoon, the better to cover his designs, Pontiac called the young men of all the tribes to a game of ball, which took place, with great noise and shouting, on the neighboring fields.   At nightfall, the garrison were startled by a burst of loud, shrill yells.   The drums beat to arms, and the troops were ordered to their posts; but the alarm was caused only by the victors in the ball play, who were announcing their success by these discordant outcries.   Meanwhile, Pontiac was in the Pottawattamie village, consulting with the chiefs of that tribe, and with the Wyandots, by what means they might compass the ruin of the English.[1]

Early on the following morning, Monday, the

[1] *Pontiac* MS.

ninth of May, the French inhabitants went in procession to the principal church of the settlement, which stood near the river bank, about half a mile above the fort. Having heard mass, they all returned before eleven o'clock, without discovering any signs that the Indians meditated an immediate act of hostility. Scarcely, however, had they done so, when the common behind the fort was once more thronged with Indians of all the four tribes; and Pontiac, advancing from among the multitude, approached the gate. It was closed and barred against him. He shouted to the sentinels, and demanded why he was refused admittance. Gladwyn himself replied, that the great chief might enter, if he chose, but that the crowd he had brought with him must remain outside. Pontiac rejoined, that he wished all his warriors to enjoy the fragrance of the friendly calumet. Gladwyn's answer was more concise than courteous, and imported that he would have none of his rabble in the fort. Thus repulsed, Pontiac threw off the mask which he had worn so long. With a grin of hate and rage, he turned abruptly from the gate, and strode towards his followers, who, in great multitudes, lay flat upon the ground, just beyond reach of gunshot. At his approach, they all leaped up and ran off, " yelping," in the words of an eye-witness, " like so many devils." [1]

Looking out from the loopholes, the garrison could see them running in a body towards the house of

---

[1] MS Letter — *Gladwyn to Amherst,* May 14. *Pontiac* MS., &c.

an old English woman, who lived, with her family, on a distant part of the common. They beat down the doors, and rushed tumultuously in. A moment more, and the mournful scalp-yell told the fate of the wretched inmates. Another large body ran, yelling, to the river bank, and, leaping into their canoes, paddled with all speed to the Isle au Cochon, where dwelt an Englishman, named Fisher, formerly a sergeant of the regulars.

They soon dragged him from the hiding-place where he had sought refuge, murdered him on the spot, took his scalp, and made great rejoicings over this miserable trophy of brutal malice. On the following day, several Canadians crossed over to the island to inter the body, which they accomplished, as they thought, very effectually. Tradition, however, relates, as undoubted truth, that when, a few days after, some of the party returned to the spot, they beheld the pale hands of the dead man thrust above the ground, in an attitude of eager entreaty. Having once more covered the refractory members with earth, they departed, in great wonder and awe; but what was their amazement, when, on returning a second time, they saw the hands protruding as before. At this, they repaired in horror to the priest, who hastened to the spot, sprinkled the grave with holy water, and performed over it the neglected rites of burial. Thenceforth, says the tradition, the corpse of the murdered soldier slept in peace.[1]

---

[1] *St. Aubin's Account*, MS.

Pontiac had borne no part in the wolfish deeds of his followers. When he saw his plan defeated, he turned towards the shore; and no' man durst approach him, for he was terrible in his rage. Pushing a canoe from the bank, he urged it with vigorous strokes, against the current, towards the Ottawa village, on the farther side. As he drew near, he shouted to the inmates. None remained in the lodges but women, children, and old men, who all came flocking out at the sound of his imperious voice. Pointing across the water, he ordered that all should prepare to move the camp to the western shore, that the river might no longer interpose a barrier between his followers and the English. The squaws labored with eager alacrity to obey him. Provisions, utensils, weapons, and even the bark covering to the lodges, were carried to the shore; and before evening all was ready for embarkation. Meantime, the warriors had come dropping in from their bloody work, until, at nightfall, nearly all had returned. Then Pontiac, hideous in his war-paint, leaped into the central area of the village. Brandishing his tomahawk, and stamping on the ground, he recounted his former exploits, and denounced vengeance on the English. The Indians flocked about him. Warrior after warrior caught the fierce contagion, and soon the ring was filled with dancers, circling round and round with frantic gesture, and startling the distant garrison with unearthly yells.[1]

The war-dance over, the work of embarkation

---

[1] *Parent's Account*, MS. *Meloche's Account*, MS.

was commenced, and long before morning the transfer was complete. The whole Ottawa population crossed the river, and pitched their wigwams on the western side, just above the mouth of the little stream then known as Parent's Creek, but since named Bloody Run, from the scenes of terror which it witnessed.[1]

During the evening, fresh tidings of disaster reached the fort. A Canadian, named Desnoyers, came down the river in a birch canoe, and, landing at the water gate, brought news that two English officers, Sir Robert Davers and Captain Robertson, had been waylaid and murdered by the Indians, above Lake St. Clair.[2] The Canadian declared, moreover, that Pontiac had just been joined by a formidable band of Ojibwas, from the Bay of Saginaw.[3] These were a peculiarly ferocious horde, and their wretched descendants still retain the character.

Every Englishman in the fort, whether trader or soldier, was now ordered under arms. No man

---

[1] *Gouin's Account.* MS.

[2] *Penn. Gaz.* Nos. 1807, 1808.

Extract from an anonymous letter — Detroit, July 9, 1763.

"You have long ago heard of our pleasant Situation, but the Storm is blown over. Was it not very agreeable to hear every Day, of their cutting, carving, boiling and eating our Companions? To see every Day dead Bodies floating down the River, mangled and disfigured? But Britons, you know, never shrink; we always appeared gay, to spite the Rascals. They boiled and eat Sir Robert Davers; and we are informed by Mr. Pauly, who escaped the other Day from one of the Stations surprised at the breaking out of the War, and commanded by himself, that he had seen an Indian have the Skin of Captain Robertson's Arm for a Tobacco-Pouch!"

[3] *Pontiac* MS.

lay down to sleep, and Gladwyn himself walked the ramparts throughout the night.

All was quiet till the approach of dawn. But as the first dim redness tinged the east, and fields and woods grew visible in the morning twilight, suddenly the war-whoop rose on every side at once. As wolves assail the wounded bison, howling their gathering cries across the wintry prairie, so the fierce Indians, pealing their terrific yells, ·came bounding naked to the assault. The men hastened to their posts. And truly it was time; for not the Ottawas alone, but the whole barbarian swarm — Wyandots, Pottawattamies, and Ojibwas — were upon them, and bullets rapped hard and fast against the palisades. The soldiers looked from the loopholes, thinking to see their assailants gathering for a rush against the feeble barrier. But, though their clamors filled the air, and their guns blazed thick and hot, yet very few were visible. Some were ensconced behind barns and fences, some skulked among bushes, and some lay flat in hollows of the ground; while those who could find no shelter were leaping about with the agility of monkeys, to dodge the shot of the fort. Each had filled his mouth with bullets, for the convenience of loading, and each was charging and firing without suspending these agile gymnastics for a moment. There was one low hill, at no great distance from the fort, behind which countless black heads of Indians alternately appeared and vanished; while, all along the ridge, their guns emitted incessant white puffs of smoke. Every loophole was a target for their bullets; but the fire was returned with steadiness, and not without effect. The Canadian *engagés* of the fur-traders retorted the Indian war-whoops with outcries not less discordant, while the British and provincials paid back the clamor of the enemy with musket and rifle balls. Within half gunshot of the palisades was a cluster of outbuildings, behind which a host of Indians found shelter. A cannon was brought to bear upon them, loaded with red-hot spikes. They were soon wrapped in flames, upon which the disconcerted savages broke away in a body, and ran off yelping, followed by a shout of laughter from the soldiers.[1]

For six hours, the attack was unabated; but as the day advanced, the assailants grew weary of their futile efforts. Their fire slackened, their clamors died away, and the garrison was left once more in peace, though from time to time a solitary shot, or lonely whoop, still showed the presence of some lingering savage, loath to be balked of his revenge. Among the garrison, only five men had been wounded, while the cautious enemy had suffered but trifling loss.

Gladwyn was still convinced that the whole affair was a sudden ebullition, which would soon subside; and being, moreover, in great want of provisions, he resolved to open negotiations with the Indians, under cover of which he might obtain the necessary supplies. The interpreter, La Butte, who, like most of his countrymen, might be said to hold

---

[1] *Pontiac MS. Penn. Gaz.* No 1808. MS. Letter— *Gladwyn to Amherst,* May 14, etc.

a neutral position between the English and the Indians, was despatched to the camp of Pontiac, to demand the reasons of his conduct, and declare that the commandant was ready to redress any real grievance of which he might complain. Two old Canadians of Detroit, Chapeton and Godefroy, earnest to forward the negotiation, offered to accompany him. The gates were opened for their departure, and many other inhabitants of the place took this opportunity of leaving it, alleging as their motive, that they did not wish to see the approaching slaughter of the English.

Reaching the Indian Camp, the three ambassadors were received by Pontiac with great apparent kindness. La Butte delivered his message, and the two Canadians labored to dissuade the chief, for his own good and for theirs, from pursuing his hostile purposes. Pontiac stood listening, armed with the true impenetrability of an Indian. At every proposal, he uttered an ejaculation of assent, partly from a strange notion of courtesy peculiar to his race, and partly from the deep dissimulation which seems native to their blood. Yet with all this seeming acquiescence, the heart of the savage was unmoved as a rock. The Canadians were completely deceived. Leaving Chapeton and Godefroy to continue the conference and push the fancied advantage, La Butte hastened back to the fort. He reported the happy issue of his mission, and added that peace might readily be had by making the Indians a few presents, for which they are always rapaciously eager. When, however he returned to the Indian camp, he found, to his chagrin, that his companions had made no progress in the negotiation. Though still professing a strong desire for peace, Pontiac had evaded every definite proposal. At La Butte's appearance, all the chiefs withdrew to consult among themselves. They returned after a short debate, and Pontiac declared that, out of their earnest desire for firm and lasting peace, they wished to hold council with their English fathers themselves. With this view, they were especially desirous that Captain Campbell, second in command, should visit their camp. This veteran officer, from his just, upright, and manly character, had gained the confidence of the Indians. To the Canadians the proposal seemed a natural one, and returning to the fort, they laid it before the commandant. Gladwyn suspected treachery, but Captain Campbell urgently asked permission to comply with the request of Pontiac. He felt, he said, no fear of the Indians, with whom he had always maintained the most friendly terms. Gladwyn, with some hesitation, acceded; and Campbell left the fort, accompanied by a junior officer, Lieutenant M'Dougal, and attended by La Butte and several other Canadians.

In the mean time, M. Gouin, anxious to learn what was passing, had entered the Indian camp, and, moving from lodge to lodge, soon saw and heard enough to convince him that the two British officers were advancing into the lion's jaws.[1] He hastened to despatch two messengers to warn them

---

[1] *Gouin's Account*, MS.

of the peril. The party had scarcely left the gate
when they were met by these men, breathless with
running; but the warning came too late. Once
embarked on the embassy, the officers would not
be diverted from it; and passing up the river road,
they approached the little· wooden bridge that
led over Parent's Creek. Crossing this bridge, and
ascending a rising ground beyond, they saw before
them the wide-spread camp of the Ottawas. A
dark multitude gathered along its outskirts, and no
sooner did they recognize the red uniform of the
officers, than they all raised at once a horrible outcry of whoops and howlings. Indeed, they seemed
disposed to give the ambassadors the reception
usually accorded to captives taken in war; for the
women seized sticks, stones, and clubs, and ran
towards Campbell and his companion, as if to make
them pass the cruel ordeal of running the gauntlet.[1]
Pontiac came forward, and his voice allayed the
tumult. He shook the officers by the hand, and,

[1] When a party returned with prisoners, the whole population of the
village turned out to receive them, armed with sticks, clubs, or even
deadlier weapons The captive was ordered to run to a given point,
usually some conspicuous lodge, or a post driven into the ground, while
his tormentors, ranging themselves in two rows, inflicted on him a mer·
ciless flagellation, which only ceased when he had reached the goal
Among the Iroquois, prisoners were led through the whole confederacy,
undergoing this martyrdom at every village, and seldom escaping without
the loss of a hand, a finger, or an eye. Sometimes the sufferer was made
to dance and sing, for the better entertainment of the crowd.

The story of General Stark is well known Being captured, in his
youth, by the Indians, and told to run the gauntlet, he instantly knocked
down the nearest warrior, snatched a club from his hands, and wielded it
with such good-will that no one dared approach him, and he reached the
goal scot free, while his more timorous companion was nearly beaten to
death

turning, led the way through the camp. It was a
confused assemblage of huts, chiefly of a conical
or half-spherical shape, and constructed of a slender framework covered with rush mats or sheets
of birch-bark. Many of the graceful birch canoes,
used by the Indians of the upper lakes, were lying
here and there among paddles, fish-spears, and
blackened kettles slung above the embers of the
fires. The camp was full of lean, wolfish dogs,
who, roused by the clamor of their owners, kept up
a discordant baying as the strangers passed. Pontiac paused before the entrance of a large lodge,
and, entering, pointed to several mats placed on
the ground, at the side opposite the opening.
Here, obedient to his signal, the two officers sat
down. Instantly the lodge was thronged with
savages. Some, and these were for the most part
chiefs, or old men, seated themselves on the ground
before the strangers; while the remaining space
was filled by a dense crowd, crouching or standing
erect, and peering over each other's shoulders. At
their first entrance, Pontiac had spoken a few
words. A pause then ensued, broken at length by
Campbell, who from his seat addressed the Indians
in a short speech. It was heard in perfect silence,
and no reply was made. For a full hour, the
unfortunate officers saw before them the same
concourse of dark, inscrutable faces, bending an
unwavering gaze upon them. Some were passing
out, and others coming in to supply their places, and
indulge their curiosity by a sight of the Englishmen.
At length, Captain Campbell, conscious, no doubt,

of the danger in which he was placed, resolved fully to ascertain his true position, and, rising to his feet, declared his intention of returning to the fort. Pontiac made a sign that he should resume his seat. " My father," he said, " will sleep to-night in the lodges of his red children." The gray-haired soldier and his companion were betrayed into the hands of their enemies.

Many of the Indians were eager to kill the captives on the spot, but Pontiac would not carry his treachery so far. He protected them from injury and insult, and conducted them to the house of M. Meloche, near Parent's Creek, where good quarters were assigned them, and as much liberty allowed as was consistent with safe custody.[1] The peril of their situation was diminished by the circumstance that two Indians, who, several days before, had been detained at the fort for some slight offence, still remained prisoners in the power of the commandant.[2]

---

[1] *Meloche's Account*, MS. *Penn. Gaz.* No. 1808 In a letter of James MacDonald, Detroit, July 12, the circumstances of the detention of the officers are related somewhat differently. Singularly enough, this letter of MacDonald is identical with a report of the events of the siege sent by Major Robert Rogers to Sir William Johnson, on the 8th of August Rogers, who was not an eye witness, appears to have borrowed the whole of his brother officer's letter without acknowledgment.

[2] Extract from a MS. Letter — *Sir J Amherst to Major Gladwyn*

" New York. 22nd June, 1763

" The Precautions you took when the Perfidious Villains came to Pay you a Visit, were Indeed very wisely Concerted ; And I Approve Entirely of the Steps you have since taken for the Defence of the Place, which, I hope, will have Enabled You to keep the Savages at Bay untill the Reinforcement, which Major Wilkins Writes me he had sent you, Arrives with you.

"I most sincerely Grieve for the Unfortunate Fate of Sir Robert

Late in the evening, La Butte, the interpreter, returned to the fort. His face wore a sad and downcast look, which sufficiently expressed the melancholy tidings that he brought. On hearing his account, some of the officers suspected, though probably without ground, that he was privy to the detention of the two ambassadors; and La Butte, feeling himself an object of distrust, lingered about the streets, sullen and silent, like the Indians among whom his rough life had been spent.

Davers, Lieut. Robertson, and the Rest of the Poor People, who have fallen into the Hands of the Merciless Villains I Trust you did not Know of the Murder of those Gentlemen, when Pontiac came with a Pipe of Peace, for if you had, you certainly would have put him, and Every Indian in your Power, to Death. Such Retaliation is the only Way of Treating such Miscreants.

"I cannot but Approve of your having Permitted Captain Campbell and Lieut. MacDougal to go to the Indians, as you had no other Method to Procure Provisions, by which means you may have been Enabled to Preserve the Garrison; for no Other Inducement should have prevailed on you to Allow those Gentlemen to Entrust themselves with the Savages. I am Nevertheless not without my Fears for them, and were it not that you have two Indians in your Hands, in Lieu of those Gentlemen, I should give them over for Lost.

"I shall Add no more at present; Capt Dalzell will Inform you of the steps taken for Reinforcing you and you may be assured — the utmost Expedition will be used for Collecting such a Force as may be Sufficient for bringing Ample Vengeance on the Treacherous and Bloody Villains who have so Perfidiously Attacked their Benefactors." MacDonald, and, after him, Rogers, says that, after the detention of the two officers, Pontiac summoned the fort to surrender, threatening, in case of refusal, to put all within to the torture The anonymous author of the *Diary of the Siege* adds that he sent word to Gladwyn that he kept the officers out of kindness, since, if they returned to the fort, he should be obliged to boil them with the rest of the garrison, the kettle being already on the fire.

CHAPTER XII.

1763.

PONTIAC AT THE SIEGE OF DETROIT.

ON the morning after the detention of the offi·
cers, Pontiac crossed over, with several of his chiefs,
to the Wyandot village. A part of this tribe, influ-
enced by Father Pothier, their Jesuit priest, had
refused to take up arms against the English; but,
being now threatened with destruction if they should
longer remain neutral, they were forced to join
the rest. They stipulate1, however, that they
should be allowed time to hear mass, before dancing the war-dance.[1] To this condition Pontiac
readily agreed, " although," observes the chronicler
in the fulness of his horror and detestation, " he
himself had no manner of worship, and cared not
for festivals or Sundays." These nominal Christians
of Father Pothier's flock, together with the other
Wyandots, soon distinguished themselves in the
war; fighting better, it was said, than all the other
Indians, — an instance of the marked superiority
of the Iroquois over the Algonquin stock.

Having secured these new allies, Pontiac pre-

---

[1] *Pontiac* MS.

pared to resume his operations with fresh vigor; and to this intent, he made an improved disposition of his forces. Some of the Pottawattamies were ordered to lie in wait along the river bank, below the fort; while others concealed themselves in the woods, in order to intercept any Englishman who might approach by land or water. Another band of the same tribe were to conceal themselves in the neighborhood of the fort, when no general attack was going forward, in order to shoot down any soldier or trader who might chance to expose his person. On the eleventh of May, when these arrangements were complete, several Canadians came early in the morning to the fort, to offer what they called friendly advice. It was to the effect that the garrison should at once abandon the place, as it would be stormed within an hour by fifteen hundred Indians. Gladwyn refused, whereupon the Canadians departed; and soon after some six hundred Indians began a brisk fusillade, which they kept up till seven o'clock in the evening. A Canadian then appeared, bearing a summons from Pontiac, demanding the surrender of the fort, and promising that the English should go unmolested on board their vessels, leaving all their arms and effects behind. Gladwyn again gave a flat refusal.[1]

On the evening of that day, the officers met to consider what course of conduct the emergency required; and, as one of them writes, the commandant was almost alone in the opinion that they

---

[1] MS. Letter — *James McDonald to* ——, Detroit, July 12.

ought still to defend the place.[1] It seemed to the rest that the only course remaining was to embark and sail for Niagara. Their condition appeared desperate; for, on the shortest allowance, they had scarcely provision enough to sustain the garrison three weeks, within which time there was little hope of succor. The houses being, moreover, of wood, and chiefly thatched with straw, might be set on fire with burning missiles. But the chief apprehensions of the officers arose from their dread that the enemy would make a general onset, and cut or burn their way through the pickets, — a mode of attack to which resistance would be unavailing. Their anxiety on this score was relieved by a Canadian in the fort, who had spent half his life among Indians, and who now assured the commandant that every maxim of their warfare was opposed to such a measure. Indeed, an Indian's idea of military honor widely differs, as before observed, from that of a white man; for he holds it to consist no less in a wary regard to his own life than in the courage and impetuosity with which he assails his enemy. His constant aim is to gain advantages without incurring loss. He sets an inestimable value on the lives of his own party, and deems a victory dearly purchased by the death of a single warrior. A war-chief attains the summit of his renown when he can boast that he has brought home a score of scalps without the loss of a man; and his reputation is wofully abridged if the mournful wailings of the

---

[1] *Penn. Gaz* No. 1808.

women mingle with the exulting yells of the warriors. Yet, with all his subtlety and caution, the
Indian is not a coward, and, in his own way of
fighting, often exhibits no ordinary courage. Stealing alone into the heart of an enemy's country, he
prowls around the hostile village, watching every
movement; and when night sets in, he enters a
lodge, and calmly stirs the decaying embers, that,
by their light, he may select his sleeping victims.
With cool deliberation he deals the mortal thrust,
kills foe after foe, and tears away scalp after scalp,
until at length an alarm is given; then, with a
wild yell, he bounds out into the darkness, and is
gone.

Time passed on, and brought little change and
no relief to the harassed and endangered garrison.
Day after day the Indians continued their attacks,
until their war-cries and the rattle of their guns
became familiar sounds. For many weeks, no
man lay down to sleep, except in his clothes,
and with his weapons by his side.[1] Parties of
volunteers sallied, from time to time, to burn the

---

[1] MS Letter from an officer at Detroit — no signature — July 31.
Extract from a letter dated Detroit, July 6

"We have been besieged here two Months, by Six Hundred Indians.
We have been upon the Watch Night and Day, from the Commanding
Officer to the lowest soldier, from the 8th of May, and have not had our
Cloaths off, nor slept all Night since it began; and shall continue so till
we have a Reinforcement up We then hope soon to give a good account of the Savages Their Camp lies about a Mile and a half from the
Fort; and that's the nearest they choose to come now. For the first
two or three Days we were attacked by three or four Hundred of them,
but we gave them so warm a Reception that now they don't care for
coming to see us, tho' they now and then get behind a House or Garden,
and fire at us about three or four Hundred yards' distance. The Day

outbuildings which gave shelter to the enemy. They cut down orchard trees, and levelled fences, until the ground about the fort was clear and open, and the enemy had no cover left from whence to fire. The two vessels in the river, sweeping the northern and southern curtains of the works with their fire, deterred the Indians from approaching those points, and gave material aid to the garrison. Still, worming their way through the grass, sheltering themselves behind every rising ground, the pertinacious savages would crawl close to the palisade, and shoot arrows, tipped with burning tow, upon the roofs of the houses; but cisterns and tanks of water were everywhere provided against such an emergency, and these attempts proved abortive. The little church, which stood near the palisade, was particularly exposed, and would probably have been set on fire, had not the priest of the settlement threatened Pontiac with the vengeance of the Great Spirit, should he be guilty of such sacrilege. Pontiac, who was filled with eagerness to get possession of the garrison, neglected no expedient that his savage tactics could supply. He went farther, and begged the French inhabitants to teach him the European method of attacking a fortified place by regular approaches; but the rude Canadians knew as little of the matter as he; or if, by chance, a few were better informed, they wisely preferred to conceal their knowledge. Soon

before Yesterday, we killed a Chief and three others, and wounded some more; yesterday went up with our Sloop, and battered their Cabins in such a Manner that they are glad to keep farther off."

after the first attack, the Ottawa chief had sent
in to Gladwyn a summons to surrender, assuring
him that, if the place were at once given up, he
might embark on board the vessels, with all his
men ; but that, if he persisted in his defence, he
would treat him as Indians treat each other ; that
is, he would burn him alive.   To this Gladwyn
made answer that he cared nothing for his threats.[1]
The attacks were now renewed with increased activity, and the assailants were soon after inspired
with fresh ardor by the arrival of a hundred and
twenty Ojibwa warriors from Grand River.   Every
man in the fort, officers, soldiers, traders, and
engagés, now slept upon the ramparts ; even in
stormy weather none were allowed to withdraw to
their quarters ;[2] yet a spirit of confidence and
cheerfulness still prevailed among the weary garrison.

Meanwhile, great efforts were made to procure a
supply of provisions.   Every house was examined,
and all that could serve for food, even grease and
tallow, was collected and placed in the public
storehouse, compensation having first been made to
the owners.   Notwithstanding these precautions
Detroit must have been abandoned or destroyed,
but for the assistance of a few friendly Canadians,
and especially of M. Baby, a prominent *habitant*,
who lived on the opposite side of the river, and
provided the garrison with cattle, hogs, and other
supplies.   These, under cover of night, were car-

---

[1] *Pontiac MS.*   [2] *Penn. Gaz.* No. 1808.

ried from his farm to the fort in boats, the Indians long remaining ignorant of what was going forward.[1]

They, on their part, began to suffer from hunger. Thinking to have taken Detroit at a single stroke, they had neglected, with their usual improvidence, to provide against the exigencies of a siege ; and now, in small parties, they would visit the Canadian families along the river shore, passing from house to house, demanding provisions, and threatening violence in case of refusal. This was the more annoying, since the food thus obtained was wasted with characteristic recklessness. Unable to endure it longer, the Canadians appointed a deputation of fifteen of the eldest among them to wait upon Pontiac, and complain of his followers' conduct. The meeting took place at a Canadian house, probably that of M. Meloche, where the great chief had made his headquarters, and where the prisoners, Campbell and M'Dougal, were confined.

[1] Extract from a MS Letter — *Major Gladwyn to Sir J. Amherst.*

"Detroit, July 8th, 1763

" Since the Commencement of this Extraordinary Affair, I have been Informed, that many of the Inhabitants of this Place, seconded by some French Traders from Montreal, have made the Indians Believe that a French Army & Fleet were in the River St. Lawrence, and that Another Army would come from the Illinois; And that when I Published the cessation of Arms, they said it was a mere Invention of Mine, purposely Calculated to Keep the Indians Quiet, as We were Affraid of them ; but they were not such Fools as to Believe me ; Which, with a thousand other Lies, calculated to Stir up Mischief, have Induced the Indians to take up Arms; And I dare say it will Appear ere long, that One Half of the Settlement merit a Gibbet, and the. Other Half ought to be Decimated ; Nevertheless, there is some Honest Men among them, to whom I am Infinitely Obliged ; I mean, Sir, Monsieur Navarre, the two Babys, & my Interpreters, St. Martin & La Bute."

When Pontiac saw the deputation' approaching along the river road, he was seized with an exceeding eagerness to know the purpose of their visit; for having long desired to gain the Canadians as allies against the English, and made several advances to that effect, he hoped that their present errand might relate to the object next his heart. So strong was his curiosity, that, forgetting the ordinary rule of Indian dignity and decorum, he asked the business on which they had come before they themselves had communicated it. The Canadians replied, that they wished the chiefs to be convened, for they were about to speak upon a matter of much importance. Pontiac instantly despatched messengers to the different camps and villages. The chiefs, soon arriving at his summons, entered the apartment. where they seated themselves upon the floor, having first gone through the necessary formality of shaking hands with the Canadian depu ties. After a suitable pause, the eldest of the French rose, and heavily complained of the outrages which they had committed. " You pretend," he said, " to be friends of the French, and yet you plunder us of our hogs and cattle, you trample upon our fields of young corn, and when you enter our houses, you enter with tomahawk raised. When your French father comes from Montreal with his great army, he will hear of what you have done, and, instead of shaking hands with you as brethren, he will punish you as enemies."

Pontiac sat with his eyes riveted upon the ground, listening to every word that was spoken.

When the speaker had concluded, he returned the following answer : —

" Brothers :

" We have never wished to do you harm, nor allow any to be done you ; but among us there are many young men who, though strictly watched, find opportunities of mischief. It is not to revenge myself alone that I make war on the English. It is to revenge you, my Brothers. When the English insulted us, they insulted you also. I know that they have taken away your arms, and made you sign a paper which they have sent home to their country. Therefore you are left defenceless ; and I mean now to revenge your cause and my own together. I mean to destroy the English, and leave not one upon our lands. You do not know the reasons from which I act. I have told you those only which concern yourselves ; but you will learn all in time. You will cease then to think me a fool. I know, my brothers, that there are many among you who take part with the English. I am sorry for it, for their own sakes ; for when our Father arrives, I shall point them out to him, and they will see whether they or I have most reason to be satisfied with the part we have acted.

" I do not doubt, my Brothers, that this war is very troublesome to you, for our warriors are continually passing and repassing through your settlement. I am sorry for it. Do not think that I approve of the damage that is done by them ; and, as a proof of this, remember the war with the Foxes, and the part which I took in it. It is now

seventeen years since the Ojibwas of Michillimackinac, combined with the Sacs and Foxes, came
down to destroy you. Who then defended you?
Was it not I and my young men ? Mickinac, great
chief of all these nations, said in council that he
would carry to his village the head of your commandant — that he would eat his heart and drink
his blood. Did I not take your part? Did I not
go to his camp, and say to him, that if he wished
to kill the French, he must first kill me and my
warriors ? Did I not assist you in routing them
and driving them away ?[1] And now you think
that I would turn my arms against you ! No,
my Brothers ; I am the same French Pontiac who
assisted you seventeen years ago. I am a Frenchman, and I wish to die a Frenchman ; and I now
repeat to you that you and I are one — that it is
for both our interests that I should be avenged.

---

[1] The annals of these remote and gloomy regions are involved in such
obscurity, that it is hard to discover the precise character of the events
to which Pontiac here refers. The only allusion to them, which the
writer has met with, is the following, inscribed on a tattered scrap of
soiled paper, found among the M'Dougal manuscripts : —

"Five miles below the mouth of Wolf River is the Great Death
Ground This took its name from the circumstance, that some years
before the Old French War, a great battle was fought between the French
troops, assisted by the Menomonies and Ottaways on the one side, and
the Sac and Fox Indians on the other. The Sacs and Foxes were nearly
all cut off; and this proved the cause of their eventual expulsion from
that country."

The M'Dougal manuscripts, above referred to, belonged to a son of the
Lieutenant M'Dougal who was the fellow-prisoner of Major Campbell.
On the death of the younger M'Dougal, the papers, which were very
voluminous, and contained various notes concerning the Indian war, and
the captivity of his father, came into the possession of a family at the
town of St Clair, in Michigan, who permitted such of them as related to
the subjects in question to be copied by the writer.

Let me alone. I do not ask you for aid, for it is not in your power to give it. I only ask provisions for myself and men. Yet, if you are inclined to assist me, I shall not refuse you. It would please me, and you yourselves would be sooner rid of your troubles; for I promise you, that, as soon as the English are driven out, we will go back to our villages, and there await the arrival of our French Father. You have heard what I have to say; remain at peace, and I will watch that no harm shall be done to you, either by my men or by the other Indians."

This speech is reported by a writer whose chief characteristic is the scrupulous accuracy with which he has chronicled minute details without interest or importance. He neglects, moreover, no opportunity of casting ignominy and contempt upon the name of Pontiac. His mind is of so dull and commonplace an order as to exclude the supposition that he himself is author of the words which he ascribes to the Ottawa chief, and the speech may probably be taken as a literal translation of the original.

As soon as the council broke up, Pontiac took measures for bringing the disorders complained of to a close, while, at the same time, he provided sustenance for his warriors; and, in doing this, he displayed a policy and forecast scarcely paralleled in the history of his race. He first forbade the commission of farther outrage.[1] He next visited in

---

[1] *Peltier's Account,* MS.

turn the families of the Canadians, and, inspecting the property belonging to them, he assigned to each the share of provisions which it must furnish for the support of the Indians.[1]   The contributions thus levied were all collected at the house of Meloche, near Parent's Creek, whence they were regularly issued, as the exigence required, to the savages of the different camps.   As the character and habits of an Indian but ill qualify him to act the part of commissary, Pontiac in this matter availed himself of French assistance.

On the river bank, not far from the house of Meloche. lived an old Canadian. named Quilleriez, a man of exceeding vanity and self-conceit, and noted in the settlement for the gayety of his attire. He wore moccasons of the most elaborate pattern, and a sash plentifully garnished with beads and wampum.   He was continually intermeddling in the affairs of the Indians, being anxious to be regarded as the leader or director among them.[2] Of this man Pontiac evidently made a tool, employing him. together with several others, to discharge, beneath his eye, the duties of his novel commissariat.   Anxious to avoid offending the

---

[1] *Gouin's Account*, MS.

[2] Tradition related by M Baby. The following is from the *Diary of the Siege:* " Mr. St Martin said . . . that one Sibbold that came here last winter with his Wife from the Illinois had told at Mr. Cuellierry's (Quilleriez) that they might expect a French Army in this Spring, and that Report took rise from him. That the Day Capt. Campbell & Lt. McDougal was detained by the Indians, *Mr. Cuellierry accepted of their Offer of being made Commandant,* if this Place was taken, to which he spoke to Mr. Cuellierry about and ask'd him if he knew what he was doing, to which Mr. Cuellierry told him, I am almost distracted, they are like so many Dogs about me. to which Mr St Martin made him no Answer."

French, yet unable to make compensation for the provisions he had exacted, Pontiac had recourse to a remarkable expedient, suggested, no doubt, by one of these European assistants. He issued promissory notes, drawn upon birch-bark, and signed with the figure of an otter, the totem to which he belonged; and we are told by a trustworthy authority that they were all faithfully redeemed.[1] In this, as in several other instances, he exhibits an openness of mind and a power of adaptation not a little extraordinary among a people whose intellect will rarely leave the narrow and deeply cut channels in which it has, run for ages, who reject instruction, and adhere with rigid tenacity to ancient ideas and usages. Pontiac always exhibited an eager desire for knowledge. Rogers represents him as earnest to learn the military art as practised among Europeans, and as inquiring curiously into the mode of making cloth, knives, and the other articles of Indian trade. Of his keen and subtle genius we have the following singular testimony from the pen of General Gage. "From a paragraph of M. D'Abbadie's letter, there is reason to judge of Pontiac, not only as a savage possessed of the most refined cunning and treachery natural to the Indians, but as a person of extraordinary abilities. He says that he keeps two secretaries, one to write for him, and the other to read the letters he receives, and he manages

---

[1] Rogers, *Account of North America*, 244. The anonymous *Diary of the Siege* says that they bore the figure of a " coon."

them so as to keep each of them ignorant of what is transacted by the other."[1]

Major Rogers, a man familiar with the Indians, and an acute judge of mankind, speaks in the highest terms of Pontiac's character and talents. "He puts on," he says, "an air of majesty and princely grandeur, and is greatly honored and revered by his subjects."[2]

In the present instance, few durst infringe the command he had given, that the property of the Canadians should be respected; indeed, it is said that none of his followers would cross the cultivated fields, but always followed the beaten paths; in such awe did they stand of his displeasure.[3]

Pontiac's position was very different from that of an ordinary military leader. When we remember that his authority, little sanctioned by law or usage, was derived chiefly from the force of his own individual mind, and that it was exercised over a people singularly impatient of restraint, we may

[1] MS. Letter — *Gage to Lord Halifax, April* 16, 1764.
Extract from a MS. Letter — *William Smith, Jr.,* to ——.

                              " New York, 22d Nov 1763

"'Tis an old saying that the Devil is easier raised than laid. Sir Jeffrey has found it so, with these Indian Demons. They have cut his little Army to Pieces, & almost if not entirely obstructed the Communication to the Detroite, where the Enemy are grown very numerous; and from whence I fancy you'll soon hear, if any survive to relate them, very tragical Accounts The Besiegers are led on by an enterprising Fellow called Pondiac. He is a Genius, for he possesses great Bravery, Art, & Oratory, & has had the Address to get himself not only at the Head of his Conquerors, but elected Generalissimo of all the confederate Forces now acting against us — Perhaps he may deserve to be called the Mithridates of the West."

[2] Rogers, *North America,* 240.
[3] *Gouin's Account,* MS.

better appreciate the commanding energy that could hold control over spirits so intractable.

The glaring faults of Pontiac's character have already appeared too clearly. He was artful and treacherous, bold, fierce, ambitious, and revengeful; yet the following anecdotes will evince that noble and generous thought was no stranger to the savage hero of this dark forest tragedy. Some time after the period of which we have been speaking, Rogers came up to Detroit, with a detachment of troops, and, on landing, sent a bottle of brandy, by a friendly Indian, as a present to Pontiac. The Indians had always been suspicious that the English meant to poison them. Those around the chief, endeavored to persuade him that the brandy was drugged. Pontiac listened to what they said, and, as soon as they had concluded, poured out a cup of the liquor, and immediately drank it, saying that the man whose life he had saved had no power to kill him. He referred to his having prevented the Indians from attacking Rogers and his party when on their way to demand the surrender of Detroit. The story may serve as a counterpart to the well-known anecdote of Alexander the Great and his physician.[1]

Pontiac had been an old friend of Baby; and one evening, at an early period of the siege, he entered his house, and, seating himself by the fire, looked for some time steadily at the embers. At length, raising his head, he said he had heard that the English had offered the Canadian a bushel of

[1] Rogers, *North America*, 244.

17

silver for the scalp of his friend. Baby declared that the story was false, and protested that he would never betray him. Pontiac for a moment keenly studied his features. " My brother has spoken the truth," he said, " and I will show that I believe him " He remained in the house through the evening, and, at its close, wrapped himself in his blanket, and lay down upon a bench, where he slept in full confidence till morning.[1]

Another anecdote, from the same source, will exhibit the power which he exercised over the minds of his followers. A few young Wyandots were in the habit of coming, night after night, to the house of Baby, to steal hogs and cattle. The latter complained of the theft to Pontiac, and desired his protection. Being at that time ignorant of the intercourse between Baby and the English, Pontiac hastened to the assistance of his friend, and, arriving about nightfall at the house, walked to and fro among the barns and enclosures. At a late hour, he distinguished the dark forms of the plunderers stealing through the gloom. " Go back to your village, you Wyandot dogs," said the Ottawa chief; " if you tread again on this man's land, you shall die." They slunk back abashed; and from that time forward the Canadian's property was safe. The Ottawas had no political connection with the Wyandots, who speak a language radically distinct. Over them he could claim no legitimate authority; yet his powerful spirit forced

---

[1] Tradition related by M François Baby.

respect and obedience from all who approached him.[1]

[1] Tradition related by M François Baby, of Windsor, U. C., the son of Pontiac's friend, who lives opposite Detroit, upon nearly the same site formerly occupied by his father's house. Though Pontiac at this time assumed the attitude of a protector of the Canadians, he had previously, according to the anonymous *Diary of the Siege*, bullied them exceedingly, compelling them to plough land for him, and do other work. Once he forced them to carry him in a sedan chair from house to house, to look for provisions.

CHAPTER XIII.

1763.

ROUT OF CUYLER'S DETACHMENT. — FATE OF THE FOREST GARRISONS.

WHILE perils were thickening around the garrison of Detroit, the British commander-in-chief at New York remained ignorant of its danger. Indeed, an unwonted quiet had prevailed, of late, along the borders and about the neighboring forts. With the opening of spring, a strong detachment had been sent up the lakes, with a supply of provisions and ammunition for the use of Detroit and the other western posts. The boats of this convoy were now pursuing their course along the northern shore of Lake Erie; and Gladwyn's garrison, aware of their approach, awaited their arrival with an anxiety which every day increased.

Day after day passed on, and the red cross of St. George still floated above Detroit. The keen-eyed watchfulness of the Indians had never abated; and woe to the soldier who showed his head above the palisades, or exposed his person before a loophole. Strong in his delusive hope of French assistance, Pontiac had sent messengers to M. Neyon, commandant at the Illinois, earnestly requesting that a force of regular troops might be sent to his aid; and Gladwyn, on his side, had ordered one of the vessels to Niagara, to hasten forward the expected convoy. The schooner set sail; but on the next day, as she lay becalmed at the entrance of Lake Erie, a multitude of canoes suddenly darted out upon her from the neighboring shores. In the prow of the foremost the Indians had placed their prisoner, Captain Campbell, with the dastardly purpose of interposing him as a screen between themselves and the fire of the English. But the brave old man called out to the crew to do their duty, without regard to him. Happily, at that moment a fresh breeze sprang up; the flapping sails stretched to the wind, and the schooner bore prosperously on her course towards Niagara, leaving the savage flotilla far behind.[1]

The fort, or rather town, of Detroit had, by this time, lost its wonted vivacity and life. Its narrow streets were gloomy and silent. Here and there strolled a Canadian, in red cap and gaudy sash;

---

[1] *Penn. Gaz.* No. 1807 MS. Letter — *Wilkins to Amherst*, June 18.

This incident may have suggested the story told by Mrs Grant, in her *Memoirs of an American Lady* A young British officer, of noble birth, had been living for some time among the Indians, and having encountered many strange adventures, he was now returning in a canoe with a party of his late associates, — none of them, it appears, were aware that hostilities existed, — and approached the schooner just before the attack commenced, expecting a friendly reception. Sir Robert D——, the young officer, was in Indian costume, and, wishing to surprise his friends, he made no answer when hailed from the vessel, whereupon he was instantly fired at and killed. — The story is without confirmation, in any contemporary document, and, indeed, is impossible in itself Sir Robert Davers was killed, as before mentioned, near Lake St Clair; but neither in his character, nor in the mode of his death, did he at all resemble the romantic adventurer whose fate is commemorated by Mrs Grant.

the weary sentinel walked to and fro before the
quarters of the commandant; an officer, perhaps,
passed along with rapid step and anxious face ; or
an Indian girl, the mate of some soldier or. trader,
moved silently by, in her finery of beads and vermilion.   Such an aspect as this the town must have
presented on the morning of the thirtieth of May,
when, at about nine o'clock, the voice of the sentinel sounded from the south-east bastion ; and loud
exclamations, in the direction of the river, roused
Detroit from its lethargy.   Instantly the place was
astir.   Soldiers, traders, and *habitants*, hurrying
through the water-gate, thronged the canoe wharf
and the narrow strand without.   The half-wild
coureurs de bois, the tall and sinewy provincials,
and the stately British soldiers, stood crowded
together, their uniforms soiled and worn, and
their faces haggard with unremitted watching.
Yet all alike wore an animated and joyous look.
The long expected convoy was full in sight.   On
the farther side of the river, at some distance below
the fort, a line of boats was rounding the woody
projection, then called Montreal Point, their oars
flashing in the sun, and the red flag of England
flying from the stern of the foremost.[1]   The toils
and dangers of the garrison were drawing to an
end.   With one accord, they broke into three
hearty cheers, again and again repeated, while a
cannon, glancing from the bastion, sent its loud
voice of defiance to the enemy, and welcome to

---

[1] *Pontiac* MS.

approaching friends.   But suddenly every cheek
grew pale with horror.   Dark naked figures were
seen rising, with wild gesture, in the boats, while,
in place of the answering salute, the distant yell
of the war-whoop fell faintly on their ears.   The
convoy was in the hands of the enemy.   The
boats had all been taken, and the troops of the detachment slain or made captive.   Officers and
men stood gazing in mournful silence, when an
incident occurred which caused them to forget the
general calamity in the absorbing interest of the
moment.

Leaving the disappointed garrison, we will pass
over to the principal victims of this deplorable
misfortune.   In each of the boats, of which there
were eighteen, two or more of the captured soldiers,
deprived of their weapons, were compelled to act
as rowers, guarded by several armed savages, while
many other Indians, for the sake of farther security,
followed the boats along the shore.[1]   In the foremost, as it happened, there were four soldiers and
only three Indians.   The larger of the two vessels
still lay anchored in the stream, about a bow-shot
from the fort, while her companion, as we have
seen, had gone down to Niagara to hasten up this
very re-enforcement.   As the boat came opposite this
vessel, the soldier who acted as steersman conceived
a daring plan of escape.   The principal Indian sat
immediately in front of another of the soldiers.   The
steersman called, in English, to his comrade to seize

---

[1] *Pontiac* MS.

the savage and throw him overboard. The man answered that he was not strong enough ; on which the steersman directed him to change places with him, as if fatigued with rowing, a movement which would excite no suspicion on the part of their guard. As the bold soldier stepped forward, as if to take his companion's oar, he suddenly seized the Indian by the hair, and, griping with the other hand the girdle at his waist, lifted him by main force, and flung him into the river. The boat rocked till the water surged over her gunwale. The Indian held fast to his enemy's clothes, and, drawing himself upward as he trailed alongside, stabbed him again and again with his knife, and then dragged him overboard. Both went down the swift current, rising and sinking; and, as some relate, perished. grappled in each other's arms.[1] The two remaining Indians leaped out of the boat. The prisoners turned, and pulled for the distant vessel, shouting aloud for aid. The Indians on shore opened a heavy fire upon them, and many canoes paddled swiftly in pursuit. The men strained with desperate strength. A fate inexpressibly horrible was the alternative. The bullets hissed thickly around their heads ; one of them was soon wounded, and the light birch canoes gained on them with fearful rapidity. Escape seemed hopeless, when the report of a cannon burst from the side of the vessel. The ball flew close past the boat, beating the water in a line of

---

[1] Another witness, Gouin, affirms that the Indian freed himself from the dying grasp of the soldier, and swam ashore.

foam, and narrowly missing the foremost canoe.
At this, the pursuers drew back in dismay; and
the Indians on shore, being farther saluted by
a second shot, ceased firing, and scattered among
the bushes. The prisoners soon reached the vessel,
where they were greeted as men snatched from
the jaws of fate; "a living monument," writes an
officer of the garrison, "that Fortune favors the
brave."[1]

They related many particulars of the catastrophe
which had befallen them and their companions.
Lieutenant Cuyler had left Fort Niagara as early
as the thirteenth of May, and embarked from Fort
Schlosser, just above the falls, with ninety-six men
and a plentiful supply of provisions and ammunition. Day after day he had coasted the northern
shore of Lake Erie, and seen neither friend nor foe
amid those lonely forests and waters, until, on the
twenty-eighth of the month, he landed at Point
Pelée, not far from the mouth of the River Detroit.
The boats were drawn on the beach, and the party
prepared to encamp. A man and a boy went to
gather firewood at a short distance from the spot,
when an Indian leaped out of the woods, seized
the boy by the hair, and tomahawked him. The
man ran into camp with the alarm. Cuyler immediately formed his soldiers into a semicircle before
the boats. He had scarcely done so when the
enemy opened their fire. For an instant, there was
a hot blaze of musketry on both sides; then the

---

[1] *Penn. Gaz* No. 1807. *St Aubin's Account*, MS. *Peltier's Account*,
MS.

Indians broke out of the woods in a body, and rushed fiercely upon the centre of the line, which gave way in every part; the men flinging down their guns, running in a blind panic to the boats, and struggling with ill-directed efforts to shove them into the water. Five were set afloat, and pushed off from the shore, crowded with the terrified soldiers. Cuyler, seeing himself, as he says, deserted by his men, waded up to his neck in the lake, and climbed into one of the retreating boats. The Indians, on their part, pushing two more afloat, went in pursuit of the fugitives, three boat-loads of whom allowed themselves to be recaptured without resistance; but the remaining two, in one of which was Cuyler himself, made their escape.[1] They rowed all night, and landed in the morning upon a small island. Between thirty and forty men, some of whom were wounded, were crowded in these two boats; the rest, about sixty in number, being killed or taken. Cuyler now made for Sandusky, which, on his arrival, he found burnt to the ground. Immediately leaving the spot, he rowed along the south shore to Presqu' Isle, from whence he proceeded to Niagara and re

---

[1] "Being abandoned by my men, I was Forced to Retreat in the best manner I could. I was left with 6 men on the Beech, Endeavoring to get off a Boat, which not being able to Effect, was Obliged to Run up to my Neck, in the Lake, to get to a Boat that had pushed off, without my Knowledge. — When I was in the Lake I saw Five Boats manned, and the Indians having manned two Boats, pursued and Brought back Three of the Five, keeping a continual Fire from off the Shore, and from the two Boats that followed us, about a Mile on the Lake; the Wind springing up fair, I and the other Remaining Boat Hoisted sail and escaped." — *Cuyler's Report*, MS.

ported his loss to Major Wilkins, the commanding officer.[1]

The actors in this bold and well-executed stroke
were the Wyandots, who, for some days, had lain
in ambush at the mouth of the river, to intercept
trading boats or parties of troops. Seeing the fright
and confusion of Cuyler's men, they had forgotten
their usual caution, and rushed upon them in the
manner described. The ammunition, provisions,
and other articles, taken in this attack, formed a
valuable prize ; but, unfortunately, there was, among
the rest, a great quantity of whiskey. This the Indians seized, and carried to their respective camps,
which, throughout the night, presented a scene of
savage revelry and riot. The liquor was poured
into vessels of birch-bark, or any thing capable of
containing it; and the Indians, crowding around,
scooped it up in their cups and ladles, and quaffed
the raw whiskey like water. While some sat

---

[1] *Cuyler's Report*, MS.

Extract from a MS Letter — *Major Wilkins to Sir J. Amherst.*

"Niagara, 6th June, 1763

"Just as I was sending off my Letter of Yesterday, Lieutenant Cuy-
ler, of the Queen's Rangers, Arrived from his Intended Voyage to the
Detroit. He has been very Unfortunate, Having been Defeated by Indians
within 30 miles of the Detroit River ; I observed that he was Wounded
and Weak, and Desired him to take the Surgeon's Assistance and some
Rest, and Recollect the Particulars of the Affair, and let me have them in
Writing, as perhaps I should find it Necessary to Transmit them to Your
Excellency, which I have now Done.

"It is probable Your Excellency will have heard of what has Happened by way of Fort Pitt, as Ensign Christie, Commanding at Presqu' Isle,
writes me he has sent an Express to Acquaint the Commanding Officer at
that Place, of Sanduskie's being Destroyed, and of Lieut. Cuyler's Defeat.

"Some Indians of the Six Nations are now with me. They seem
very Civil ; The Interpreter has just told them I was writing to Your
Excellency for Rum, and they are very glad."

apart, wailing and moaning in maudlin drunkenness, others were maddened to the ferocity of wild
beasts.   Dormant jealousies were awakened, old
forgotten quarrels kindled afresh, and, had not the
squaws taken the precaution of hiding all the
weapons they could find before the debauch began,
much blood would, no doubt, have been spilt.   As
it was, the savages were not entirely without means
of indulging their drunken rage.   Many were
wounded, of whom two died in the morning; and
several others had their noses bitten off,—a singular
mode of revenge, much in vogue upon similar occasions, among the Indians of the upper lakes.   The
English were gainers by this scene of riot; for late
in the evening, two Indians, in all the valor and
vain-glory of drunkenness, came running directly
towards the fort, boasting their prowess in a loud
voice; but being greeted with two rifle bullets, they
leaped into the air like a pair of wounded bucks,
and fell dead on their tracks.

It will not be proper to pass over in silence the
fate of the unfortunate men taken prisoners in this
affair.   After night had set in, several Canadians
came to the fort, bringing vague and awful reports
of the scenes that had been enacted at the Indian
camp.   The soldiers gathered round them, and,
frozen with horror, listened to the appalling narrative.   A cloud of deep gloom sank down upon the
garrison, and none could help reflecting how thin
and frail a barrier protected them from a similar
fate.   On the following day, and for several succeeding days, they beheld frightful confirmation of the

rumors they had heard. Naked corpses, gashed with knives and scorched with fire, floated down on the pure waters of the Detroit, whose fish came up to nibble at the clotted blood that clung to their ghastly faces.[1]

[1] "The Indians, fearing that the other barges might escape as the first had done, changed their plan of going to the camp. They landed their prisoners, tied them, and conducted them by land to the Ottawas village, and then crossed them to Pondiac's camp, where they were all butchered. As soon as the canoes reached the shore, the barbarians landed their prisoners, one after the other, on the beach. They made them strip themselves, and then sent arrows into different parts of their bodies. These unfortunate men wished sometimes to throw themselves on the ground to avoid the arrows; but they were beaten with sticks and forced to stand up until they fell dead; after which those who had not fired fell upon their bodies, cut them in pieces, cooked, and ate them. On others they exercised different modes of torment by cutting their flesh with flints, and piercing them with lances. They would then cut their feet and hands off, and leave them weltering in their blood till they were dead. Others were fastened to stakes, and children employed in burning them with a slow fire. No kind of torment was left untried by these Indians. Some of the bodies were left on shore; others were thrown into the river. Even the women assisted their husbands in torturing their victims. They slitted them with their knives, and mangled them in various ways. There were, however, a few whose lives were saved, being adopted to serve as slaves." — *Pontiac* MS.

"The remaining barges proceeded up the river, and crossed to the house of Mr. Meloche, where Pontiac and his Ottawas were encamped. The barges were landed, and, the women having arranged themselves in two rows, with clubs and sticks, the prisoners were taken out, one by one, and told to run the gauntlet to Pontiac's lodge. Of sixty-six persons who were brought to the shore, sixty-four ran the gauntlet, and were all killed. One of the remaining two, who had had his thigh broken in the firing from the shore, and who was tied to his seat and compelled to row, had become by this time so much exhausted that he could not help himself. He was thrown out of the boat and killed with clubs. The other, when directed to run for the lodge, suddenly fell upon his knees in the water, and having dipped his hand in the water, he made the sign of the cross on his forehead and breast, and darted out in the stream. An expert swimmer from the Indians followed him, and, having overtaken him, seized him by the hair, and crying out, 'You seem to love water; you shall have enough of it,' he stabbed the poor fellow, who sunk to rise no more.' — *Gouin's Account*, MS.

Late one afternoon, at about this period of the siege, the garrison were again greeted with the dismal cry of death, and a line of naked warriors was seen issuing from the woods, which, like a wall of foliage, rose beyond the pastures in rear of the fort. Each savage was painted black, and each bore a scalp fluttering from the end of a pole. It was but too clear that some new disaster had befallen; and in truth, before nightfall, one La Brosse, a Canadian, came to the gate with the tidings that Fort Sandusky had been taken, and all its garrison slain or made captive.[1] This post had been attacked by the band of Wyandots living in its neighborhood, aided by a detachment of their brethren from Detroit. Among the few survivors of the slaughter was the commanding officer, Ensign Paully, who had been brought prisoner to Detroit, bound hand and foot, and solaced on the passage with the expectation of being burnt alive. On landing near the camp of Pontiac, he was surrounded by a crowd of Indians, chiefly squaws and children, who pelted him with stones, sticks, and gravel, forcing him to dance and sing, though by no means in a cheerful strain. A worse infliction seemed in store for him, when happily an old woman, whose husband had lately died, chose to adopt him in place of the deceased warrior. Seeing no alternative but the stake, Paully accepted the proposal; and, having been first plunged in the river, that the white blood might be washed from his veins, he was conducted

---

[1] *Pontiac MS.*

to the lodge of the widow, and treated thenceforth with all the consideration due to an Ottawa warrior.

Gladwyn soon received a letter from him, through one of the Canadian inhabitants, giving a full account of the capture of Fort Sandusky. On the sixteenth of May — such was the substance of the communication — Paully was informed that seven Indians were waiting at the gate to speak with him. As several of the number were well known to him, he ordered them, without hesitation, to be admitted. Arriving at his quarters, two of the treacherous visitors seated themselves on each side of the commandant, while the rest were disposed in various parts of the room. The pipes were lighted, and the conversation began, when an Indian, who stood in the doorway, suddenly made a signal by raising his head. Upon this, the astonished officer was instantly pounced upon and disarmed; while, at the same moment, a confused noise of shrieks and yells, the firing of guns, and the hurried tramp of feet, sounded from the area of the fort without. It soon ceased, however, and Paully, led by his captors from the room, saw the parade ground strown with the corpses of his murdered garrison. At nightfall, he was conducted to the margin of the lake, where several birch canoes lay in readiness; and as, amid thick darkness, the party pushed out from shore, the captive saw the fort, lately under his command, bursting on all sides into sheets of flame.[1]

---

[1] MS. Official Document — *Report of the Loss of the Posts in the Indian Country*, enclosed in a letter from Major Gladwyn to Sir Jeffrey Amherst, July 8, 1763.

Soon after these tidings of the loss of Sandusky, Gladwyn's garrison heard the scarcely less unwelcome news that the strength of their besiegers had been re-enforced by two strong bands of Ojibwas. Pontiac's forces in the vicinity of Detroit now amounted, according to Canadian computation, to about eight hundred and twenty warriors. Of these, two hundred and fifty were Ottawas, commanded by himself in person; one hundred and fifty were Pottawattamies, under Ninivay; fifty were Wyandots, under Takee; two hundred were Ojibwas, under Wasson; and added to these were a hundred and seventy of the same tribe, under their chief, Sekahos.[1] As the warriors brought their squaws and children with them, the whole number of savages congregated about Detroit no doubt exceeded three thousand; and the neighboring fields and meadows must have presented a picturesque and stirring scene.

The sleepless garrison, worn by fatigue and ill fare, and harassed by constant petty attacks, were yet farther saddened by the news of disaster which thickened from every quarter. Of all the small posts scattered at intervals through the vast wilderness to the westward of Niagara and Fort Pitt, it soon appeared that Detroit alone had been able to sustain itself. For the rest, there was but one unvaried tale of calamity and ruin. On the fifteenth of June, a number of Pottawattamies were seen approaching the gate of the fort, bringing with them four English prisoners, who proved to

[1] *Pontiac* MS.

be Ensign Schlosser, lately commanding at St. Joseph's, together with three private soldiers. The Indians wished to exchange them for several of their own tribe, who had been for nearly two months prisoners in the fort. After some delay, this was effected; and the garrison then learned the unhappy fate of their comrades at St. Joseph's. This post stood at the mouth of the River St. Joseph's, near the head of Lake Michigan, a spot which had long been the site of a Roman Catholic mission. Here, among the forests, swamps, and ocean-like waters, at an unmeasured distance from any abode of civilized man, the indefatigable Jesuits had labored more than half a century for the spiritual good of the Pottawattamies, who lived in great numbers near the margin of the lake. As early as the year 1712, as Father Marest informs us, the mission was in a thriving state, and around it had gathered a little colony of the forest-loving Canadians. Here, too, the French government had established a military post, whose garrison, at the period of our narrative, had been supplanted by Ensign Schlosser, with his command of fourteen men, a mere handful, in the heart of a wilderness swarming with insidious enemies. They seem, however, to have apprehended no danger, when, on the twenty-fifth of May, early in the morning, the officer was informed that a large party of the Pottawattamies of Detroit had come to pay a visit to their relatives at St. Joseph's. Presently, a chief, named Washashe, with three or four followers, came to his quarters, as if to hold a friendly " talk ; " and immediately after a Canadian came in with intelligence that the fort was surrounded by Indians, who evidently had hostile intentions. At this, Schlosser ran out of the apartment, and crossing the parade, which was full of Indians and Canadians, hastily entered the barracks. These were also crowded with savages, very insolent and disorderly. Calling upon his sergeant to get the men under arms, he hastened out again to the parade, and endeavored to muster the Canadians together ; but while busying himself with these somewhat unwilling auxiliaries, he heard a wild cry from within the barracks. Instantly all the Indians in the fort rushed to the gate, tomahawked the sentinel, and opened a free passage to their comrades without. In less than two minutes, as the officer declares, the fort was plundered, eleven men were killed, and himself, with the three survivors, made prisoners, and bound fast. They then conducted him to Detroit, where he was exchanged as we have already seen.[1]

[1] *Loss of the Posts in the Indian Country*, MS. Compare *Diary of the Siege*, 25.

The following is from a curious letter of one Richard Winston, a trader at St. Joseph's, to his fellow-traders at Detroit, dated 19 June, 1763 : —

" Gentlemen, I address myself to you all, not knowing who is alive or who is dead. I have only to inform you that by the blessing of God and the help of M. Louison Chevalie, I escaped being killed when the unfortunate garrison was massacred, Mr. Hambough and me being hid in the house of the said Chevalie for 4 days and nights. Mr Hambough is brought by the Savages to the Illinois, likewise Mr. Chim. Unfortunate me remains here Captive with the Savages. I must say that I met with no bad usage ; however, I would that I was (with) some Christian or other. I am quite naked, & Mr. Castacrow, who is indebted to Mr. Cole, would not give me one inch to save me from death."

Three days after these tidings reached Detroit, Father Jonois, a Jesuit priest of the Ottawa mission near Michillimackinac, came to Pontiac's camp, together with the son of Minavavana, great chief of the Ojibwas, and several other Indians. On the following morning, he appeared at the gate of the fort, bringing a letter from Captain Etherington, commandant at Michillimackinac. The commencement of the letter was as follows: —

"Michillimackinac, 12 June, 1763.

"Sir:

"Notwithstanding what I wrote you in my last, that all the savages were arrived, and that every thing seemed in perfect tranquillity, yet on the second instant the Chippeways, who live in a plain near this fort, assembled to play ball, as they had done almost every day since their arrival. They played from morning till noon; then, throwing their ball close to the gate, and observing Lieutenant Lesley and me a few paces out of it, they came behind us, seized and carried us into the woods.

"In the mean time, the rest rushed into the fort, where they found their squaws, whom they had previously planted there, with their hatchets hid under their blankets, which they took, and in an instant killed Lieutenant Jamet, and fifteen rank and file, and a trader named Tracy. They wounded two, and took the rest of the garrison prisoners, five of whom they have since killed.

"They made prisoners all the English traders, and robbed them of every thing they had; but they offered no violence to the persons or property of any of the Frenchmen."

Captain Etherington next related some particulars of the massacre at Michillimackinac, sufficiently startling, as will soon appear. He spoke in high terms of the character and conduct of Father Jonois, and requested that Gladwyn would send all the troops he could spare up Lake Huron, that the post might be recaptured from the Indians, and garrisoned afresh. Gladwyn, being scarcely able to defend himself, could do nothing for the relief of his brother officer, and the Jesuit set out on his long and toilsome canoe voyage back to Michillimackinac.[1] The loss of this place was a very serious misfortune, for, next to Detroit, it was the most important post on the upper lakes.

The next news which came in was that of the loss of Ouatanon, a fort situated upon the Wabash, a little below the site of the present town of La Fayette. Gladwyn received a letter from its commanding officer, Lieutenant Jenkins, informing him that, on the first of June, he and several of his men had been made prisoners by stratagem, on which the rest of the garrison had surrendered. The Indians, however, apologized for their conduct, declaring that they acted contrary to their own inclinations, and that the surrounding tribes compelled them to take up the hatchet.[2] These

---

[1] *Pontiac* MS.

[2]   "Ouatanon, June 1st, 1763.

"Sir:

"I have heard of your situation, which gives me great Pain, indeed, we are not in much better, for this morning the Indians sent for me, to

excuses, so consolatory to the sufferers, might probably have been founded in truth, for these savages
were of a character less ferocious than many of the
others, and as they were farther removed from the
settlements, they had not felt to an equal degree
the effects of English insolence and encroachment.

Close upon these tidings came the news that
Fort Miami was taken. This post, standing on the
River Maumee, was commanded by Ensign Holmes.
And here I cannot but remark on the forlorn situation of these officers, isolated in the wilderness,
hundreds of miles, in some instances, from any
congenial associates, separated from every human
being except the rude soldiers under their com-

speak to me, and Immediately bound me, when I got to their Cabbin, and
I soon found some of my Soldiers in the same Condition : They told me
Detroit, Miamis, and all them Posts were cut off, and that it was a Folly
to make any Resistance, therefore desired me to make the few Soldiers,
that were in the Fort, surrender, otherwise they would put us all to
Death, in case one man was killed They were to have fell on us and
killed us all, last night, but Mr. Maisongville and Lorain gave them wampum not to kill us, & when they told the Interpreter that we were all to
be killed, & he knowing the condition of the Fort, beg'd of them to make
us prisoners. They have put us into French houses, & both Indians and
French use us very well : All these Nations say they are very sorry, but
that they were obliged to do it by the Other Nations. The Belt did not
Arrive here 'till last night about Eight o'Clock. Mr. Lorain can inform
you of all Just now Received the News of St Joseph's being taken,
Eleven men killed and three taken Prisoners with the Officer I have
nothing more to say, but that I sincerely wish you a speedy succour, and
that we may be able to Revenge ourselves on those that Deserve it.

    " I Remain, with my Sincerest wishes for your safety,
        " Your most humble servant,
                                                " EDW⁰ JENKINS.

    " N B We expect to set off in a day or two for the Illinois."

    This expectation was not fulfilled, and Jenkins remained at Ouatanon.
A letter from him is before me, written from thence to Gladwyn on the
29th July, in which he complains that the Canadians were secretly advis-
ing the Indians to murder all the English in the West.

mand, and the white or red savages who ranged the surrounding woods. Holmes suspected the intention of the Indians, and was therefore on his guard, when, on the twenty-seventh of May, a young Indian girl, who lived with him, came to tell him that a squaw lay dangerously ill in a wigwam near the fort, and urged him to come to her relief. Having confidence in the girl, Holmes forgot his caution and followed her out of the fort. Pitched at the edge of a meadow, hidden from view by an intervening spur of the woodland, stood a great number of Indian wigwams. When Holmes came in sight of them, his treacherous conductress pointed out that in which the sick woman lay. He walked on without suspicion; but, as he drew near, two guns flashed from behind the hut, and stretched him lifeless on the grass. The shots were heard at the fort, and the sergeant rashly went out to learn the reason of the firing. He was immediately taken prisoner, amid exulting yells and whoopings. The soldiers in the fort climbed upon the palisades, to look out, when Godefroy, a Canadian, and two other white men, made their appearance, and summoned them to surrender; promising that, if they did so, their lives should be spared, but that otherwise they would all be killed without mercy. The men, being in great terror, and without a leader, soon threw open the gate, and gave themselves up as prisoners.[1]

---

[1] *Loss of the Posts*, MS. Compare *Diary of the Siege*, 22, 26.

It appears by a deposition taken at Detroit on the 11th June, that Godefroy, mentioned above, left Detroit with four other Canadians three or four days after the siege began. Their professed object was to bring a French officer from the Illinois to induce Pontiac to abandon his hostile

Had detachments of Rogers's Rangers garrisoned these posts, or had they been held by such men as the Rocky Mountain trappers of the present day, wary, skilful, and almost ignorant of fear, some of them might, perhaps, have been saved; but the soldiers of the 60th Regiment, though many of them were of provincial birth, were not suited by habits and discipline for this kind of service.

The loss of Presqu' Isle will close this catalogue of calamity. Rumors of it first reached Detroit on the twentieth of June, and, two days after, the garrison heard those dismal cries announcing scalps and prisoners, which, of late, had grown mournfully familiar to their ears. Indians were seen passing in numbers along the opposite bank of the river, leading several English prisoners, who proved to be Ensign Christie, the commanding officer at Presqu' Isle, with those of his soldiers who survived.

On the third of June, Christie, then safely ensconced in the fort which he commanded, had written as follows to his superior officer, Lieutenant Gordon, at Venango: " This morning Lieutenant Cuyler of Queen's Company of Rangers came here, and gave me the following melancholy account of his whole party being cut off by a large body of Indians at the mouth of the Detroit River." Here follows the story of Cuyler's disaster, and Christie

designs. At the mouth of the Maumee they met John Welsh, an English trader, with two canoes, bound for Detroit. They seized him, and divided his furs among themselves and a party of Indians who were with them They then proceeded to Fort Miami, and aided the Indians to capture it. Welsh was afterwards carried to Detroit, where the Ottawas murdered him.

closes as follows : " I have sent to Niagara a letter to the Major, desiring some more ammunition and provisions, and have kept six men of Lieutenant Cuyler's, as I expect a visit from the hellhounds. I have ordered everybody here to move into the blockhouse, and shall be ready for them, come when they will."

Fort Presqu' Isle stood on the southern shore of Lake Erie, at the site of the present town of Erie. It was an important post to be commanded by an Ensign, for it controlled the communication between the lake and Fort Pitt; but the blockhouse, to which Christie alludes, was supposed to make it impregnable against Indians. This blockhouse, a very large and strong one, stood at an angle of the fort, and was built of massive logs, with the projecting upper story usual in such structures, by means of which a vertical fire could be had upon the heads of assailants, through openings in the projecting part of the floor, like the *machicoulis* of a mediæval castle. It had also a kind of bastion, from which one or more of its walls could be covered by a flank fire. The roof was of shingles, and might easily be set on fire; but at the top was a sentry-box or look-out, from which water could be thrown. On one side was the lake, and on the other a small stream which entered it. Unfortunately, the bank of this stream rose in a high steep ridge within forty yards of the blockhouse, thus affording a cover to assailants, while the bank of the lake offered them similar advantages on another side.

After his visit from Cuyler, Christie, whose garrison now consisted of twenty-seven men, prepared for a stubborn defence. The doors of the block-house, and the sentry-box at the top, were lined to make them bullet-proof; the angles of the roof were covered with green turf as a protection against fire-arrows, and gutters of bark were laid in such a manner that streams of water could be sent to every part. His expectation of a " visit from the hell-hounds " proved to be perfectly well founded. About two hundred of them had left Detroit expressly for this object. At early dawn on the fifteenth of June, they were first dis covered stealthily crossing the mouth of the little stream, where the bateaux were drawn up, and crawling under cover of the banks of the lake and of the adjacent saw-pits. When the sun rose, they showed themselves, and began their customary yelling. Christie, with a very unnecessary reluctance to begin the fray, ordered his men not to fire till the Indians had set the example. The consequence was, that they were close to the blockhouse before they received the fire of the garrison; and many of them sprang into the ditch, whence, being well sheltered, they fired at the loop-holes, and amused themselves by throwing stones and handfuls of gravel, or, what was more to the purpose, fire-balls of pitch. Some got into the fort and sheltered themselves behind the bakery and other buildings, whence they kept up a brisk fire; while others pulled down a small out-house of plank, of which they made a movable breastwork, and approached under cover of it by pushing it before them.   At the same time, great numbers of them lay close behind the ridges by the stream, keeping up a rattling fire into every loophole, and shooting burning arrows against the roof and sides of the blockhouse.   Some were extinguished with water, while many dropped out harmless after burning a small hole.   The Indians now rolled logs to the top of the ridges, where they made three strong breastworks, from behind which they could discharge their shot and throw their fireworks with greater effect.   Sometimes they would try to dart across the intervening space and shelter themselves with their companions in the ditch, but all who attempted it were killed or wounded.   And now the hard-beset little garrison could see them throwing up earth and stones behind the nearest breastwork.   Their implacable foes were undermining the blockhouse.   There was little time to reflect on this new danger; for another, more imminent, soon threatened them. The barrels of water, always kept in the building, were nearly emptied in extinguishing the frequent fires; and though there was a well close at hand, in the parade ground, it was death to approach it.   The only resource was to dig a subterranean passage to it.   The floor was torn up; and while some of the men fired their heated muskets from the loopholes, the rest labored stoutly at this cheerless task.   Before it was half finished, the roof was on fire again, and all the water that remained was poured down to extinguish it.   In a few moments, the cry of fire was again raised, when a soldier, at imminent risk of his life, tore off the burning shingles and averted the danger.

By this time it was evening. The garrison had had not a moment's rest since the sun rose. Darkness brought little relief, for guns flashed all night from the Indian intrenchments. In the morning, however, there was a respite. The Indians were ominously quiet, being employed, it seems, in pushing their subterranean approaches, and preparing fresh means for firing the blockhouse. In the afternoon the attack began again. They set fire to the house of the commanding officer, which stood close at hand, and which they had reached by means of their trenches. The pine logs blazed fiercely, and the wind blew the flame against the bastion of the blockhouse, which scorched, blackened, and at last took fire; but the garrison had by this time dug a passage to the well, and, half stifled as they were, they plied their water-buckets with such good will that the fire was subdued, while the blazing house soon sank to a glowing pile of embers. The men, who had behaved throughout with great spirit, were now, in the words of their officer, " exhausted to the greatest extremity; " yet they still kept up their forlorn defence, toiling and fighting without pause within the wooden walls of their dim prison, where the close and heated air was thick with the smoke of gunpowder. The firing on both sides lasted through the rest of the day, and did not cease till midnight, at which hour a voice was heard to call out, in French, from the enemy's intrenchments,

warning the garrison that farther resistance would
be useless, since preparations were made for setting
the blockhouse on fire, above and below at once.
Christie demanded if there were any among them
who spoke English; upon which, a man in the
Indian dress came out from behind the breastwork.
He was a soldier, who, having been made prisoner early in the French war, had since lived
among the savages, and now espoused their cause,
fighting with them against his own countrymen.
He said that if they yielded, their lives should be
spared; but if they fought longer, they must all be
burnt alive. Christie told them to wait till morning for his answer. They assented, and suspended
their fire. Christie now asked his men, if we may
believe the testimony of two of them, " whether
they chose to give up the blockhouse, or remain
in it and be burnt alive?" They replied that they
would stay as long as they could bear the heat, and
then fight their way through.[1] A third witness,
Edward Smyth, apparently a corporal, testifies that
all but two of them were for holding out. He says
that when his opinion was asked, he replied that,
having but one life to lose, he would be governed
by the rest; but that at the same time he reminded
them of the recent treachery at Detroit, and of the
butchery at Fort William Henry, adding that, in his
belief, they themselves could expect no better usage.

[1] *Evidence of Benjamin Gray, soldier in the 1st Battalion of the 60th Regiment, before a Court of Inquiry held at Fort Pitt, 12th Sept. 1763. Evidence
of David Smart, soldier in the 60th Regiment, before a Court of Inquiry held at
Fort Pitt, 24th Dec., 1763, to take evidence relative to the loss of Presqu' Isle
which did not appear when the last court sat.*

When morning came, Christie sent out two soldiers as if to treat with the enemy, but, in reality,
as he says, to learn the truth of what they had
told him respecting their preparations to burn
the blockhouse. On reaching the breastwork, the
soldiers made a signal, by which their officer saw
that his worst fears were well founded. In pursuance of their orders, they then demanded that
two of the principal chiefs should meet with
Christie midway between the breastwork and the
blockhouse. The chiefs appeared accordingly; and
Christie, going out, yielded up the blockhouse; having first stipulated that the lives of all the garrison
should be spared, and that they might retire unmo
lested to the nearest post. The soldiers, pale and
haggard, like men who had passed through a fiery
ordeal, now issued from their scorched and bullet-
pierced stronghold. A scene of plunder instantly
began. Benjamin Gray, a Scotch soldier, who had
just been employed, on Christie's order, in carrying
presents to the Indians, seeing the confusion, and
hearing a scream from a sergeant's wife, the only
woman in the garrison, sprang off into the woods
and succeeded in making his way to Fort Pitt with
news of the disaster. It is needless to say that no
faith was kept with the rest, and they had good cause
to be thankful that they were not butchered on the
spot. After being detained for some time in the
neighborhood, they were carried prisoners to Detroit, where Christie soon after made his escape,
and gained the fort in safety.[1]

[1] *Loss of the Posts*, MS. *Pontiac* MS *Report of Ensign Christie*, MS.
Testimony of Edward Smyth, MS. This last evidence was taken by order

After Presqu' Isle was taken, the neighboring
posts of Le Bœuf and Venango shared its fate;
while farther southward, at the forks of the Ohio,
a host of Delaware and Shawanoe warriors were
gathering around Fort Pitt, and blood and havoc
reigned along the whole frontier.

of Colonel Bouquet, commanding the battalion of the Royal American
Regiment to which Christie belonged.   Christie's surrender had been
thought censurable both by General Amherst and by Bouquet.   According to Christie's statements, it was unavoidable; but according to those
of Smyth, and also of the two soldiers, Gray and Smart, the situation,
though extremely critical, seems not to have been desperate.   Smyth's
testimony bears date 30 March, 1765, nearly two years after the event.
Some allowance is therefore to be made for lapses of memory.   He places
the beginning of the attack on the twenty-first of June, instead of the
fifteenth, — an evident mistake   The *Diary of the Siege of Detroit* says
that Christie did not make his escape, but was brought in and surrendered
by six Huron chiefs on the ninth of July.   In a letter of Bouquet dated
June 18th, 1760, is enclosed a small plan of Presqu' Isle

CHAPTER XIV.

1763.

THE INDIANS CONTINUE TO BLOCKADE DETROIT.

WE return once more to Detroit and its belea
guered garrison. On the nineteenth of June, a
rumor reached them that one of the vessels had
been seen near Turkey Island, some miles below
the fort, but that, the wind failing her, she had
dropped down with the current, to wait a more
favorable opportunity. It may be remembered
that this vessel had, several weeks before, gone
down Lake Erie to hasten the advance of Cuyler's
expected detachment. Passing these troops on her
way, she had held her course to Niagara; and here
she had remained until the return of Cuyler, with
the remnant of his men, made known the catastrophe that had befallen him. This officer, and
the survivors of his party, with a few other troops
spared from the garrison of Niagara, were ordered
to embark in her, and make the best of their way
back to Detroit. They had done so, and now, as
we have seen, were almost within sight of the fort;
but the critical part of the undertaking yet remained. The river channel was in some places

narrow, and more than eight hundred Indians were on the alert to intercept their passage.

For several days, the officers at Detroit heard nothing farther of the vessel, when, on the twenty-third, a great commotion was visible among the Indians, large parties of whom were seen to pass along the outskirts of the woods, behind the fort. The cause of these movements was unknown till evening, when M. Baby came in with intelligence that the vessel was again attempting to ascend the river, and that all the Indians had gone to attack her. Upon this, two cannon were fired, that those on board might know that the fort still held out. This done, all remained in much anxiety awaiting the result.

The schooner, late that afternoon, began to move slowly upward, with a gentle breeze, between the main shore and the long-extended margin of Fighting Island. About sixty men were crowded on board, of whom only ten or twelve were visible on deck; the officer having ordered the rest to lie hidden below, in hope that the Indians, encouraged by this apparent weakness, might make an open attack. Just before reaching the narrowest part of the channel, the wind died away, and the anchor was dropped. Immediately above, and within gunshot of the vessel, the Indians had made a breastwork of logs, carefully concealed by bushes, on the shore of Turkey Island. Here they lay in force, waiting for the schooner to pass. Ignorant of this, but still cautious and wary, the crew kept a strict watch from the moment the sun went down.

Hours wore on, and nothing had broken the deep repose of the night. The current gurgled with a monotonous sound around the bows of the schooner, and on either hand the wooded shores lay amid the obscurity, black and silent as the grave. At length, the sentinel could discern, in the distance, various moving objects upon the dark surface of the water. The men were ordered up from below, and all took their posts in perfect silence. The blow of a hammer on the mast was to be the signal to fire. The Indians, gliding stealthily over the water in their birch canoes, had, by this time, approached within a few rods of their fancied prize, when suddenly the dark side of the slumbering vessel burst into a blaze of cannon and musketry, which illumined the night like a flash of lightning. Grape and musket shot flew tearing among the canoes, destroying several of them, killing fourteen Indians, wounding as many more, and driving the rest in consternation to the shore.[1] Recovering from their surprise, they began to fire upon the vessel from behind their breastwork ; upon which she weighed anchor, and dropped down once more beyond their reach, into the broad river below. Several days afterwards, she again attempted to ascend. This time, she met with better success ; for, though the Indians fired at her constantly from the shore, no man was hurt, and at length she left behind her the perilous channels of the Islands. As she passed the Wyandot village, she sent a shower of grape among its yelp·

---

[1] *Pontiac* MS.

ing inhabitants, by which several were killed; and then, furling her sails, lay peacefully at anchor by the side of her companion vessel, abreast of the fort.

The schooner brought to the garrison a much-needed supply of men, ammunition, and provisions. She brought, also, the important tidings that peace was at length concluded between France and England. The bloody and momentous struggle of the French war, which had shaken North America since the year 1755, had indeed been virtually closed by the victory on the Plains of Abraham, and the junction of the three British armies at Montreal. Yet up to this time, its embers had continued to burn, till at length peace was completely established by formal treaty between the hostile powers. France resigned her ambitious project of empire in America, and ceded Canada and the region of the lakes to her successful rival. By this treaty, the Canadians of Detroit were placed in a new position. Hitherto they had been, as it were, prisoners on capitulation, neutral spectators of the quarrel between their British conquerors and the Indians; but now their allegiance was transferred from the crown of France to that of Britain, and they were subjects of the English king. To many of them the change was extremely odious, for they cordially hated the British. They went about among the settlers and the Indians, declaring that the pretended news of peace was only an invention of Major Gladwyn; that the king of France would never abandon his children; and

that a great French army was even then ascending
the St. Lawrence, while another was approaching
from the country of the Illinois.[1] This oft-repeated
falsehood was implicitly believed by the Indians,
who continued firm in the faith that their Great
Father was about to awake from his sleep, and
wreak his vengeance upon the insolent English,
who had intruded on his domain.

Pontiac himself clung fast to this delusive hope;
yet he was greatly vexed at the safe arrival of the
vessel, and the assistance she had brought to the
obstinate defenders of Detroit. He exerted himself with fresh zeal to gain possession of the place,
and attempted to terrify Gladwyn into submission.
He sent a message, in which he strongly urged him
to surrender, adding, by way of stimulus, that eight
hundred more Ojibwas were every day expected,
and that, on their arrival, all his influence could
not prevent them from taking the scalp of every
Englishman in the fort. To this friendly advice
Gladwyn returned a brief and contemptuous answer.

Pontiac, having long been anxious to gain the
Canadians as auxiliaries in the war, now determined on a final effort to effect his object. For
this purpose, he sent messages to the principal
inhabitants, inviting them to meet him in council.
In the Ottawa camp, there was a vacant spot, quite
level, and encircled by the huts of the Indians.
Here mats were spread for the reception of the
deputies, who soon convened, and took their seats

---

[1] MS. Letter — *Gladwyn to Amherst*, July 8.

in a wide ring. One part was occupied by the Canadians, among whom were several whose withered, leathery features proclaimed them the patriarchs of the secluded little settlement. Opposite these sat the stern-visaged Pontiac, with his chiefs on either hand, while the intervening portions of the circle were filled by Canadians and Indians promiscuously mingled. Standing on the outside, and looking over the heads of this more dignified assemblage, was a motley throng of Indians and Canadians, half breeds, trappers, and voyageurs, in wild and picturesque, though very dirty attire, Conspicuous among them were numerous Indian dandies, a large class in every aboriginal community, where they hold about the same relative position as do their counterparts in civilized society. They were wrapped in the gayest blankets, their necks adorned with beads, their cheeks daubed with vermilion, and their ears hung with pendants. They stood sedately looking on, with evident self-complacency, yet ashamed and afraid to take their places among the aged chiefs and warriors of repute.

All was silent, and several pipes were passing round from hand to hand, when Pontiac rose, and threw down a war-belt at the feet of the Canadians.

" My brothers," he said, " how long will you suffer this bad flesh to remain upon your lands? I have told you before, and I now tell you again, that when I took up the hatchet, it was for your good. This year the English must all perish throughout Canada. The Master of Life commands it; and you, who know him better than we, wish to oppose his will. Until now I have said nothing on this matter. I have not urged you to take part with us in the war. It would have been enough had you been content to sit quiet on your mats, looking on, while we were fighting for you. But you have not done so. You call yourselves our friends, and yet you assist the English with provisions, and go about as spies among our villages. This must not continue. You must be either wholly French or wholly English. If you are French, take up that war-belt, and lift the hatchet with us; but if you are English, then we declare war upon you. My brothers, I know this is a hard thing. We are all alike children of our Great Father the King of France, and it is hard to fight among brethren for the sake of dogs. But there is no choice. Look upon the belt, and let us hear your answer." [1]

One of the Canadians, having suspected the purpose of Pontiac, had brought with him, not the treaty of peace, but a copy of the capitulation of Montreal with its dependencies, including Detroit. Pride, or some other motive, restrained him from confessing that the Canadians were no longer children of the King of France, and he determined to keep up the old delusion that a French army was on its way to win back Canada, and chastise the English invaders. He began his speech in reply to Pontiac by professing great love for the Indians, and a strong desire to aid them in the war. "But, my brothers," he added, holding out the articles of

[1] *Pontiac* MS

capitulation, "you must first untie the knot with
which our Great Father, the King, has bound us.
In this paper, he tells all his Canadian children to
sit quiet and obey the English until he comes,
because he wishes to punish his enemies himself.
We dare not disobey him, for he would then be
angry with us. And you, my brothers, who speak
of making war upon us if we do not do as you
wish, do you think you could escape his wrath, if
you should raise the hatchet against his French
children? He would treat you as enemies, and
not as friends, and you would have to fight both
English and French at once. Tell us, my brothers,
what can you reply to this?"

Pontiac for a moment sat silent, mortified, and
perplexed; but his purpose was not destined to be
wholly defeated. "Among the French," says the
writer of the diary, "were many infamous characters, who, having no property, cared nothing what
became of them." Those mentioned in these opprobrious terms were a collection of trappers, voyageurs, and nondescript vagabonds of the forest,
who were seated with the council, or stood looking on, variously attired in greasy shirts, Indian
leggins, and red woollen caps. Not a few among
them, however, had thought proper to adopt the
style of dress and ornament peculiar to the red
men, who were their usual associates, and appeared among their comrades with paint rubbed
on their cheeks. and feathers dangling from their
hair. Indeed, they aimed to identify themselves
with the Indians, a transformation by which they

gained nothing; for these renegade whites were
held in light esteem, both by those of their own
color and the savages themselves. They were for
the most part a light and frivolous crew, little to
be relied on for energy or stability; though among
them were men of hard and ruffian features, the
ringleaders and bullies of the voyageurs, and even
a terror to the *Bourgeois*[1] himself. It was one of
these who now took up the war belt, and declared

[1] This name is always applied, among the Canadians of the North-
west, to the conductor of a trading party, the commander in a trading
fort, or, indeed, to any person in a position of authority.

Extract from a Letter — *Detroit, July 9, 1763* (*Penn Gaz No.* 1808)

"Judge of the Conduct of the Canadians here, by the Behaviour of
these few Sacres Bougres, I have mentioned; I can assure you, with
much Certainty, that there are but very few in the Settlement who are
not engaged with the Indians in their damn'd Design, in short, Monsieur
is at the Bottom of it; we have not only convincing Proofs and Circumstances, but undeniable Proofs of it. There are four or five sensible, honest Frenchmen in the Place, who have been of a great deal of Service to
us, in bringing us Intelligence and Provisions, even at the Risque of their
own Lives; I hope they will be rewarded for their good Services; I hope
also to see the others exalted on High, to reap the Fruits of their Labours,
as soon as our Army arrives; the Discoveries we have made of their
horrid villianies, are almost incredible. But to return to the Terms of
Capitulation. Pondiac proposes that we should immediately give up the
Garrison, lay down our Arms, as the French, their Fathers, were obliged
to do, leave the Cannon, Magazines, Merchants' Goods, and the two
Vessels, and be escorted in Battoes, by the Indians, to Niagara The
Major returned Answer, that the General had not sent him there to
deliver up the Fort to Indians, or anybody else; and that he would
defend it whilst he had a single man to fight alongside of him Upon
this, Hostilities recommenced, since which Time, being two months, the
whole Garrison, Officers, Soldiers, Merchants, and Servants, have been
upon the Ramparts every Night, not one having slept in a House, except
the Sick and Wounded in the Hospital.

"Our Fort is extremely large, considering our Numbers, the Stockade
being above 1000 Paces in Circumference, judge what a Figure we make
on the Works"

The writer of the above letter is much too sweeping and indiscriminate in his denunciation of the French.

that he and his comrades were ready to raise the
hatchet for Pontiac. The better class of Canadians were shocked at this proceeding, and vainly
protested against it. Pontiac, on his part, was
much pleased at such an accession to his forces,
and he and his chiefs shook hands, in turn, with
each of their new auxiliaries. The council had
been protracted to a late hour. It was dark before
the assembly dissolved, " so that," as the chronicler
observes, " these new Indians had no opportunity
of displaying their exploits that day." They remained in the Indian camp all night, being afraid
of the reception they might meet among their
fellow-whites in the settlement. The whole of
the following morning was employed in giving them
a feast of welcome. For this entertainment a large
number of dogs were killed, and served up to the
guests ; none of whom, according to the Indian
custom on such formal occasions, were permitted
to take their leave until they had eaten the whole
of the enormous portion placed before them.

Pontiac derived little advantage from his Canadian allies, most of whom, fearing the resentment
of the English and the other inhabitants, fled, before the war was over, to the country of the Illinois.[1]
On the night succeeding the feast, a party of the
renegades, joined by about an equal number of
Indians, approached the fort, and intrenched themselves, in order to fire upon the garrison. At daybreak, they were observed, the gate was thrown
open, and a file of men, headed by Lieutenant Hay,

---

[1] Croghan, *Journal.* See Butler, *Hist. Kentucky,* 463.

sallied to dislodge them. This was effected without much difficulty. The Canadians fled with such despatch, that all of them escaped unhurt, though two of the Indians were shot.

It happened that among the English was a soldier who had been prisoner, for several years, among the Delawares, and who, while he had learned to hate the whole race, at the same time had acquired many of their habits and practices. He now ran forward, and, kneeling on the body of one of the dead savages, tore away the scalp, and shook it, with an exultant cry, towards the fugitives.[1] This act, as afterwards appeared, excited great rage among the Indians.

Lieutenant Hay and his party, after their successful sally, had retired to the fort; when, at about four o'clock in the afternoon, a man was seen running towards it, closely pursued by Indians. On his arriving within gunshot, they gave over the chase, and the fugitive came panting beneath the stockade, where a wicket was flung open to receive him. He proved to be the commandant of Sandusky, who, having, as before mentioned, been adopted by the Indians, and married to an old squaw, now seized the first opportunity of escaping from her embraces.

Through him, the garrison learned the unhappy tidings that Captain Campbell was killed. This gentleman, from his high personal character, no less than his merit as an officer, was held in general esteem; and his fate excited a feeling

[1] *Pontiac* MS.

of anger and grief among all the English in Detroit. It appeared that the Indian killed and scalped, in the skirmish of that morning was nephew to Wasson, chief of the Ojibwas. On hearing of his death, the enraged uncle had immediately blackened his face in sign of revenge, called together a party of his followers, and repairing to the house of Meloche, where Captain Campbell was kept prisoner, had seized upon him, and bound him fast to a neighboring fence, where they shot him to death with arrows. Others say that they tomahawked him on the spot; but all agree that his body was mutilated in a barbarous manner. His heart is said to have been eaten by his murderers, to make them courageous; a practice not uncommon among Indians, after killing an enemy of acknowledged bravery. The corpse was thrown into the river, and afterwards brought to shore and buried by the Canadians. According to one authority, Pontiac was privy to this act; but a second, equally credible, represents him as ignorant of it, and declares that Wasson fled to Saginaw to escape his fury; while a third affirms that the Ojibwas carried off Campbell by force from before the eyes of the great chief.[1] The other captive, M'Dougal, had previously escaped.

---

[1] *Gouin's Account*, MS. *St. Aubin's Account*, MS. *Diary of the Siege.*
James MacDonald writes from Detroit on the 12th of July. " Half an hour afterward the savages carried (the body of) the man they had lost before Capt. Campbell, stripped him naked, and directly murthered him in a cruel manner, which indeed gives me pain beyond expression, and I am sure cannot miss but to affect sensibly all his acquaintances. Although he is now out of the question, I must own I never had, nor never shall

The two armed schooners, anchored opposite the
fort, were now become objects of awe and aversion
to the Indians.   This is not to be wondered at, for,
besides aiding in the defence of the place, by sweeping two sides of it with their fire, they often caused
great terror and annoyance to the besiegers.   Several times they had left their anchorage, and, taking
up a convenient position, had battered the Indian
camps and villages with no little effect.   Once in
particular, — and this was the first attempt of the
kind, — Gladwyn himself, with several of his officers, had embarked on board the smaller vessel,
while a fresh breeze was blowing from the north-
west.   The Indians, on the banks, stood watching
her as she tacked from shore to shore, and pressed
their hands against their mouths in amazement,
thinking that magic power alone could enable her
thus to make her way against wind and current.[1]
Making a long reach from the opposite shore, she
came on directly towards the camp of Pontiac, her
sails swelling, her masts leaning over till the black
muzzles of her guns almost touched the river.   The
Indians watched her in astonishment.   On she
came, till their fierce hearts exulted in the idea
that she would run ashore within their clutches,
when suddenly a shout of command was heard on
board, her progress was arrested, she rose upright,
and her sails flapped and fluttered as if tearing

have, a Friend or Acquaintance that I valued more than he. My present
comfort is, that if Charity, benevolence, innocence, and integrity are a
sufficient dispensation for all mankind, that entitles him to happiness in
the world to come."
    [1] *Penn. Gaz.* No. 1808.

loose from their fastenings. Steadily she came round, broadside to the shore; then, leaning once more to the wind, bore away gallantly on the other tack. She did not go far. The wondering spectators, quite at a loss to understand her movements, soon heard the hoarse rattling of her cable, as the anchor dragged it out, and saw her furling her vast white wings. As they looked unsuspectingly on, a puff of smoke was emitted from her side; a loud report followed; then another and another; and the balls, rushing over their heads, flew through the midst of their camp, and tore wildly among the forest-trees beyond. All was terror and consternation. The startled warriors bounded away on all sides; the squaws snatched up their children, and fled screaming; and, with a general chorus of yells, the whole encampment scattered in such haste, that little damage was done, except knocking to pieces their frail cabins of bark.[1]

This attack was followed by others of a similar kind; and now the Indians seemed resolved to turn all their energies to the destruction of the vessel which caused them such annoyance. On the night of the tenth of July, they sent down a blazing raft, formed of two boats, secured together with a rope, and filled with pitch-pine, birch-bark, and other combustibles, which, by good fortune, missed the vessel, and floated down the stream without doing injury. All was quiet throughout the following night; but about two o'clock on the morning of the twelfth, the sentinel on duty saw a glowing

[1] *Pontiac* MS.

spark of fire on the surface of the river, at some
distance above. It grew larger and brighter; it
rose in a forked flame, and at length burst forth
into a broad conflagration. In this instance, too,
fortune favored the vessel; for the raft, which was
larger than the former, passed down between her
and the fort, brightly gilding her tracery of ropes
and spars, lighting up the old palisades and bastions
of Detroit, disclosing the white Canadian farms and
houses along the shore, and revealing the dusky
margin of the forest behind. It showed, too, a
dark group of naked spectators, who stood on the
bank to watch the effect of their artifice, when a
cannon flashed, a loud report broke the stillness,
and before the smoke of the gun had risen, these
curious observers had vanished. The raft floated
down, its flames crackling and glaring wide through
the night, until it was burnt to the water's edge,
and its last hissing embers were quenched in the
river.

Though twice defeated, the Indians would not
abandon their plan, but, soon after this second
failure, began another raft, of different construction
from the former, and so large that they thought it
certain to take effect. Gladwyn, on his part, provided boats which were moored by chains at some
distance above the vessels, and made other preparations of defence, so effectual that the Indians, after
working four days upon the raft, gave over their
undertaking as useless. About this time, a party
of Shawanoe and Delaware Indians arrived at Detroit, and were received by the Wyandots with a

salute of musketry, which occasioned some alarm among the English, who knew nothing of its cause. They reported the progress of the war in the south and east; and, a few days after, an Abenaki, from Lower Canada, also made his appearance, bringing to the Indians the flattering falsehood that their Great Father, the King of France, was at that moment advancing up the St. Lawrence with his army. It may here be observed, that the name of Father, given to the Kings of France and England, was a mere title of courtesy or policy; for, in his haughty independence, the Indian yields submission to no man.

It was now between two and three months since the siege began; and if one is disposed to think slightingly of the warriors whose numbers could avail so little against a handful of half-starved English and provincials, he has only to recollect, that where barbarism has been arrayed against civilization, disorder against discipline, and ungoverned fury against considerate valor, such has seldom failed to be the result.

At the siege of Detroit, the Indians displayed a high degree of comparative steadiness and perseverance; and their history cannot furnish another instance of so large a force persisting so long in the attack of a fortified place. Their good conduct may be ascribed to their deep rage against the English, to their hope of speedy aid from the French, and to the controlling spirit of Pontiac, which held them to their work. The Indian is but ill qualified for such attempts, having too much caution for an assault by storm, and too little patience for a blockade. The Wyandots and Pottawattamies had shown, from the beginning, less zeal than the other nations; and now, like children, they began to tire of the task they had undertaken. A deputation of the Wyandots came to the fort, and begged for peace, which was granted them; but when the Pottawattamies came on the same errand, they insisted, as a preliminary, that some of their people, who were detained prisoners by the English, should first be given up. Gladwyn demanded, on his part, that the English captives known to be in their village should be brought to the fort, and three of them were accordingly produced. As these were but a small part of the whole, the deputies were sharply rebuked for their duplicity, and told to go back for the rest. They withdrew angry and mortified; but, on the following day, a fresh deputation of chiefs made their appearance, bringing with them six prisoners. Having repaired to the council-room, they were met by Gladwyn, attended only by one or two officers. The Indians detained in the fort were about to be given up, and a treaty concluded, when one of the prisoners declared that there were several others still remaining in the Pottawattamie village. Upon this, the conference was broken off, and the deputies ordered instantly to depart. On being thus a second time defeated, they were goaded to such a pitch of rage, that, as afterwards became known, they formed the desperate resolution of killing Gladwyn on the spot, and then making their escape in the best way they could ; but, happily, at that moment the commandant observed an Ottawa among them, and, resolving to seize him, called upon the guard without to assist in doing so. A file of soldiers entered, and the chiefs, seeing it impossible to execute their design, withdrew from the fort, with black and sullen brows. A day or two afterwards, however, they returned with the rest of the prisoners, on which peace was granted them, and their people set at liberty.[1]

---

[1] Whatever may have been the case with the Pottawattamies, there were indications from the first that the Wyandots were lukewarm or even reluctant in taking part with Pontiac. As early as May 22. some of them complained that he had forced them into the war. *Diary of the Siege. Johnson* MSS.

CHAPTER XV.

1763.

THE FIGHT OF BLOODY BRIDGE.

FROM the time when peace was concluded with the Wyandots and Pottawattamies until the end of July, little worthy of notice took place at Detroit. The fort was still watched closely by the Ottawas and Ojibwas, who almost daily assailed it with petty attacks. In the mean time, unknown to the garrison, a strong re-enforcement was coming to their aid. Captain Dalzell had left Niagara with twenty-two barges, bearing two hundred and eighty men, with several small cannon, and a fresh supply of provisions and ammunition.[1]

[1] Extract from a MS. Letter — *Sir J. Amherst to Sir W. Johnson.*

"New York, 16th June, 1763

" Sir :

" I am to thank you for your Letter of the 6th Instant, which I have this moment Received, with some Advices from Niagara, concerning the Motions of the Indians that Way, they having attacked a Detachment under the Command of Lieut Cuyler of Hopkins's Rangers, who were on their Route towards the Detroit, and Obliged him to Return to Niagara, with (I am sorry to say) too few of his Men.

" Upon this Intelligence, I have thought it Necessary to Dispatch Captain Dalyell, my Aid de Camp, with Orders to Carry with him all such Reinforcements as can possibly be collected (having, at the same time, a due Attention to the Safety of the Principal Forts), to Niagara, and to proceed to the Detroit, if Necessary, and Judged Proper "

20

Coasting the south shore of Lake Erie, they soon reached Presqu' Isle, where they found the scorched and battered blockhouse captured a few weeks before, and saw with surprise the mines and intrenchments made by the Indians in assailing it.[1]   Thence, proceeding on their voyage, they reached Sandusky on the twenty-sixth of July; and here they marched inland to the neighboring village of the Wyandots, which they burnt to the ground, at the same time destroying the corn, which this tribe, more provident than most of the others, had planted there in the spring.   Dalzell then steered northward for the mouth of the Detroit, which he reached on the evening of the twenty-eighth, and cautiously ascended under cover of night.   "It was fortunate," writes Gladwyn, "that they were not discovered, in which case they must have been destroyed or taken, as the Indians, being emboldened by their late successes, fight much better than we could have expected."

On the morning of the twenty-ninth, the whole country around Detroit was covered by a sea of fog, the precursor of a hot and sultry day; but at sunrise its surface began to heave and toss, and, parting at intervals, disclosed the dark and burnished surface of the river; then lightly rolling, fold upon fold, the mists melted rapidly away, the last remnant clinging sluggishly along the margin of the forests.   Now, for the first time, the garrison could discern the approaching convoy.[2]   Still they remained in suspense, fearing

[1] *Penn Gaz.* No. 1811.   [2] *Pontiac* MS

lest it might have met the fate of the former detachment; but a salute from the fort was answered by a swivel from the boats, and at once all apprehension passed away. The convoy soon reached a point in the river midway between the villages of the Wyandots and the Pottawatta-mies. About a fortnight before, as we have seen, these capricious savages had made a treaty of peace, which they now saw fit to break, opening a hot fire upon the boats from either bank.[1] It was answered by swivels and musketry; but before the short engagement was over, fifteen of the English were killed or wounded. This danger passed, boat after boat came to shore, and landed its men amid the cheers of the garrison. The detachment was composed of soldiers from the 55th and 80th Regiments, with twenty independent rangers, com-manded by Major Rogers; and as the barracks in the place were too small to receive them, they were all quartered upon the inhabitants.

Scarcely were these arrangements made, when a great smoke was seen rising from the Wyandot village across the river, and the inhabitants, appar-ently in much consternation, were observed pad-dling down stream with their household utensils, and even their dogs. It was supposed that they had abandoned and burned their huts; but in truth, it was only an artifice of these Indians, who had set fire to some old canoes and other refuse piled in front of their village, after which the war-riors, having concealed the women and children,

---

[1] MS. Letter — *Major Rogers to* ——, Aug. 5.

returned and lay in ambush among the bushes, hoping to lure some of the English within reach of their guns. None of them, however, fell into the snare.[1]

Captain Dalzell was the same officer who was the companion of Israel Putnam in some of the most adventurous passages of that rough veteran's life; but more recently he had acted as aide-de-camp to Sir Jeffrey Amherst. On the day of his arrival, he had a conference with Gladwyn, at the quarters of the latter, and strongly insisted that the time was come when an irrecoverable blow might be struck at Pontiac. He requested permission to march out on the following night, and attack the Indian camp. Gladwyn, better acquainted with the position of affairs, and perhaps more cautious by nature, was averse to the attempt; but Dalzell urged his request so strenuously that the commandant yielded to his representations, and gave a tardy consent.[2]

Pontiac had recently removed his camp from its old position near the mouth of Parent's Creek, and was now posted several miles above, behind a great marsh, which protected the Indian huts from the

---

[1] *Pontiac* MS.

[2] Extract from a MS. Letter — *Major Gladwyn to Sir J. Amherst.*

"Detroit, Aug. 8th, 1763

"On the 31st, Captain Dalyell Requested, as a particular favor, that I would give him the Command of a Party, in order to Attempt the Surprizal of Pontiac's Camp, under cover of the Night, to which I answered that I was of opinion he was too much on his Guard to Effect it; he then said he thought I had it in my power to give him a Stroke, and that if I did not Attempt it now, he would Run off, and I should never have another Opportunity; this induced me to give in to the Scheme, contrary to my Judgement."

cannon of the vessel. On the afternoon of the thirtieth, orders were issued and preparations made for the meditated attack. Through the inexcusable carelessness of some of the officers, the design became known to a few Canadians, the bad result of which will appear in the sequel.

About two o'clock on the morning of the thirty first of July, the gates were thrown open in silence, and the detachment, two hundred and fifty in number, passed noiselessly out. They filed two deep along the road, while two large bateaux, each bearing a swivel on the bow, rowed up the river abreast of them. Lieutenant Brown led the advance guard of twenty-five men; the centre was commanded by Captain Gray, and the rear by Captain Grant. The night was still, close, and sultry, and the men marched in light undress. On their right was the dark and gleaming surface of the river with a margin of sand intervening, and on their left a succession of Canadian houses, with barns, orchards, and cornfields, from whence the clamorous barking of watch-dogs saluted them as they passed. The inhabitants, roused from sleep, looked from the windows in astonishment and alarm. An old man has told the writer how, when a child, he climbed on the roof of his father's house, to look down on the glimmering bayonets, and how, long after the troops had passed, their heavy and measured tramp sounded from afar, through the still night. Thus the English moved forward to the attack, little thinking that, behind houses and enclosures, Indian scouts watched every yard of their progress — little suspecting that Pontiac, apprised by the Canadians of their plan, had broken up his camp, and was coming against them with all his warriors, armed and painted for battle.

A mile and a half from the fort, Parent's Creek, ever since that night called Bloody Run, descended through a wild and rough hollow, and entered the Detroit amid a growth of rank grass and sedge. Only a few rods from its mouth, the road crossed it by a narrow wooden bridge, not existing at the present day. Just beyond this bridge, the land rose in abrupt ridges, parallel to the stream. Along their summits were rude intrenchments made by Pontiac to protect his camp, which had formerly occupied the ground immediately beyond. Here, too, were many piles of firewood belonging to the Canadians, besides strong picket fences, enclosing orchards and gardens connected with the neighboring houses. Behind fences, wood-piles, and intrenchments, crouched an unknown number of Indian warriors with levelled guns. They lay silent as snakes, for now they could hear the distant tramp of the approaching column.

The sky was overcast, and the night exceedingly dark. As the English drew near the dangerous pass, they could discern the oft-mentioned house of Meloche upon a rising ground to the left, while in front the bridge was dimly visible, and the ridges beyond it seemed like a wall of undistinguished blackness. They pushed rapidly forward, not wholly unsuspicious of danger. The advance guard were half way over the bridge, and the main body just entering upon it, when a horrible . burst of yells rose in their front, and the Indian guns blazed forth in a general discharge. Half the advanced party were shot down; the appalled survivors shrank back aghast. The confusion reached even the main body, and the whole recoiled together; but Dalzell raised his clear voice above the din, advanced to the front, rallied the men, and led them forward to the attack.[1] Again the Indians poured in their volley, and again the English hesitated; but Dalzell shouted from the van, and, in the madness of mingled rage and fear, they charged at a run across the bridge and up the heights beyond. Not an Indian was there to oppose them. In vain the furious soldiers sought their enemy behind fences and intrenchments. The active savages had fled; yet still their guns flashed thick through the gloom, and their war-cry rose with undiminished clamor. The English pushed forward amid the pitchy darkness, quite ignorant of their way, and soon became involved in a maze of out-houses and enclosures. At every pause they made, the retiring enemy would gather to renew the attack, firing back hotly upon the front and flanks. To advance farther would be useless, and the only alternative was to withdraw and wait for daylight. Captain Grant, with his company, recrossed the bridge, and took up his station on the road. The rest followed, a small party remaining to hold the enemy in check while the dead and

[1] *Penn. Gaz.* No. 1811.

wounded were placed on board the two bateaux which had rowed up to the bridge during the action. This task was commenced amid a sharp fire from both sides; and before it was completed, heavy volleys were heard from the rear, where Captain Grant was stationed. A great force of Indians had fired upon him from the house of Meloche and the neighboring orchards. Grant pushed up the hill, and drove them from the orchards at the point of the bayonet — drove them, also, from the house, and, entering it, found two Canadians within. These men told him that the Indians were bent on cutting off the English from the fort, and that they had gone in great numbers to occupy the houses which commanded the road below.[1] It was now evident that instant retreat was necessary; and the command being issued to that effect, the men fell back into marching order, and slowly began their retrograde movement. Grant was now in the van, and Dalzell at the rear. Some of the Indians followed, keeping up a scattering and distant fire; and from time to time the rear faced about, to throw back a volley of musketry at the pursuers Having proceeded in this manner for half a mile they reached a point where, close upon the right, were many barns and outhouses, with strong picket fences. Behind these, and in a newly dug cellar close at hand, lay concealed a great multitude of Indians. They suffered the advanced party to pass unmolested; but when the centre and rear came opposite their ambuscade, they raised a frightful

[1] *Detail of the Action of the 31st of July* See *Gent. Mag* XXXIII 486.

yell, and poured a volley among them. The men had well-nigh fallen into a panic. The river ran close on their left, and the only avenue of escape lay along the road in front. Breaking their ranks, they crowded upon one another in blind eagerness to escape the storm of bullets; and but for the presence of Dalzell, the retreat would have been turned into a flight. "The enemy," writes an officer who was in the fight, "marked him for his extraordinary bravery;" and he had already received two severe wounds. Yet his exertions did not slacken for a moment. Some of the soldiers he rebuked, some he threatened, and some he beat with the flat of his sword; till at length order was partially restored, and the fire of the enemy returned with effect. Though it was near daybreak, the dawn was obscured by a thick fog, and little could be seen of the Indians, except the incessant flashes of their guns amid the mist, while hundreds of voices, mingled in one appalling yell, confused the faculties of the men, and drowned the shout of command. The enemy had taken possession of a house, from the windows of which they fired down upon the English. Major Rogers, with some of his provincial rangers, burst the door with an axe, rushed in, and expelled them. Captain Gray was ordered to dislodge a large party from behind some neighboring fences. He charged them with his company, but fell, mortally wounded in the attempt.[1] They gave way, however; and now, the fire of the Indians being much diminished,

---

[1] *Penn. Gaz.* No. 1811.

the retreat was resumed.   No sooner had the men
faced about, than the savages came darting through
the mist upon their flank and rear, cutting down
stragglers, and scalping the fallen.   At a little
distance lay a sergeant of the 55th, helplessly
wounded, raising himself on his hands, and gazing with a look of despair after his retiring comrades.   The sight caught the eye of Dalzell.   That
gallant soldier, in the true spirit of heroism, ran
out, amid the firing, to rescue the wounded man,
when a shot struck him, and he fell dead.   Few
observed his fate, and none durst turn back to
recover his body.   The detachment pressed on,
greatly harassed by the pursuing Indians.   Their
loss would have been much more severe, had not
Major Rogers taken possession of another house,
which commanded the road, and covered the retreat
of the party.

He entered it with some of his own men, while
many panic-stricken regulars broke in after him, in
their eagerness to gain a temporary shelter.   The
house was a large and strong one, and the women
of the neighborhood had crowded into the cellar
for refuge.   While some of the soldiers looked in
blind terror for a place of concealment, others
seized upon a keg of whiskey in one of the
rooms, and quaffed the liquor with eager thirst;
while others, again, piled packs of furs, furniture,
and all else within their reach, against the windows,
to serve as a barricade.   Panting and breathless,
their faces moist with sweat and blackened with
gunpowder, they thrust their muskets through

the openings, and fired out upon the whooping assailants. At intervals, a bullet flew sharply whizzing through a crevice, striking down a man, perchance, or rapping harmlessly against the partitions. Old Campau, the master of the house, stood on a trap-door to prevent the frightened soldiers from seeking shelter among the women in the cellar. A ball grazed his gray head, and buried itself in the wall, where a few years since it might still have been seen. The screams of the half-stifled women below, the quavering war-whoops without, the shouts and curses of the soldiers, mingled in a scene of clamorous confusion, and it was long before the authority of Rogers could restore order.[1]

In the mean time, Captain Grant, with his advanced party, had moved forward about half a mile, where he found some orchards and enclosures, by means of which he could maintain himself until the centre and rear should arrive. From this point he detached all the men he could spare to occupy the houses below; and as soldiers soon began to come in from the rear, he was enabled to re-enforce these detachments, until a complete line of communication was established with the fort, and the retreat effectually secured. Within an hour, the whole party had arrived, with the exception of Rogers and his men, who were quite unable to come off, being besieged in the house of Campau,

---

[1] Many particulars of the fight at the house of Campau were related to me, on the spot, by John R. Williams, Esq., of Detroit, a connection of the Campau family.

by full two hundred Indians.   The two armed
bateaux had gone down to the fort, laden with the
dead and wounded.   They now returned, and, in
obedience to an order from Grant, proceeded up
the river to a point opposite Campau's house, where
they opened a fire of swivels, which swept the
ground above and below it, and completely scattered the assailants.   Rogers and his party now
came out, and marched down the road, to unite
themselves with Grant.   The two bateaux accompanied them closely, and, by a constant fire, restrained the Indians from making an attack.
Scarcely had Rogers left the house at one door,
when the enemy entered it at another, to obtain the
scalps from two or three corpses left behind.   Foremost of them all, a withered old squaw rushed in,
with a shrill scream, and, slashing open one of the
dead bodies with her knife, scooped up the blood
between her hands, and quaffed it with a ferocious
ecstasy.

Grant resumed his retreat as soon as Rogers had
arrived, falling back from house to house, joined
in succession by the parties sent to garrison each.
The Indians, in great numbers, stood whooping
and yelling, at a vain distance, unable to make an
attack, so well did Grant choose his positions, and
so steadily and coolly conduct the retreat.   About
eight o'clock, after six hours of marching and com-
bat, the detachment entered once more within the
sheltering palisades of Detroit.

In this action, the English lost fifty-nine men
killed and wounded.   The loss of the Indians

could not be ascertained, but it certainly did not exceed fifteen or twenty.   At the beginning of the fight, their numbers were probably much inferior to those of the English ; but fresh parties were continually joining them, until seven or eight hundred warriors must have been present.

The Ojibwas and Ottawas alone formed the ambuscade at the bridge, under Pontiac's command ; for the Wyandots and Pottawattamies came later to the scene of action, crossing the river in their canoes, or passing round through the woods behind the fort, to take part in the fray.[1]

In speaking of the fight of Bloody Bridge, an able writer in the Annual Register for the year 1763 observes, with justice, that although in European warfare it would be deemed a mere skirmish, yet in a conflict with the American savages, it rises to the importance of a pitched battle ; since these people, being thinly scattered over a great extent of country, are accustomed to conduct their warfare by detail, and never take the field in any great force.

The Indians were greatly elated by their success. Runners were sent out for several hundred miles, through the surrounding woods, to spread tidings

[1] MS. Letters — *MacDonald to Dr. Campbell*, Aug 8. *Gage to Lord Halifax*, Oct 12. *Amherst to Lord Egremont*, Sept. 3. *Meloche's Account*, MS   *Gouin's Account*, MS   *St Aubin's Account*, MS. *Peltier's Account*, MS. *Maxwell's Account*, MS , etc. In the *Diary of the Siege* is the following, under date of August 1st   "Young Mr Campo (Campau) brought in the Body of poor Capt. Dalyel (Dalzell) about three o'clock to-day, which was mangled in such a horrid Manner that it was shocking to human nature ; the Indians wip'd his Heart about the Faces of our Prisoners."

of the victory; and re-enforcements soon began to come in to swell the force of Pontiac. "Fresh warriors," writes Gladwyn, "arrive almost every day, and I believe that I shall soon be besieged by upwards of a thousand." The English, on their part, were well prepared for resistance, since the garrison now comprised more than three hundred effective men; and no one entertained a doubt of their ultimate success in defending the place. Day after day passed on; a few skirmishes took place, and a few men were killed, but nothing worthy of notice occurred, until the night of the fourth of September, at which time was achieved one of the most memorable feats which the chronicles of that day can boast.

The schooner Gladwyn, the smaller of the two armed vessels so often mentioned, had been sent down to Niagara with letters and despatches. She was now returning, having on board Horst, her master, Jacobs, her mate, and a crew of ten men, all of whom were provincials, besides six Iroquois Indians, supposed to be friendly to the English. On the night of the third, she entered the River Detroit; and in the morning the six Indians asked to be set on shore, a request which was foolishly granted. They disappeared in the woods, and probably reported to Pontiac's warriors the small numbers of the crew. The vessel stood up the river until nightfall, when, the wind failing, she was compelled to anchor about nine miles below the fort. The men on board watched with anxious vigilance; and as night came on, they listened to every sound which broke the stillness, from the strange cry of the nighthawk, wheeling above their heads, to the bark of the fox from the woods on shore. The night set in with darkness so complete, that at the distance of a few rods nothing could be discerned. Meantime, three hundred and fifty Indians, in their birch canoes, glided silently down with the current, and were close upon the vessel before they were seen. There was only time to fire a single cannon-shot among them, before they were beneath her bows, and clambering up her sides, holding their knives clinched fast between their teeth. The crew gave them a close fire of musketry, without any effect; then, flinging down their guns, they seized the spears and hatchets with which they were all provided, and met the assailants with such furious energy and courage, that in the space of two or three minutes they had killed and wounded more than twice their own number. But the Indians were only checked for a moment. The master of the vessel was killed, several of the crew were disabled, and the assailants were leaping over the bulwarks, when Jacobs, the mate, called out to blow up the schooner. This desperate command saved her and her crew. Some Wyandots, who had gained the deck, caught the meaning of his words, and gave the alarm to their companions. Instantly every Indian leaped overboard in a panic, and the whole were seen diving and swimming off in all directions, to escape the threatened explosion. The schooner was cleared of her assailants, who did not dare to renew the attack; and on the following morning she sailed for the fort, which she reached without molestation. Six of her crew escaped unhurt. Of the remainder, two were killed, and four seriously wounded, while the Indians had seven men killed upon the spot, and nearly twenty wounded, of whom eight were known to have died within a few days after. As the action was very brief, the fierceness of the struggle is sufficiently apparent from the loss on both sides. "The appearance of the men," says an eye-witness who saw them on their arrival, " was enough to convince every one of their bravery; they being as bloody as butchers, and their bayonets, spears, and cutlasses, blood to the hilt." The survivors of the crew were afterwards rewarded as their courage deserved.[1]

And now, taking leave, for a time, of the garri-.

[1] MS. Letter— *Gladwyn to Amherst*, Sept. 9. Carver, 164 *Relation of the Gallant Defence of the Schooner near Detroit*, published by order of General Amherst, in the New York papers. *Penn. Gaz* No. 1816. MS. Letter— *Amherst to Lord Egremont*, Oct. 13. *St. Aubin's Account*, MS. *Peltier's Account*, MS. *Relation of some Transactions at the Detroit in Sept. and Oct* 1763, MS.

The Commander-in-chief ordered a medal to be struck and presented to each of the men. Jacobs, the mate of the schooner, appears to have been as rash as he was brave; for Captain Carver says, that several years after, when in command of the same vessel, he was lost, with all his crew, in a storm on Lake Erie, in consequence of having obstinately refused to take in ballast enough

As this affair savors somewhat of the marvellous, the following evidence is given touching the most remarkable features of the story. The document was copied from the archives of London.

Extract from " *A Relation of the Gallant Defence made by the Crew of the Schooner on Lake Erie, when Attacked by a Large Body of Indians; as Published by Order of Sir Jeffrey Amherst in the New York Papers.*"

" The Schooner Sailed from Niagara, loaded with Provisions, some time in August last: Her Crew consisted of the Master and Eleven Men, with Six Mohawk Indians, who were Intended for a particular

son of Detroit, whose fortunes we have followed so long, we will turn to observe the progress of events in a quarter of the wilderness yet more wild and remote.

Service. She entered the Detroit River, on the 3d September; And on the 4th in the Morning, the Mohawks seemed very Desirous of being put on Shore, which the Master, very Inconsiderately, agreed to   The Wind proved contrary all that Day; and in the Evening, the Vessell being at Anchor, about Nine o'Clock, the Boat-swain discovered a Number of Canoes coming down the River, with about Three Hundred and Fifty Indians ; Upon which the Bow Gun was Immediately Fired , but before the other Guns could be brought to Bear, the Enemy got under the Bow and Stern, in Spite of the Swivels & Small Arms, and Attempted to Board the Vessell ; Whereupon the Men Abandoned their Small Arms, and took to their Spears, with which they were provided ; And, with Amazing Resolution and Bravery, knocked the Savages in the Head ; Killed many ; and saved the Vessell. . . It is certain Seven of the Savages were Killed on the Spot, and Eight had Died of those that were Wounded, when the Accounts came away The Master and One Man were Killed, and four Wounded, on Board the Schooner, and the other Six brought her Safe to the Detroit."

It is somewhat singular that no mention is here made of the command to blow up the vessel The most explicit authorities on this point are Carver, who obtained his account at Detroit, three years after the war, and a letter published in the *Pennsylvania Gazette*, No. 1816. This letter is dated at Detroit, five days after the attack The circumstance is also mentioned in several traditional accounts of the Canadians.

CHAPTER XVI.

1763.

MICHILLIMACKINAC.

In the spring of the year 1763, before the war broke out, several English traders went up to Michillimackinac, some adopting the old route of the Ottawa, and others that of Detroit and the lakes. We will follow one of the latter on his adventurous progress. Passing the fort and settlement of Detroit, he soon enters Lake St. Clair, which seems like a broad basin filled to overflowing, while, along its far distant verge, a faint line of forest separates the water from the sky. He crosses the lake, and his voyageurs next urge his canoe against the current of the great river above. At length, Lake Huron opens before him, stretching its liquid expanse, like an ocean, to the farthest horizon. His canoe skirts the eastern shore of Michigan, where the forest rises like a wall from the water's edge; and as he advances northward, an endless line of stiff and shaggy fir-trees, hung with long mosses, fringes the shore with an aspect of monotonous desolation. In the space of two or three weeks, if his Canadians labor well, and no accident occur, the trader approaches the end of his voyage.   Passing on his right the extensive Island of Bois Blanc, he sees, nearly in front, the beautiful Mackinaw, rising, with its white cliffs and green foliage, from the broad breast of the waters.   He does not steer towards it, for at that day the Indians were its only tenants, but keeps along the main shore to the left, while his voyageurs raise their song and chorus.   Doubling a point, he sees before him the red flag of England swelling lazily in the wind, and the palisades and wooden bastions of Fort Michillimackinac standing close upon the margin of the lake.   On the beach, canoes are drawn up, and Canadians and Indians are idly lounging.   A little beyond the fort is a cluster of the white Canadian houses, roofed with bark, and protected by fences of strong round pickets.

The trader enters at the gate, and sees before him an extensive square area, surrounded by high palisades.   Numerous houses, barracks, and other buildings, form a smaller square within, and in the vacant space which they enclose appear the red uniforms of British soldiers, the gray coats of Canadians, and the gaudy Indian blankets, mingled in picturesque confusion; while a multitude of squaws, with children of every hue, stroll restlessly about the place.   Such was Fort Michillimackinac in 1763.[1]   Its name, which, in the Algonquin tongue, signifies the Great Turtle, was first, from

---

1 This description is drawn from traditional accounts aided by a personal examination of the spot, where the stumps of the pickets and the foundations of the houses may still be traced

a fancied resemblance, applied to the neighboring island, and thence to the fort.

Though buried in a wilderness, Michillimackinac was still of no recent origin. As early as 1671, the Jesuits had established a mission near the place, and a military force was not long in following ; for, under the French dominion, the priest and the soldier went hand in hand. Neither toil, nor suffering, nor all the terrors of the wilderness, could damp the zeal of the undaunted missionary ; and the restless ambition of France was always on the alert to seize every point of vantage, and avail itself of every means to gain ascendency over the forest tribes. Besides Michillimackinac, there were two other posts in this northern region, Green Bay, and the Sault Ste. Marie. Both were founded at an early period, and both presented the same characteristic features — a mission-house, a fort, and a cluster of Canadian dwellings. They had been originally garrisoned by small parties of militia, who, bringing their families with them, settled on the spot, and were founders of these little colonies. Michillimackinac, much the largest of the three, contained thirty families within the palisades of the fort, and about as many more without. Besides its military value, it was important as a centre of the fur-trade ; for it was here that the traders engaged their men, and sent out their goods in canoes, under the charge of subordinates, to the more distant regions of the Mississippi and the North-west.

During the greater part of the year, the garrison

and the settlers were completely isolated — cut off
from all connection with the world ; and, indeed,
so great was the distance, and so serious the perils,
which separated the three sister posts of the northern lakes, that often, through the whole winter, all
intercourse was stopped between them.[1]

It is difficult for the imagination adequately to
conceive the extent of these fresh-water oceans,
and vast regions of forest. which, at the date of
our narrative, were the domain of nature, a mighty
hunting and fishing ground, for the sustenance of a
few wandering tribes.   One might journey among
them for days, and even weeks together, without
beholding a human face.   The Indians near Mich-
illimackmac were the Ojibwas and Ottawas, the
former of whom claimed the eastern section of
Michigan, and the latter the western, their respective portions being separated by a line drawn
southward from the fort itself.[2]   The principal
village of the Ojibwas contained about a hundred
warriors, and stood upon the Island of Michillimackinac, now called Mackinaw.   There was
another smaller village near the head of Thunder
Bay.   The Ottawas, to the number of two hundred and fifty warriors, lived at the settlement of
L'Arbre Croche, on the shores of Lake Michigan,
some distance west of the fort.   This place was
then the seat of the old Jesuit mission of St. Ig-
nace, originally placed, by Father Marquette, on the
northern side of the straits.   Many of the Ottawas

1 MS. *Journal of Lieutenant Gorell*, commanding at Green Bay, 1761–63.
2 Carver, *Travels*, 29.

were nominal Catholics. They were all somewhat improved from their original savage condition, living in log houses, and cultivating corn and vegetables to such an extent as to supply the fort with provisions, besides satisfying their own wants. The Ojibwas, on the other hand, were not in the least degree removed from their primitive barbarism.[1]

These two tribes, with most of the other neighboring Indians, were strongly hostile to the English. Many of their warriors had fought against them in the late war, for France had summoned allies from the farthest corners of the wilderness, to aid her in her struggle. This feeling of hostility was excited to a higher pitch by the influence of the Canadians, who disliked the English, not merely as national enemies, but also as rivals in the fur-trade, and were extremely jealous of their intrusion upon the lakes. The following incidents, which occurred in the autumn of the year 1761, will illustrate the state of feeling which prevailed: —

At that time, although Michillimackinac had been surrendered, and the French garrison removed, no English troops had yet arrived to supply their place, and the Canadians were the only tenants of the fort. An adventurous trader, Alexander Henry, who, with one or two others, was the pioneer of the English fur-trade in this region, came to Michillimackinac by the route of the Ottawa. On the way, he was several times warned to turn back,

---

[1] Many of these particulars are derived from memoranda furnished by Henry R. Schoolcraft, Esq.

and assured of death if he proceeded; and, at length, was compelled for safety to assume the disguise of a Canadian voyageur. When his canoes, laden with goods, reached the fort, he was very coldly received by its inhabitants, who did all in their power to alarm and discourage him. Soon after his arrival, he received the very unwelcome information, that a large number of Ojibwas, from the neighboring villages, were coming, in their canoes, to call upon him. Under ordinary circumstances, such a visitation, though disagreeable enough, would excite neither anxiety nor surprise; for the Indians, when in their villages, lead so monotonous an existence, that they are ready to snatch at the least occasion of excitement, and the prospect of a few trifling presents, and a few pipes of tobacco, is often a sufficient inducement for a journey of several days. But in the present instance there was serious cause of apprehension, since Canadians and Frenchmen were alike hostile to the solitary trader. The story could not be better told than in his own words.

" At two o'clock in the afternoon, the Chippewas (Ojibwas) came to the house, about sixty in number, and headed by Minavavana, their chief. They walked in single file, each with his tomahawk in one hand and scalping-knife in the other. Their bodies were naked from the waist upward, except in a few examples, where blankets were thrown loosely over the shoulders. Their faces were painted with charcoal, worked up with grease, their bodies with white clay, in patterns of various fancies. Some had feathers thrust through their noses. and their heads decorated with the same. It is unnecessary to dwell on the sensations with which I beheld the approach of this uncouth, if not frightful assemblage.

" The chief entered first, and the rest followed without noise. On receiving a sign from the former, the latter seated themselves on the floor.

" Minavavana appeared to be about fifty years of age. He was six feet in height, and had in his countenance an indescribable mixture of good and evil. Looking steadfastly at me, where I sat in ceremony, with an interpreter on either hand, and several Canadians behind me, he entered, at the same time, into conversation with Campion, inquiring how long it was since I left Montreal, and observing that the English, as it would seem, were brave men, and not afraid of death, since they dared to come, as I had done, fearlessly among their enemies.

" The Indians now gravely smoked their pipes, while I inwardly endured the tortures of suspense. At length, the pipes being finished. as well as a long pause, by which they were succeeded, Minavavana, taking a few strings of wampum in his hand, began the following speech : —

" ' Englishman, it is to you that I speak, and I demand your attention.

" ' Englishman, you know that the French King is our father. He promised to be such ; and we, in return, promised to be his children. This promise we have kept.

" ' Englishman, it is you that have made war with this our father. You are his enemy; and how, then, could you have the boldness to venture among us, his children? You know that his enemies are ours.

" ' Englishman, we are informed that our father, the King of France, is old and infirm; and that, being fatigued with making war upon your nation, he is fallen asleep. During his sleep you have taken advantage of him, and possessed yourselves of Canada. But his nap is almost at an end. I think I hear him already stirring, and inquiring for his children, the Indians; and when he does awake, what must become of you? He will de stroy you utterly.

" ' Englishman, although you have conquered the French, you have not yet conquered us. We are not your slaves. These lakes, these woods and mountains, were left to us by our ancestors. They are our inheritance; and we will part with them to none. Your nation supposes that we, like the white people, cannot live without bread, and pork, and beef! But you ought to know that He, the Great Spirit and Master of Life, has provided food for us in these spacious lakes, and on these woody mountains.

" ' Englishman, our father, the King of France, employed our young men to make war upon your nation. In this warfare many of them have been killed; and it is our custom to retaliate until such time as the spirits of the slain are satisfied. But the spirits of the slain are to be satisfied in either of two ways; the first is by the spilling of the blood of the nation by which they fell; the other, by *covering the bodies of the dead*, and thus allaying the resentment of their relations. This is done by making presents.

" ' Englishman. your king has never sent us any presents, nor entered into any treaty with us; wherefore he and we are still at war; and, until he does these things, we must consider that we have no other father nor friend, among the white men, than the King of France; but for you, we have taken into consideration that you have ventured your life among us, in the expectation that we should not molest you. You do not come armed, with an intention to make war; you come in peace, to trade with us, and supply us with necessaries, of which we are in much want. We shall regard you, therefore, as a brother; and you may sleep tranquilly, without fear of the Chippewas. As a token of our friendship, we present you this pipe to smoke.'

" As Minavavana uttered these words, an Indian presented me with a pipe, which, after I had drawn the smoke three times, was carried to the chief, and after him to every person in the room. This ceremony ended, the chief arose, and gave me his hand, in which he was followed by all the rest."[1]

These tokens of friendship were suitably acknowledged by the trader, who made a formal reply to Minavavana's speech. To this succeeded a request for whiskey on the part of the Indians,

[1] Henry, *Travels*, 45.

with which Henry unwillingly complied ; and, having distributed several small additional presents, he
beheld, with profound satisfaction, the departure
of his guests.   Scarcely had he ceased to congratu-
late himself on having thus got rid of the Ojibwas,
or, as he calls them, the Chippewas, when a more
formidable invasion once more menaced him with
destruction.   Two hundred L'Arbre Croche Ottawas came in a body to the fort, and summoned
Henry, together with Goddard and Solomons, two
other traders, who had just arrived, to meet them
in council.   Here they informed their startled
auditors that they must distribute their goods
among the Indians, adding a worthless promise to
pay them in the spring, and threatening force in
case of a refusal.   Being allowed until the next
morning to reflect on what they had heard, the
traders resolved on resistance, and, accordingly,
arming about thirty of their men with muskets,
they barricaded themselves in the house occupied
by Henry, and kept strict watch all night.   The
Ottawas, however, did not venture an attack.   On
the following day, the Canadians, with pretended
sympathy, strongly advised compliance with the demand ; but the three traders resolutely held out, and
kept possession of their stronghold till night. when,
to their surprise and joy, the news arrived that the
body of troops known to be on their way towards the
fort were, at that moment, encamped within a few
miles of it.   Another night of watching and anxiety
succeeded ; but at sunrise, the Ottawas launched
their canoes and departed, while, immediately after,

the boats of the English detachment were seen
to approach the landing-place. Michillimackinac
received a strong garrison; and for a time, at least,
the traders were safe.

Time passed on, and the hostile feelings of the
Indians towards the English did not diminish. It
necessarily follows, from the extremely loose character of Indian government, — if indeed the name
government be applicable at all, — that the separate members of the same tribe have little political
connection, and are often united merely by the
social tie of totemship. Thus the Ottawas at
L'Arbre Croche were quite independent of those
at Detroit. They had a chief of their own, who by
no means acknowledged the authority of Pontiac,
though the high reputation of this great warrior
everywhere attached respect and influence to his
name. The same relations subsisted between the
Ojibwas of Michillimackinac and their more southern tribesmen; and the latter might declare war
and make peace, without at all involving the former.

The name of the Ottawa chief at L'Arbre Croche
has not survived in history or tradition. The chief
of the Ojibwas, however, is still remembered by the
remnants of his people, and was the same whom
Henry calls Minavavana, or, as the Canadians
entitled him, by way of distinction, *Le Grand
Sauteur*, or the Great Ojibwa. He lived in the
little village of Thunder Bay, though his power
was acknowledged by the Indians of the neighboring islands. That his mind was of no common
order is sufficiently evinced by his speech to Henry;

but he had not the commanding spirit of Pontiac. His influence seems not to have extended beyond his own tribe. He could not, or at least he did not, control the erratic forces of an Indian community, and turn them into one broad current of steady and united energy. Hence, in the events about to be described, the natural instability of the Indian character was abundantly displayed.

In the spring of the year 1763, Pontiac, in compassing his grand scheme of hostility, sent, among the rest, to the Indians of Michillimackinac, inviting them to aid him in the war. His messengers, bearing in their hands the war-belt of black and purple wampum, appeared before the assembled warriors, flung at their feet a hatchet painted red, and delivered the speech with which they had been charged. The warlike auditory answered with ejaculations of applause, and, taking up the blood-red hatchet, pledged themselves to join in the contest. Before the end of May, news reached the Ojibwas that Pontiac had already, struck the English at Detroit. This wrought them up to a high pitch of excitement and emulation, and they resolved that peace should last no longer. Their numbers were at this time more than doubled by several bands of their wandering people, who had gathered at Michillimackinac from far and near, attracted probably by rumors of impending war. Being, perhaps, jealous of the Ottawas, or willing to gain all the glory and plunder to themselves, they determined to attack the fort, without communicating the design to their neighbors of L'Arbre Croche.

At this time there were about thirty-five men, with their officers, in garrison at Michillimackinac.[1] Warning of the tempest that impended had been clearly given; enough, had it been heeded, to have averted the fatal disaster. Several of the Canadians least hostile to the English had thrown out hints of approaching danger, and one of them had even told Captain Etherington, the commandant, that the Indians had formed a design to destroy, not only his garrison, but all the English on the lakes. With a folly, of which, at this period, there were several parallel instances among the British officers in America, Etherington not only turned a deaf ear to what he heard, but threatened to send prisoner to Detroit the next person who should disturb the fort with such tidings. Henry, the trader, who was at this time in the place, had also seen occasion to distrust the Indians; but on communicating his suspicions to the commandant, the latter treated them with total disregard. Henry accuses himself of sharing this officer's infatuation. That his person was in danger, had been plainly intimated to him, under the following curious circumstances: —

An Ojibwa chief, named Wawatam, had conceived for him one of those friendly attachments which often form so pleasing a feature in the Indian character. It was about a year since Henry had first met with this man. One morning, Wa-

---

[1] This appears from the letters of Captain Etherington. Henry states the number at ninety. It is not unlikely that he meant to include all the inhabitants of the fort, both soldiers and Canadians, in his enumeration

watam had entered his house, and placing before
him, on the ground, a large present of furs and
dried meat, delivered a speech to the following
effect: Early in life, he said, he had withdrawn,
after the ancient usage of his people, to fast and
pray in solitude, that he might propitiate the Great
Spirit, and learn the future career marked out for
him. In the course of his dreams and visions on
this occasion, it was revealed to him that, in after
years, he should meet a white man, who should be
to him a friend and brother. No sooner had he
seen Henry, than the irrepressible conviction rose
up within him, that he was the man whom the
Great Spirit had indicated, and that the dream was
now fulfilled. Henry replied to the speech with
suitable acknowledgments of gratitude, made a
present in his turn, smoked a pipe with Wawatam,
and, as the latter soon after left the fort, speedily
forgot his Indian friend and brother altogether.
Many months had elapsed since the occurrence of
this very characteristic incident, when, on the
second of June, Henry's door was pushed open
without ceremony, and the dark figure of Wawatam glided silently in. He said that he was just
returned from his wintering ground. Henry, at
length recollecting him, inquired after the success
of his hunt; but the Indian, without replying, sat
down with a dejected air, and expressed his surprise and regret at finding his brother still in the
fort. He said that he was going on the next day
to the Sault Ste. Marie, and that he wished Henry
to go with him. He then asked if the English had

heard no bad news, and said that through the winter he himself had been much disturbed by the singing of evil birds. Seeing that Henry gave little attention to what he said, he at length went away with a sad and mournful face. On the next morning he came again, together with his squaw, and, offering the trader a present of dried meat, again pressed him to go with him, in the afternoon, to the Sault Ste. Marie. When Henry demanded his reason for such urgency, he asked if his brother did not know that many bad Indians, who had never shown themselves at the fort, were encamped in the woods around it. To-morrow, he said, they are coming to ask for whiskey, and would all get drunk, so that it would be dangerous to remain. Wawatam let fall, in addition, various other hints, which, but for Henry's imperfect knowledge of the Algonquin language, could hardly have failed to draw his attention. As it was, however, his friend's words were spoken in vain; and at length, after long and persevering efforts, he and his squaw took their departure, but not, as Henry declares, before each had let fall some tears. Among the Indian women, the practice of weeping and wailing is universal upon all occasions of sorrowful emotion; and the kind-hearted squaw, as she took down her husband's lodge, and loaded his canoe for departure, did not cease to sob and moan aloud.

On this same afternoon, Henry remembers that the fort was full of Indians, moving about among the soldiers with a great appearance of friendship. Many of them came to his house, to purchase knives and small hatchets, often asking to see silver bracelets, and other ornaments, with the intention, as afterwards appeared, of learning their places of deposit, in order the more easily to lay hand on them at the moment of pillage.   As the afternoon drew to a close, the visitors quietly went away; and many of the unhappy garrison saw for the last time the sun go down behind the waters of Lake Michigan.

CHAPTER XVII.

1763.

THE MASSACRE.

THE following morning was warm and sultry. It was the fourth of June, the birthday of King George. The discipline of the garrison was relaxed, and some license allowed to the soldiers.[1] Encamped in the woods, not far off, were a large number of Ojibwas, lately arrived; while several bands of the Sac Indians, from the River Wisconsin, had also erected their lodges in the vicinity. Early in the morning, many Ojibwas came to the fort, inviting officers and soldiers to come out and see a grand game of ball, which was to be played between their nation and the Sacs. In consequence, the place was soon deserted by half its tenants. An outline of Michillimackinac, as far as tradition has preserved its general features, has already been given; and it is easy to conceive, with sufficient accuracy, the appearance it must have presented on this eventful morning. The houses and barracks were so ranged as to form a quadrangle, enclosing an extensive area, upon which their doors

---

[1] The above is Henry's date. Etherington says, the second.

all opened, while behind rose the tall palisades, forming a large external square. The picturesque Canadian houses, with their rude porticoes, and projecting roofs of bark, sufficiently indicated the occupations of their inhabitants; for birch canoes were lying near many of them, and fishing-nets were stretched to dry in the sun. Women and children were moving about the doors; knots of Canadian voyageurs reclined on the ground, smoking and conversing; soldiers were lounging listlessly at the doors and windows of the barracks, or strolling in careless undress about the area.

Without the fort the scene was of a very different character. The gates were wide open, and soldiers were collected in groups under the shadow of the palisades, watching the Indian ball play. Most of them were without arms, and mingled among them were a great number of Canadians, while a multitude of Indian squaws, wrapped in blankets. were conspicuous in the crowd.

Captain Etherington and Lieutenant Leslie stood near the gate, the former indulging his inveterate English propensity; for, as Henry informs us, he had promised the Ojibwas that he would bet on their side against the Sacs. Indian chiefs and warriors were also among the spectators, intent, apparently, on watching the game, but with thoughts, in fact, far otherwise employed.

The plain in front was covered by the ball players. The game in which they were engaged, called *baggattaway* by the Ojibwas, is still, as it always has been, a favorite with many Indian tribes. At either extremity of the ground, a tall post was planted, marking the stations of the rival parties. The object of each was to defend its own post, and drive the ball to that of its adversary. Hundreds of lithe and agile figures were leaping and bounding upon the plain. Each was nearly naked, his loose black hair flying in the wind, and each bore in his hand a bat of a form peculiar to this game. At one moment the whole were crowded together, a dense throng of combatants, all struggling for the ball; at the next, they were scattered again, and running over the ground like hounds in full cry. Each, in his excitement, yelled and shouted at the height of his voice. Rushing and striking, tripping their adversaries, or hurling them to the ground, they pursued the animating contest amid the laughter and applause of the spectators. Suddenly, from the midst of the multitude, the ball soared into the air, and, descending in a wide curve, fell near the pickets of the fort. This was no chance stroke. It was part of a preconcerted stratagem to insure the surprise and destruction of the garrison. As if in pursuit of the ball, the players turned and came rushing, a maddened and tumultuous throng, towards the gate. In a moment they had reached it. The amazed English had no time to think or act. The shrill cries of the ball-players were changed to the ferocious war-whoop. The warriors snatched from the squaws the hatchets, which the latter, with this design, had concealed beneath their blankets. Some of the Indians assailed the spectators without, while others rushed into the fort, and all was carnage and confusion. At the outset, several strong hands had fastened their gripe upon Etherington and Leslie, and led them away from the scene of massacre towards the woods.[1] Within the area of the fort, the men were slaughtered without mercy. But here the task of description may well be resigned to the pen of the trader, Henry.

"I did not go myself to see the match which was now to be played without the fort, because, there being a canoe prepared to depart on the following day for Montreal, I employed myself in writing letters to my friends; and even when a fellow-trader, Mr. Tracy, happened to call upon me, saying that another canoe had just arrived from Detroit, and proposing that I should go with him to the beach, to inquire the news, it so happened that I still remained to finish my letters; promising to follow Mr. Tracy in the course of a few minutes. Mr. Tracy had not gone more than twenty paces from my door, when I heard an Indian war-cry, and a noise of general confusion.

"Going instantly to my window, I saw a crowd of Indians, within the fort, furiously cutting down and scalping every Englishman they found: in particular, I witnessed the fate of Lieutenant Jamette.

"I had, in the room in which I was, a fowling-piece, loaded with swan shot. This I immediately seized, and held it for a few minutes, waiting to hear the drum beat to arms. In this dreadful

---

[1] MS. Letter — *Etherington to Gladwyn, June* 12. See Appendix, C.

interval I saw several of my countrymen fall, and more than one struggling between the knees of an Indian, who, holding him in this manner, scalped him while yet living.

" At length, disappointed in the hope of seeing resistance made to the enemy, and sensible, of course, that no effort of my own unassisted arm could avail against four hundred Indians, I thought only of seeking shelter amid the slaughter which was raging. I observed many of the Canadian inhabitants of the fort calmly looking on, neither opposing the Indians nor suffering injury; and from this circumstance, I conceived a hope of finding security in their houses.

" Between the yard door of my own house and that of M. Langlade,[1] my next neighbor, there was only a low fence, over which I easily climbed. At my entrance, I found the whole family at the windows, gazing at the scene of blood before them. I addressed myself immediately to M. Langlade, begging that he would put me into some place of safety until the heat of the affair should be over; an act of charity by which he might, perhaps, preserve me from the general massacre; but while I uttered my petition, M. Langlade, who had looked for a moment at me, turned again to the window,

---

[1] CHARLES LANGLADE, who is praised by Etherington, though spoken of in equivocal terms by Henry, was the son of a Frenchman of good family and an Ottawa squaw. He was born at Mackinaw in 1724, and served with great reputation as a partisan officer in the old French war. He and his father, Augustin Langlade, were the first permanent settlers within the present State of Wisconsin. He is said to have saved Etherington and Leslie from the torture. See the *Recollections of Augustin Grignon*, his grandson, in *Collections of the Hist. Soc. of Wisconsin*, III. 197.

shrugging his shoulders, and intimating that he could do nothing for me — ' *Que voudriez-vous que j'en ferais ?* '

" This was a moment for despair ; but the next a Pani[1] woman, a slave of M. Langlade's, beckoned me to follow her. She brought me to a door, which she opened, desiring me to enter, and telling me that it led to the garret, where I must go and conceal myself. I joyfully obeyed her directions ; and she, having followed me up to the garret door, locked it after me, and, with great presence of mind, took away the key.

" This shelter obtained, if shelter I could hope to find it, I was naturally anxious to know what might still be passing without. Through an aperture, which afforded me a view of the area of the fort, I beheld, in shapes the foulest and most terrible, the ferocious triumphs of barbarian conquerors. The dead were scalped and mangled ; the dying were writhing and shrieking under the unsatiated knife and tomahawk ; and from the bodies of some, ripped open, their butchers were drinking the blood, scooped up in the hollow of joined hands, and quaffed amid shouts of rage and victory. I was shaken not only with horror, but with fear. The sufferings which I witnessed I seemed on the point of experiencing. No long time elapsed before

---

[1] This name is commonly written *Pawnee.* The tribe who bore it lived west of the Mississippi. They were at war with many surrounding nations, and, among the rest, with the Sacs and Foxes, who often brought their prisoners to the French settlements for sale   It thus happened that Pawnee slaves were to be found in the principal families of Detroit and Michillimackinac.

every one being destroyed who could be found, there was a general cry of ' All is finished.' At the same instant I heard some of the Indians enter the house where I was.

" The garret was separated from the room below only by a layer of single boards, at once the flooring of the one and the ceiling of the other. I could, therefore, hear every thing that passed ; and the Indians no sooner came in than they inquired whether or not any Englishmen were in the house. M. Langlade replied, that ' he could not say, he did not know of any,' answers in which he did not exceed the truth ; for the Pani woman had not only hidden me by stealth, but kept my secret and her own. M. Langlade was, therefore, as I presume, as far from a wish to destroy me as he was careless about saving me, when he added to these answers, that ' they might examine for themselves, and would soon be satisfied as to the object of their question.' Saying this, he brought them to the garret door.

" The state of my mind will be imagined. Arrived at the door, some delay was occasioned by the absence of the key ; and a few moments were thus allowed me, in which to look around for a hiding-place. In one corner of the garret was a heap of those vessels of birch bark used in maple-sugar making.

" The door was unlocked and opening, and the Indians ascending the stairs, before I had completely crept into a small opening which presented itself at one end of the heap. An instant after, four Indians entered the room, all armed with tomahawks, and all besmeared with blood, upon every part of their bodies.

" The die appeared to be cast. I could scarcely breathe; but I thought the throbbing of my heart occasioned a noise loud enough to betray me. The Indians walked in every direction about the garret; and one of them approached me so closely, that, at a particular moment had he put forth his hand, he must have touched me. Still I remained undiscovered; a circumstance to which the dark color of my clothes, and the want of light, in a room which had no window in the corner in which I was, must have contributed. In a word, after taking several turns in the room, during which they told M. Langlade how many they had killed, and how many scalps they had taken, they returned downstairs; and I, with sensations not to be expressed, heard the door, which was the barrier between me and my fate, locked for the second time.

" There was a feather bed on the floor; and on this, exhausted as I was by the agitation of my mind, I threw myself down and fell asleep. In this state I remained till the dusk of the evening, when I was awakened by a second opening of the door. The person that now entered was M. Langlade's wife, who was much surprised at finding me, but advised me not to be uneasy, observing that the Indians had killed most of the English, but that she hoped I might myself escape. A shower of rain having begun to fall, she had come to stop a hole in the roof. On her going away, I begged her to send me a little water to drink, which she did.

" As night was now advancing, I continued to lie on the bed, ruminating on my condition, but unable to discover a resource from which I could hope for life. A flight to Detroit had no probable chance of success. The distance from Michilli-mackinac was four hundred miles; I was without provisions, and the whole length of the road lay through Indian countries, countries of an enemy in arms, where the first man whom I should meet would kill me. To stay where I was, threatened nearly the same issue. As before, fatigue of mind, and not tranquillity, suspended my cares, and pro-cured me farther sleep.

" The respite which sleep afforded me during the night was put an end to by the return of morn-ing. I was again on the rack of apprehension. At sunrise, I heard the family stirring; and, pres-ently after, Indian voices, informing M. Langlade that they had not found my hapless self among the dead, and they supposed me to be somewhere concealed. M. Langlade appeared, from what followed, to be, by this time, acquainted with the place of my retreat; of which, no doubt, he had been informed by his wife. The poor woman, as soon as the Indians mentioned me, declared to her husband, in the French tongue, that he should no longer keep me in his house, but deliver me up to my pursuers; giving as a reason for this meas-ure, that, should the Indians discover his instru-mentality in my concealment, they might revenge

it on her children, and that it was better that I
should die than they. M. Langlade resisted, at
first, this sentence of his wife, but soon suffered
her to prevail, informing the Indians that he had
been told I was in his house; that I had come
there without his knowledge, and that he would
put me into their hands. This was no sooner
expressed than he began to ascend the stairs, the
Indians following upon his heels.

" I now resigned myself to the fate with which
I was menaced; and, regarding every effort at
concealment as vain, I rose from the bed, and
presented myself full in view to the Indians, who
were entering the room. They were all in a state
of intoxication, and entirely naked, except about
the middle. One of them, named Wenniway,
whom I had previously known, and who was
upwards of six feet in height, had his entire face
and body covered with charcoal and grease, only
that a white spot, of two inches in diameter, encircled either eye. This man, walking up to me,
seized me, with one hand, by the collar of the coat,
while in the other he held a large carving-knife, as
if to plunge it into my breast; his eyes, meanwhile,
were fixed steadfastly on mine. At length, after
some seconds of the most anxious suspense, he
dropped his arm, saying, ' I won't kill you!' To
this he added, that he had been frequently engaged
in wars against the English, and had brought away
many scalps; that, on a certain occasion, he had
lost a brother, whose name was Musinigon, and that
I should be called after him.

"A reprieve, upon any terms, placed me among the living. and gave me back the sustaining voice of hope; but Wenniway ordered me downstairs, and there informing me that I was to be taken to his cabin, where, and indeed everywhere else, the Indians were all mad with liquor, death again was threatened, and not as possible only, but as certain. I mentioned my fears on this subject to M. Langlade, begging him to represent the danger to my master. M. Langlade, in this instance, did not withhold his compassion; and Wenniway immediately consented that I should remain where I was, until he found another opportunity to take me away."

Scarcely, however, had he been gone an hour, when an Indian came to the house, and directed Henry to follow him to the Ojibwa camp. Henry knew this man, who was largely in his debt, and some time before, on the trader's asking him for payment, the Indian had declared, in a significant tone, that he would pay him soon. There seemed at present good ground to suspect his intention; but, having no choice, Henry was obliged to follow him. The Indian led the way out of the gate; but, instead of going towards the camp, he moved with a quick step in the direction of the bushes and sand-hills behind the fort. At this, Henry's suspicions were confirmed. He refused to proceed farther, and plainly told his conductor that he believed he meant to kill him. The Indian coolly replied that he was quite right in thinking so, and at the same time, seizing the prisoner by the arm, raised his knife to strike him in the breast. Henry parried the blow, flung the Indian from him, and ran for his life. He gained the gate of the fort, his enemy close at his heels, and, seeing Wenniway standing in the centre of the area, called upon him for protection. The chief ordered the Indian to desist; but the latter, who was foaming at the mouth with rage, still continued to pursue Henry, vainly striking at him with his knife. Seeing the door of Langlade's house wide open, the trader darted in, and at length found himself in safety. He retired once more to his garret, and lay down, feeling, as he declares, a sort of conviction that no Indian had power to harm him.

This confidence was somewhat shaken when, early in the night, he was startled from sleep by the opening of the door. A light gleamed in upon him, and he was summoned to descend. He did so, when, to his surprise and joy, he found, in the room below, Captain Etherington, Lieutenant Leslie, and Mr. Bostwick, a trader, together with Father Jonois, the Jesuit priest from L'Arbre Croche. The Indians were bent on enjoying that night a grand debauch upon the liquor they had seized; and the chiefs, well knowing the extreme danger to which the prisoners would be exposed during these revels, had conveyed them all into the fort, and placed them in charge of the Canadians.

Including officers, soldiers, and traders, they amounted to about twenty men, being nearly all who had escaped the massacre.

When Henry entered the room, he found his three companions in misfortune engaged in anxious

debate. These men had supped full of horrors;
yet they were almost on the point of risking a
renewal of the bloodshed from which they had
just escaped. The temptation was a strong one
The fort was this evening actually in the hands of
the white men. The Indians, with their ordinary
recklessness and improvidence, had neglected even
to place a guard within the palisades. They were
now, one and all, in their camp, mad with liquor,
and the fort was occupied by twenty Englishmen,
and about three hundred Canadians, principally
voyageurs. To close the gates, and set the Indians
at defiance, seemed no very difficult matter. It
might have been attempted, but for the dissuasions
of the Jesuit, who had acted throughout the part
of a true friend of humanity, and who now strongly
represented the probability that the Canadians would
prove treacherous, and the certainty that a failure
would involve destruction to every Englishman in
the place. The idea was therefore abandoned,
and Captain Etherington, with his companions,
that night shared Henry's garret, where they
passed the time in condoling with each other on
their common misfortune.

A party of Indians came to the house in the
morning, and ordered Henry to follow them out.
The weather had changed, and a cold storm had
set in. In the dreary and forlorn area of the fort
were a few of the Indian conquerors, though the
main body were still in their camp, not yet recovered from the effects of their last night's carouse.
Henry's conductors led him to a house, where in a

room almost dark, he saw two traders and a soldier imprisoned. They were released, and directed to follow the party. The whole then proceeded together to the lake shore, where they were to embark for the Isles du Castor. A chilling wind blew strongly from the north-east, and the lake was covered with mists, and tossing angrily. Henry stood shivering on the beach, with no other upper garment than a shirt, drenched with the cold rain. He asked Langlade, who was near him, for a blanket, which the latter refused unless security were given for payment. Another Canadian proved more merciful, and Henry received a covering from the weather. With his three companions, guarded by seven Indians, he embarked in the canoe, the soldier being tied by his neck to one of the cross-bars of the vessel. The thick mists and the tempestuous weather compelled them to coast the shore, close beneath the wet dripping forests. In this manner they had proceeded about eighteen miles, and were approaching L'Arbre Croche, when an Ottawa Indian came out of the woods, and called. to them from the beach, inquiring the news, and asking who were their prisoners. Some conversation followed, in the course of which the canoe approached the shore, where the water was very shallow. All at once, a loud yell was heard, and a hundred Ottawas, rising from among the trees and bushes, rushed into the water, and seized upon the canoe and prisoners. The astonished Ojibwas remonstrated in vain. The four Englishmen were taken from them, and led in safety to the shore.

Good will to the prisoners, however, had by no means prompted the Ottawas to this very unexpected proceeding. They were jealous and angry that the Ojibwas should have taken the fort without giving them an opportunity to share in the plunder; and they now took this summary mode of asserting their rights.

The chiefs, however, shook Henry and his companions by the hand, professing great good will, assuring them, at the same time, that the Ojibwas were carrying them to the Isles du Castor merely to kill and eat them. The four prisoners, the sport of so many changing fortunes, soon found themselves embarked in an Ottawa canoe, and on their way back to Michillimackinac. They were not alone. A flotilla of canoes accompanied them, bearing a great number of Ottawa warriors; and before the day was over, the whole had arrived at the fort. At this time, the principal Ojibwa encampment was near the woods, in full sight of the landing-place. Its occupants, astonished at this singular movement on the part of their rivals, stood looking on in silent amazement, while the Ottawa warriors, well armed, filed into the fort, and took possession of it.

This conduct is not difficult to explain, when we take into consideration the peculiarities of the Indian character. Pride and jealousy are always strong and active elements in it. The Ottawas deemed themselves insulted because the Ojibwas had undertaken an enterprise of such importance without consulting them, or asking their assistance. It may be added, that the Indians of L'Arbre Croche were somewhat less hostile to the English than the neighboring tribes ; for the great influence of the priest Jonois seems always to have been exerted on the side of peace.

The English prisoners looked upon the new-comers as champions and protectors, and conceived hopes from their interference not destined to be fully realized. On the morning after their arrival, the Ojibwa chiefs invited the principal men of the Ottawas to hold a council with them, in a building within the fort. They placed upon the floor a valuable present of goods, which were part of the plunder they had taken ; and their great war-chief, Minavavana, who had conducted the attack, rose and addressed the Ottawas.

Their conduct, he said, had greatly surprised him. They had betrayed the common cause, and opposed the will of the Great Spirit, who had decreed that every Englishman must die. Excepting them, all the Indians had raised the hatchet. Pontiac had taken Detroit, and every other fort had also been destroyed. The English were meeting with destruction throughout the whole world, and the King of France was awakened from his sleep. He exhorted them, in conclusion, no longer to espouse the cause of the English, but, like their brethren, to lift the hatchet against them.

When Minavavana had concluded his speech, the council adjourned until the next day ; a custom common among Indians, in order that the auditors may have time to ponder with due deliberation

28

upon what they have heard. At the next meeting, the Ottawas expressed a readiness to concur with the views of the Ojibwas. Thus the difference between the two tribes was at length amicably adjusted. The Ottawas returned to the Ojibwas some of the prisoners whom they had taken from them; still, however, retaining the officers and several of the soldiers. These they soon after carried to L'Arbre Croche. where they were treated with kindness, probably owing to the influence of Father Jonois.[1] The priest went down to Detroit with a letter from Captain Etherington, acquainting Major Gladwyn with the loss of Michillimackinac, and entreating that a force might be sent immediately to his aid. The letter, as we have seen, was safely delivered; but Gladwyn was, of course, unable to render the required assistance.

Though the Ottawas and Ojibwas had come to terms, they still looked on each other with distrust, and it is said that the former never forgot the slight that had been put upon them. The Ojibwas took the prisoners who had been returned to them from the fort, and carried them to one of their small villages, which stood near the shore, at no great distance to the south-east. Among the other lodges was a large one, of the kind often seen in Indian villages, erected for use on public occasions, such as dances, feasts, or councils. It was now to serve as a prison. The soldiers were bound together, two and two, and farther secured by long ropes tied round their necks, and fastened to the pole which supported the lodge in the centre.

[1] MS. Letter — *Etherington to Gladwyn, June 28.*

Henry and the other traders escaped this rigorous treatment. The spacious lodge was soon filled with Indians, who came to look at their captives, and gratify themselves by deriding and jeering at them. At the head of the lodge sat the great war-chief Minavavana, side by side with Henry's master, Wenniway. Things had remained for some time in this position, when Henry observed an Indian stooping to enter at the low aperture which served for a door, and, to his great joy, recognized his friend and brother, Wawatam, whom he had last seen on the day before the massacre. Wawatam said nothing; but, as he passed the trader, he shook him by the hand, in token of encouragement, and, proceeding to the head of the lodge, sat down with Wenniway and the war-chief. After he had smoked with them for a while in silence, he rose and went out again. Very soon he came back, followed by his squaw, who brought in her hands a valuable present, which she laid at the feet of the two chiefs. Wawatam then addressed them in the following speech:—

•" Friends and relations, what is it that I shall say? You know what I feel. You all have friends, and brothers, and children, whom as your selves you love; and you, — what would you ex perience, did you, like me, behold your dearest friend — your brother — in the condition of a slave; a slave, exposed every moment to insult, and to menaces of death? This case, as you all know, is mine. See there, [pointing to Henry,] my friend and brother among slaves, — himself a slave!

" You all well know that, long before the war began, I adopted him as my brother. From that moment he became one of my family, so that no change of circumstances could break the cord which fastened us together.

" He is my brother; and because I am your relation, he is therefore your relation too; and how, being your relation, can he be your slave?

" On the day on which the war began, you were fearful lest, on this very account, I should reveal your secret. You requested, therefore, that I would leave the fort, and even cross the lake. I did so; but I did it with reluctance. I did it with reluctance, notwithstanding that you, Minavavana, who had the command in this enterprise, gave me your promise that you would protect my friend, delivering him from all danger, and giving him safely to me.

" The performance of this promise I now claim. I come not with empty hands to ask it. You, Minavavana, best know whether or not, as it respects yourself, you have kept your word; but I bring these goods to buy off every claim which any man among you all may have on my brother as his prisoner." [1]

To this speech the war-chief returned a favorable answer. Wawatam's request was acceded to,

---

[1] Henry, *Travels*, 102. The authenticity of this very interesting book has never been questioned. Henry was living at Montreal as late as the year 1809. In 1797 he, with others, claimed, in virtue of Indian grants, a large tract of land west of the River Cuyahoga, in the present State of Ohio. A letter from him is extant, dated in April of that year, in which he offers this land to the Connecticut Land Company, at one-sixth of a dollar an acre.

the present was accepted, and the prisoner released. Henry soon found himself in the lodge of his friend, where furs were spread for him to lie upon, food and drink brought for his refreshment, and every thing done to promote his comfort that Indian hospitality could suggest. As he lay in the lodge, on the day after his release, he heard a loud noise from within the prison-house, which stood close at hand, and, looking through a crevice in the bark, he saw the dead bodies of seven soldiers dragged out. It appeared that a noted chief had just arrived from his wintering ground. Having come too late to take part in the grand achievement of his countrymen, he was anxious to manifest to all present his entire approval of what had been done, and with this design he had entered the lodge and despatched seven of the prisoners with his knife.

The Indians are not habitual cannibals. After a victory, however, it often happens that the bodies of their enemies are consumed at a formal war-feast — a superstitious rite, adapted, as they think, to increase their courage and hardihood. Such a feast took place on the present occasion, and most of the chiefs partook of it, though some of them, at least, did so with repugnance.

About a week had now elapsed since the massacre, and a revulsion of feeling began to take place among the Indians. Up to this time all had been triumph and exultation; but they now began to fear the consequences of their conduct. Indefinite and absurd rumors of an approaching attack from the English were afloat in the camp, and, in their growing uneasiness, they thought it expedient to shift their position to some point more capable of defence. Three hundred and fifty warriors, with their families and household effects, embarked in canoes for the Island of Michillimackinac, seven or eight miles distant. Wawatam, with his friend Henry, was of the number. Strong gusts of wind came from the north, and when the fleet of canoes was half way to the Island, it blew a gale, the waves pitching and tossing with such violence, that the frail and heavy-laden vessels were much endangered. Many voices were raised in prayer to the Great Spirit, and a dog was thrown into the lake, as a sacrifice to appease the angry manitou of the waters. The canoes weathered the storm, and soon drew near the island. Two squaws, in the same canoe with Henry, raised their voices in mournful wailing and lamentation. Late events had made him sensible to every impression of horror, and these dismal cries seemed ominous of some new disaster, until he learned that they were called forth by the recollection of dead relatives, whose graves were visible upon a neighboring point of the shore.

The Island of Michillimackinac, or Mackinaw, owing to its situation, its beauty, and the fish which the surrounding water supplied, had long been a favorite resort of Indians. It is about three miles wide. So clear are the waters of Lake Huron, which wash its shores, that one may count the pebbles at an incredible depth. The island is fenced round by white limestone cliffs, beautifully contrast ing with the green foliage that half covers them, and in the centre the land rises in woody heights. The rock which forms its foundation assumes fantastic shapes — natural bridges, caverns, or sharp pinnacles, which at this day are pointed out as the curiosities of the region. In many of the caves have been found quantities of human bones, as if, at some period, the island had served as a grand depository for the dead; yet of these remains the present race of Indians can give no account. Legends and superstitions attached a mysterious celebrity to the place, and here, it was said, the fairies of Indian tradition might often be seen dancing upon the white rocks, or basking in the moonlight.[1]

The Indians landed at the margin of a little bay. Unlading their canoes, and lifting them high and dry upon the beach, they began to erect their lodges, and before night had completed the work.

---

[1] Tradition, preserved by Henry Conner. See also Schoolcraft, *Algic Researches*, II 159

"Their tradition concerning the name of this little island is curious. They say that Michapous, the chief of spirits, sojourned long in that vicinity. They believed that a mountain on the border of the lake was the place of his abode, and they called it by his name. It was here, say they, that he first instructed man to fabricate nets for taking fish, and where he has collected the greatest quantity of these finny inhabitants of the waters. On the island he left spirits, named Imakinakos; and from these aerial possessors it has received the appellation of Michillimakinac.

"When the savages, in those quarters, make a feast of fish, they invoke the spirits of the island, thank them for their bounty, and entreat them to continue their protection to their families. They demand of them to preserve their nets and canoes from the swelling and destructive billows, when the lakes are agitated by storms. All who assist in the ceremony lengthen their voices together, which is an act of gratitude. In the observance of this duty of their religion, they were formerly very punctual and scrupulous; but the French rallied them so much upon the subject, that they became ashamed to practise it openly." — Heriot, *Travels in Canada*, 185.

Messengers arrived on the next day from Pontiac, informing them that he was besieging Detroit, and urging them to come to his aid. But their warlike ardor had well-nigh died out. A senseless alarm prevailed among them, and they now thought more of securing their own safety than of injuring the enemy. A vigilant watch was kept up all day, and the unusual precaution taken of placing guards at night. Their fears, however, did not prevent them from seizing two English trading canoes, which had come from Montreal by way of the Ottawa. Among the booty found in them was a quantity of whiskey, and a general debauch was the immediate result. As night closed in, the dolorous chanting of drunken songs was heard from within the lodges, the prelude of a scene of riot; and Wawatam, knowing that his friend Henry's life would be in danger, privately led him out of the camp to a cavern in the hills, towards the interior of the island. Here the trader spent the night, in a solitude made doubly dreary by a sense of his forlorn and perilous situation. On waking in the morning, he found that he had been lying on human bones, which covered the floor of the cave. The place had anciently served as a charnel-house. Here he spent another solitary night, before his friend came to apprise him that he might return with safety to the camp.

Famine soon began among the Indians, who were sometimes without food for days together. No complaints were heard; but with faces blackened, in sign of sorrow, they patiently endured

the privation with that resignation under inevitable suffering, which distinguishes the whole Indian race.   They were at length compelled to
cross over to the north shore of Lake Huron,
where fish were more abundant; and here they
remained until the end of summer, when they
gradually dispersed, each family repairing to its
winter hunting-grounds.   Henry, painted and attired like an Indian, followed his friend Wawatam,
and spent a lonely winter among the frozen forests,
hunting the bear and moose for subsistence.[1]

The posts of Green Bay and the Sault Ste. Marie
did not share the fate of Michillimackinac.   During
the preceding winter, Ste. Marie had been partially
destroyed by an accidental fire, and was therefore
abandoned, the garrison withdrawing to Michillimackinac, where many of them perished in the

---

[1] The following description of Minavavana, or the Grand Sauteur, who
was the leader of the Ojibwas at the massacre of Michillimackinac, is
drawn from Carver's *Travels :* —

"The first I accosted were Chipeways, inhabiting near the Ottowaw
lakes, who received me with great cordiality, and shook me by the hand,
in token of friendship. At some little distance behind these stood a chief
remarkably tall and well made, but of so stern an aspect that the most
undaunted person could not behold him without feeling some degree of
terror. He seemed to have passed the meridian of life, and by the mode
in which he was painted and tatowed, I discovered that he was of high
rank   However, I approached him in a courteous manner, and expected
to have met with the same reception I had done from the others ; but, to
my great surprise, he withheld his hand, and looking fiercely at me, said,
in the Chipeway tongue, ' *Cawin nishishin saganosh*,' that is, ' The English
are no good.' As he had his tomahawk in his hand, I expected that this
laconick sentence would have been followed by a blow ; to prevent which
I drew a pistol from my belt, and, holding it in a careless position, passed
close by him, to let him see I was not afraid of him. . . . Since I came
to England, I have been informed, that the Grand Sautor, having rendered himself more and more disgustful to the English by his inveterate
enmity towards them, was at length stabbed in his tent, as he encamped
near Michillimackinac, by a trader." — Carver, 96.

massacre.   The fort at Green Bay first received an English garrison in the year 1761, at the same time with the other posts of this region.   The force consisted of seventeen men, of the 60th or Royal American regiment, commanded by Lieutenant Gorell.   Though so few in number, their duties were of a very important character.   In the neighborhood of Green Bay were numerous and powerful Indian tribes.   The Menomonies lived at the mouth of Fox River, close to the fort.   The Winnebagoes had several villages on the lake which bears their name, and the Sacs and Foxes were established on the River Wisconsin, in a large village composed of houses neatly built of logs and bark, and surrounded by fields of corn and vegetables.[1]   West of the Mississippi was the powerful nation of the Dahcotah, whose strength was loosely estimated at thirty thousand fighting men, and who, in the excess of their haughtiness, styled the surrounding tribes their dogs and slaves.[2]   The commandant of Green Bay was the representative of the British government, in communication with all these tribes.   It devolved upon him to secure their friendship, and keep them at peace; and he was also intrusted, in a great measure, with the power of regulating the fur-trade among them.   In the course of each season, parties of Indians, from every quarter, would come to the fort, each expecting to be received with speeches and presents.

[1] Carver, *Travels*, 47.

[2] Gorell, *Journal*, MS.   The original manuscript is preserved in the library of the Maryland Historical Society, to which it was presented by Robert Gilmor, Esq.

Gorell seems to have acquitted himself with great judgment and prudence. On first arriving at the fort, he had found its defences decayed and ruinous, the Canadian inhabitants unfriendly, and many of the Indians disposed to hostility. His good conduct contributed to allay their irritation, and he was particularly successful in conciliating his immediate neighbors, the Menomonies. They had taken an active part in the late war between France and England, and their spirits were humbled by the losses they had sustained, as well as by recent ravages of the small-pox. Gorell summoned them to a council, and delivered a speech, in which he avoided wounding their pride, but at the same time assumed a tone of firmness and decision, such as can alone command an Indian's respect. He told them that the King of England had heard of their ill conduct, but that he was ready to forget all that had passed. If, however, they should again give him cause of complaint, he would send an army, numerous as the trees of the forest, and utterly destroy them. Flattering expressions of confidence and esteem succeeded, and the whole was enforced by the distribution of a few presents. The Meno monies replied by assurances of friendship, more sincerely made and faithfully kept than could have been expected. As Indians of the other tribes came from time to time to the fort, they met with a similar reception; and, in his whole intercourse with them, the constant aim of the commandant was to gain their good will. The result was most happy for himself and his garrison.

On the fifteenth of June, 1763, an Ottawa Indian brought to Gorell the following letter from Captain Etherington: —

" Michillimackinac, June 11, 1763.

" Dear Sir :

" This place was taken by surprise, on the second instant, by the Chippeways, [Ojibwas.] at which time Lieutenant Jamet and twenty [fifteen] more were killed, and all the rest taken prisoners; but our good friends, the Ottawas, have taken Lieutenant Lesley, me, and eleven men, out of their hands, and have promised to reinstate us again. You'll therefore, on the receipt of this, which I send by a canoe of Ottawas, set out with all your garrison, and what English traders you have with you, and come with the Indian who gives you this, who will conduct you safe to me. You must be sure to follow the instruction you receive from the bearer of this, as you are by no means to come to this post before you see me at the village, twenty miles from this. . . . I must once more beg you'll lose no time in coming to join me ; at the same time, be very careful, and always be on your guard. I long much to see you, and am, dear sir,

" Your most humble serv't.
" GEO. ETHERINGTON.

" J. GORELL,
" Royal Americans."

On receiving this letter, Gorell summoned the Menomonies to a council, told them what the Ojibwas had done, and said that he and his soldiers were going to Michillimackinac to restore order; adding, that during his absence he commended the fort to their care. Great numbers of the Winnebagoes and of the Sacs and Foxes afterwards arrived, and Gorell addressed them in nearly the same words. Presents were given them, and it soon appeared that the greater part were well disposed towards the English, though a few were inclined to prevent their departure, and even to threaten hostility. At this juncture, a fortunate incident occurred. A Dahcotah chief arrived with a message from his people to the following import: They had heard, he said, of the bad conduct of the Ojibwas. They hoped that the tribes of Green Bay would not follow their example, but, on the contrary, would protect the English garrison. Unless they did so, the Dahcotah would fall upon them, and take ample revenge. This auspicious interference must, no doubt, be ascribed to the hatred with which the Dahcotah had long regarded the Ojibwas. That the latter should espouse one side of the quarrel, was abundant reason to the Dahcotah for adopting the other.

Some of the Green Bay Indians were also at enmity with the Ojibwas, and all opposition to the departure of the English was now at an end. Indeed, some of the more friendly offered to escort the garrison on its way; and on the twenty-first of June, Gorell's party embarked in several bateaux, accompanied by ninety warriors in canoes. Approaching Isle du Castor, near the mouth of Green Bay, an alarm was given that the Ojibwas were lying there in ambush; on which the Menomonies raised the war-song, stripped themselves, and prepared to do battle in behalf of the English. The alarm, however, proved false, and, having crossed Lake Michigan in safety, the party arrived at the village of L'Arbre Croche on the thirtieth. The Ottawas came down to the beach, to salute them with a discharge of guns; and, on landing, they were presented with the pipe of peace. Captain Etherington and Lieutenant Leslie, with eleven men, were in the village, detained as prisoners, though treated with kindness. It was thought that the Ottawas intended to disarm the party of Gorell also; but the latter gave out that he would resist such an attempt, and his soldiers were permitted to retain their weapons.

Several succeeding days were occupied by the Indians in holding councils. Those from Green Bay requested the Ottawas to set their prisoners at liberty, and they at length assented. A difficulty still remained, as the Ojibwas had declared that they would prevent the English from passing down to Montreal. Their chiefs were therefore summoned; and being at this time, as we have seen, in a state of much alarm, they at length reluctantly yielded the point. On the eighteenth of July, the English, escorted by a fleet of Indian canoes, left L'Arbre Croche, and reaching, without interruption, the portage of the River Ottawa,

descended to Montreal, where they all arrived in
safety, on the thirteenth of August.[1] Except the
garrison of Detroit, not a British soldier now
remained in the region of the lakes.

[1] Gorell, *Journal*, MS.

END OF VOL. I.

CPSIA information can be obtained at www.ICGtesting.com
Printed in the USA
BVOW09s1748310515

402586BV00009B/70/P

9 781298 316677